INTERNATIONAL LAW AND
INTERNATIONAL RELATIONS

International Relations for the Twenty-first Century

Series Editors: R. J. Barry Jones (University of Reading), Charles Hauss (George Mason University) and Mary Durfee (Michigan Technical University)

Ranging from international political economy to security, migration, human rights and the environment, this series is designed to explore the issues that make International Relations such an exciting, controversial and, at times, confusing field in a world undergoing unprecedented change.

The books are designed as core texts for advanced undergraduate and specialized graduate courses, and each volume follows a standard format. The first section is devoted to general theories and concepts. The second includes carefully selected case studies which students can use to deepen their understanding of the theoretical issues. The books include, as an integral part of the text, addresses of particularly helpful websites, and the series also has its own website with links to Internet-based resources in International Relations.

Forthcoming titles in the series:

International Conflict and Conflict Resolution – Charles Hauss
Global Migration – Joanne Van Selm
The Global Environment – Elizabeth De Sombre
The EU Enters the Twenty-first Century – Michael Huelshoff

INTERNATIONAL LAW AND INTERNATIONAL RELATIONS

J. CRAIG BARKER

CONTINUUM
London and New York

Continuum
The Tower Building, 11 York Road, London SE1 7NX
370 Lexington Avenue, New York, NY 10017–6503

First published 2000

British Library Cataloguing-in-Publication Data
A catalogue record for this book is available from the British Library.

ISBN 0–8264–5029–6 (hardback)
     0–8264–5028–8 (paperback)

Typeset by YHT Ltd, London
Printed and bound in Great Britain by Biddles Ltd, *www.biddles.co.uk*

CONTENTS

PREFACE

This book is part of a series examining the academic discipline of international relations at the beginning of the Twenty-first century. As will become apparent during the reading of this book, the subject of international law, while undoubtedly a relevant consideration for scholars of international relations, has become marginalized by those theoretical explanations of how states behave which focus on the relative power of states and the structure of the international system. Theoretical approaches to international relations, including, in particular, realist, neo-realist and structural realist approaches, regard international law as weak and ineffective and, therefore, of only limited interest. Recent developments in the theory of international relations have, however, resulted in a newly found interest among international relations scholars for the subject of international law. The primary purpose of this book is to seek to explain the way in which international law works in order that students of international relations can properly understand such developments. However, the book will also be of interest to students of international law who understand that international law is only one of the factors that states will take into account in deciding on a particular course of action in their relations with other states.

The structure of the book follows that of other books in the series by examining in the first part of the book the theoretical considerations surrounding international law and its relation to the discipline of international relations. Chapters 1 and 2 set out the basic principles of international law. In particular, Chapter 1 examines the historical development and nature of international law. Particular consideration is given therein to questions of why international law is binding and how international law is enforced. Chapter 2 examines the general principles of international law, focusing on the primacy of states as subjects of international law and the sources of international law. Chapter 3 examines international relations approaches to international law. This discussion will compare and contrast realist assumptions as to the nature of international law with approaches taken by institutionalists, liberals and constructivists. While these theories do not encompass the full extent of theorizing on the subject of international relations, they are, nevertheless, the theories which have been identified as contributing most to the re-establishment of international law as a factor to be taken into account in considering vital issues in the relations of states.

The second part of the book is made up of four case studies. My own research interests have dictated the choice of case studies. Thus, two case studies focus on the use and threat of force while the remaining two studies focus on the question of immunities from jurisdiction. Nevertheless, it is hoped that the chosen case studies will illustrate many of the issues relating to the nature and relevance of international law raised in the first part of the book. The development of the case studies in this book may differ from other books in the series. The reason for this is two-fold. First, the nature of legal analysis is such that it does not easily lend itself to the type of case study with which international relations students may be familiar. Secondly, and more importantly, I decided at an early stage that students unfamiliar with legal analysis would benefit from a detailed exposition of legal approaches to various international incidents. While the book is clearly in favour of promoting interdisciplinary analysis of such incidents, the case studies present only an explanation of legal considerations. It is left to the readers to take that analysis and attempt to apply it to their own understanding of how the international system works. It is hoped that the analyses contained in the case studies will encourage students to consider more fully the relevance of international law to international relations. To that end, the conclusions set out a number of assumptions about international law as illustrated by the various case studies.

Considerable thanks are due to a number of individuals and organizations for their assistance in the preparation of this book. I should like to thank the University of Reading and, in particular, the Faculty of Letters and Social Sciences, for support and financial assistance in the preparation of this work through its Research Endowment Trust Fund, and the Department of Law for their generous funding of my research assistant. I am deeply indebted to all the students who have studied the subject of international law with me at many different universities. I have relied on many of their contributions in the, often lively, discussions I have had with them over the years. The following individuals have assisted me greatly at different stages of my work and I should like to thank them all: Tony Downes, Duncan French, Sandy Ghandhi, Jennifer James, Carl Stychin and Colin Warbrick. Thanks are also due to the series editors including, in particular, Chip Hauss and Barry Jones for getting me started on this project, and for their helpful comments on various drafts of this work. Particular thanks are due also to Heather McIlveen, my research assistant, who did all that I asked of her and more. Finally, I should like to thank my wife Kim, my daughter Megan, and my son Mackenzie, for putting up with me through all the trials and tribulations involved in the preparation of this work. I have sought to take account of the law as of 1 January 2000. In particular it should be noted that since the manuscript was completed General Pinochet has been allowed to return to Chile on medical grounds.

To Kim,
with love

GLOSSARY

acts jure imperii   acts that are performed in the exercise of sovereign or governmental functions

aggression   'the use of armed force by a state against the territorial integrity or political independence of another state' General Assembly Resolution 3314 (XXIX)

anarchy   the absence of government or a political superior within a society. Regarded as being of particular significance to the society of states

anticipatory self-defence   a controversial concept within international law which posits that states are entitled to use military force in self-defence in the face of a threat of force by other states. See also *Self-defence*

amnesty   general pardon especially for a political offence

Austinian handicap   phrase used to refer to the claim by Austin, a nineteenth-century English jurist, that international law was not law 'properly so-called' because it was not commanded by a sovereign and was not supported by sanctions

basic norm (grundnorm)   fundamental governing principle of a legal system, similar to the concept of a rule of recognition

binding obligation   a requirement to do or to refrain from doing a particular act under penalty of the law

black-letter law   a strict textual approach to the study of law

coercion   controlling of action of another state by force, be it political, economic or military

common law   unwritten law purporting to be derived from ancient usage

compliance theory   a theory existing in both international law and international relations that focuses on building measures with which states are able and willing to comply

constitutional law   the study of the fundamental principles according to which a state or other organization is governed

constructivism   a critical branch of international relations theory that focuses on the social relationships of states within the international system, arguing that state identities and interests are constructed by intersubjective social structures

convention   formal treaty instrument of a multilateral character on a topic which is generally of considerable importance

countermeasures   retaliatory measures taken by one state against another which may be lawful insofar as they are proportionate and do not involve the use of force

crime against humanity   term used to refer to criminal acts which offend against the whole of mankind and which, accordingly, attract universal jurisdiction (see also *Universal jurisdiction*)

customary international law   a primary source of international law deriving from the practice of states coupled with a general belief that the practice in question is legally binding

diplomatic immunity   the immunity of diplomatic agents from the civil and administrative and criminal jurisdiction of the state to which they have been sent to represent their country (the receiving state). See Vienna Convention on Diplomatic Relations 1961, Article 31

diplomatic privileges   exemptions enjoyed by diplomatic personnel from the substantive law of the receiving state. Examples include exemption from taxation and customs duties

direct applicability   phrase used to describe a rule of law that is automatically operative without the need for further enactment

direct effect   phrase used, particularly in relation to European Union Law, to describe the way in which law is able to confer rights and duties directly upon individuals

domestic jurisdiction   the right of a state to have primary responsibility for all matters which occur within its territorial boundaries

double criminality   a requirement of the law of extradition that an extraditable crime be recognized as a crime within the jurisdiction of both the extraditing and the requesting state

enforcement action   within the context of international law, each state is entitled to enforce its own rights as against other states insofar as it acts within the law in doing so. A form of centralized enforcement action is provided for under the auspices of the United Nations Security Council in Chapter VII (Articles 39–51) of the UN Charter

executive   branch of government concerned with executing laws

expropriation   unlawful seizure of property by a state from its lawful owner

exterritoriality   a now discredited theory of diplomatic law which traces diplomatic immunity back to the fiction that the diplomatic mission and all diplomatic representatives were deemed not to be on the territory of the receiving state

extra-territorial offences   offences over which a state has jurisdiction notwithstanding the fact that they occurred outside the territory of that state

forum state   state in which a particular court of law is situated and has the authority to act

functional necessity   the principal theoretical basis for the granting of diplomatic privileges and immunities which has regard to the ability of the diplomatic agent fully to perform his functions without fear of interference

general principles of law   a category of sources of international law which identifies the existence of legal principles common to the domestic law of 'civilized' states and which are capable of being applied to international law

genocide   deliberate extermination of a race, nation or other identifiable grouping of individuals

head of state immunity   the immunity of the head of one state from the civil and administrative and criminal jurisdiction of another state

hegemony   leadership; pre-eminence of one state in the relations between sovereign, equal states

idealism   a theory of international relations developed in the immediate aftermath of World War I which was based on the assertion that international law and international organizations possessed the power to prevent future wars

immunity ratione materiae   immunity, be it state or diplomatic, which attaches to an individual by virtue of the official nature of his acts

immunity ratione personae   immunity, be it state or diplomatic, which attaches to an individual by reason of his office

idealists   proponents of the theory of idealism (see also *Idealism*)

institutionalism   a theory of international relations that seeks to move away from the realist paradigms concerning the significance of power and the centrality of the state by focusing on appreciation for law, rules and institutions. 'The focus of institutionalists is broader than formal international organisations but narrower than the structure of the international system' (Beck *et al.*, 1996)

internalization   the process, central to transnational and liberal theories of international relations, by which international legal rules become recognized within the domestic legal structures of states

inviolability   specifically in relation to diplomatic law, the right of a diplomatic agent or mission not to be violated

iteration   repeated action or omission of a state within a legal process. See, in particular, Setear (1997)

judiciary   collective name for the judges of a state

juridical   relating to the law

jurisdiction the right of a state to prescribe and enforce laws. The primary basis of jurisdiction is territorial which allows a state to make and enforce rules within its own boundaries. However, jurisdiction may also exist over non-resident nationals on the basis of the nationality principle, or indeed, over non-resident, non-nationals on the basis of universality or more controversially on the basis of the security and passive personality principles

jurisprudence science or philosophy of law

jus cogens a peremptory norm of general international law, which has the effect of overriding all other norms of international law. See further Vienna Convention on the Law of Treaties 1969, Article 53

law-habit idea that states follow international law out of habit or, more precisely, out of the law's current acceptability and the interest of the international community in vindicating it

liberalism a branch of international relations theory, which focuses on individuals and private groups as the fundamental actors in international relations and emphasizes the role of democracy in contributing to peace and stability in international politics

legal personality the existence of rights and duties together with the procedural capacity to enforce those rights and duties in a legal system

legislation law created by a legislative body, that is a body given the power to make such law

legislature body within a state that is given the power to make law in respect of that state

natural law (naturalism) a theory of law, developed from divine law, which is identified with reason and man's innate ability to identify what is right and just. Law is, accordingly based on the innate moral sense

neo-realism a development of realist theorizing in international relations which, while accepting many of the core realist assumptions, argues that states are capable of cooperation in pursuit of absolute gains

non-intervention principle of international law enshrined in Article 2(7) of the UN Charter which prohibits the involvement by one state in the affairs of another state

norm a standard or indicator of behaviour

obligation a binding agreement or duty

pacta sunt servanda requirement or acceptance by states that they should perform their obligations in good faith. Particularly relevant to the law of treaties – see, e.g. Vienna Convention on Law of Treaties Article 26, which provides that: 'every treaty in force is binding upon the parties to it and must be performed by them in good faith.'

par in parem non habet imperium Latin maxim which specifically means that 'no state can be expected to submit to the laws of another'. It forms the cornerstone of the doctrine of state immunity (see also *State immunity*)

persona non grata the right of a state receiving a diplomatic agent to declare the agent to be no longer acceptable and to request his withdrawal

positivism theory of international law that suggests that law emanates from the free will of independent sovereign states. At its most extreme, the theory denies the possibility of any legal restraints on a state other than those to which it has expressly consented

primary rules rules identified by the legal philosopher H.L.A. Hart as the rules that directly regulate the conduct of the members of a society

proportionality principal requirement of the right of a state to take lawful countermeasures against another state. The concept is particularly relevant in relation to the right of self-defence

provisional measures non-binding measures that may be imposed on a state by the International Court of Justice prior to a hearing on the merits of a case

quasi-universal jurisdiction a form of universal jurisdiction which is created by treaty and so is dependent upon the specific consent of states to that jurisdiction through the signing and ratification of the relevant treaty (see also *Universal jurisdiction*)

realism the dominant theory of international relations which regards states, the primary actors on the world stage, as existing in a state of permanent anarchy where power and the pursuit thereof is the dominant consideration

realists proponents of the theory of realism (see also *Realism*)

reciprocity principle or practice of give-and-take in interchange between states

recognition political act with legal consequences acknowledging validity or genuineness of a new state or government

regime term used by international relations scholars to identify 'the principles, norms, rules and decision-making procedures that pattern state expectations and behaviour' (Slaughter Burley, 1993)

regime theory the study of international regimes

representative character theory a theory of diplomatic law which traces the privileges and immunities of a diplomatic agent back to the rights of the sovereign or state he represents

responsibility liability of states under international law for injurious acts

rule of recognition general agreement among those to whom a legal system is addressed that the law is binding on them

secondary rules criteria by which primary rules of a legal system are identified, altered and applied *self-defence*   basic principle of international law, found in customary international law and confirmed in the UN Charter Article 51, allowing states to defend themselves in the face of an armed attack by another state

shared expectations   a concept similar to *opinio juris* by which states agree on what the lawful course of action is in a given situation

sovereignty   a legal concept, central to the question of statehood, associated with the idea of supreme law-making power within a state and which, when translated into the international sphere has given rise to claims of states to be above the law. (See further discussion of this concept in Chapter 2.)

state immunity   the immunity of a state from the civil and administrative and criminal jurisdiction of another

structural realism   a development of realist theory of international relations which focuses more upon the structure of the international community and structural causes of conflict rather than the characteristics of states which may lead to conflict. 'Structural realists consider states to be positional actors, motivated not so much by the prospect of absolute gains as the need to maintain or enhance their position vis-à-vis other states in order to ensure survival.' (Beck *et al.*, 1996, p. 145)

transnational law   a concept, first coined by Phillip Jessup, which asserts that the domestic–international distinction in law no longer exists and that there exists instead a system of transnational legal rules created by private actors as well as governments which can be enforced by domestic as well as international tribunals

treaty   'an international agreement concluded between states in written form and governed by international law, whether embodied in a single instrument or in two or more related instruments and whatever its particular designation.' Vienna Convention on Law of Treaties, Article 2(1)

universality   see *Universal jurisdiction*

universal jurisdiction   the right, or indeed the duty, established under customary international law, of all states to prosecute or extradite an individual accused of certain crimes under international law

veto   specifically with reference to the voting procedure of the UN Security Council, the veto is the exercise by one of the five permanent members of a vote against a resolution of the Security Council on all matters other than simply procedural matters

CHAPTER 1

THE DEVELOPMENT AND NATURE OF INTERNATIONAL LAW

INTRODUCTION

International law, in various forms, has governed the relations between different social groupings, including tribes, cities, sovereigns and, ultimately, states for many thousands of years. Throughout that time, the influence of the law has been apparent to a greater or lesser extent at different times. Yet, despite the longevity of the discipline, the international lawyer has traditionally been regarded as an intellectual outcast, a misfit who is unable to offer sufficient certainty, clarity and obligation to be accepted by traditional legal thinkers whose doctrinal approach to the law is built upon interpretation and precedent. Similarly, political scientists have been quick to reject notions of international law as inadequate in a world of power politics, concluding that, if international law exists at all, it is irrelevant to modern international relations. And yet, international law not only continues to exist, but also, it continues to bind states in their relations with one another. Indeed, as the twenty-first century dawns, there is increased willingness, particularly amongst political scientists, to defend rather than attack the role of international law.

In this first chapter, it is intended briefly to examine the historical development of international law before moving to introduce the two fundamental questions mentioned above, that is: is international law really law? And, is international law relevant? In examining each of these questions consideration will be given first to the question of whether international law is binding on states and secondly to the related but separate question of the enforcement of international law.

THE HISTORICAL DEVELOPMENT OF
INTERNATIONAL LAW

Clearly, there was no such thing as international law in prehistoric times. However, at least one writer has suggested that tribes of cave dwelling anthropoid apes may have had dealings with one another on such matters as drawing the limits of their respective hunting grounds and bringing to an end a day's battle.[1] If that were the case, one of the first rules governing that type of relationship, and hence, one of the first rules of inter-tribal law, might have been the inviolability of the messenger or negotiator; an early form of diplomatic immunity. While this is pure speculation, it is not unreasonable. Certainly, by the time of the ancients, a form of international law had been firmly established in a number of disparate civilizations including the Ancient Indians,[2] Chinese,[3] Egyptians,[4] Greeks[5] and, perhaps most notably, the Romans.[6]

As empires grew and began to interact with one another, the need for more formalized relations began to emerge. This process led to the enactment of the first known international treaty, which dates from approximately 3100 BC, and was a peace treaty between two Mesopotamian city-states.[7] Many similar treaties of peace and friendship were entered into between the ancients. Georg Schwarzenberger, for example, refers to the Treaty of Kadesh, which was a Treaty of Eternal Peace and Alliance between Ramases II of Egypt and the Hittite King Hattusilis dating from around 1284–3 BC.[8] As with other treaties of the time, the primary object was to establish a state of lasting peace between the two empires. Remarkably, many of the principles of modern international law were reflected in the treaty, which recognized the principles of sovereignty, recognition, responsibility, consent and good faith.[9]

---

1. Nicolson (1954), p. 2.
2. See Viswanatha (1925) and Chatterjee (1958).
3. See Britton (1935) and Whyte (1928).
4. See Breasted (1927).
5. See Phillipson (1979).
6. *Idem.*
7. Nussbaum (1962), p. 1.
8. Schwarzenberger (1972), pp. 229–31. See also Schwarzenberger (1976), pp. 40–51.
9. Schwarzenberger (1972), p. 242.

The practice of dealing with other empires by means of treaties of peace and friendship continued into the mediaeval period and beyond.[10] However, by the beginning of the twelfth century, such treaties were no longer concluded between empires; rather, they were agreements between sovereign rulers aimed at asserting the independence of such sovereigns from one another and the equality between them.[11] For example, the Declaration of Arbroath in 1320 took the form of a Petition from the Barons of Scotland to Pope John XXII containing a request by Scotland to be treated by England on a footing of sovereign equality. This led to the truce of 1328 in which King Edward III finally recognized the independence of Scotland and the position of Robert the Bruce as King of Scotland. In a subsequent truce of 1381 between King Richard II and King Robert of Scotland, the two nations, or, in effect, the two sovereigns, were recognized as being equal in the absence of a common superior.

As the interrelationship of sovereigns and their sovereign nations increased, the need for a delimitation of the rules of such relationships increased with it. Beginning in the middle of the fifteenth century, the so-called classical writers began to formulate the rules of international law which, to a greater or lesser extent, were accepted first by the independent sovereigns and, latterly, by states, in their relations with one another. The sources of this 'law of nations' were broad and disparate, a point made most clearly by W. W. Bishop who writes:

> Building upon what to us seems a curious hodgepodge of recorded practice, ideas of ethics and morals, accounts in imaginative literature, legal doctrines of Roman law and of the canon law, theological speculations, and whatever else came to hand, these writers formulated the principles and rules of international law.[12]

Undoubtedly, religion was of fundamental importance to the early writers on international law as it had been to the early practitioners.[13] For example, Francisco de Vitoria, one of the earliest classical writers, saw the

---

10. For example, the Treaties of Eternal Peace of AD 532 and AD 562 between the Byzantine and Persian Empires (Schwarzenberger, 1976, p. 48).
11. See, for example, the Treaty of Subsidy between King Henry I of England and Count Robert of Flanders (1101) (*Idem*).
12. Bishop (1971), p. 15.
13. Referring to the Treaty of Kadesh, Schwarzenberger notes that 'ultimately, the binding character of the Treaty rests on non-legal foundations: a thousand gods invoked by each Contracting Party as the witnesses and guarantors of the treaty' (Schwarzenberger, 1976, pp. 47–8).

binding nature of pacts among men as lying in the law which governed the whole world, the law of God, to the extent that those who violated international rules were regarded as having committed a mortal sin.[14] Such reliance on theology continued until the time of Alberico Gentili, an Italian jurist, who became Professor of Civil Law at Oxford. Gentili separated the treatment of international law from that of theology but continued to rely on an extension of Roman law doctrines as a basis of international law.[15]

The most famous and respected of all the classical writers on international law is Hugo de Groot, or, more commonly, Grotius. The basis of Grotius' philosophy of law is to be found in the *Prolegomena* to his definitive work on the law of war and peace, *De Jure Belli ac Pacis*, written in 1625. Grotius believed the basis of international law was to be found in the law of nature which man, above all other species, is able to discover through 'the maintenance of social order ... which is consonant with human intelligence'.[16] He was able therefore to dispel the myth that 'all creatures, men as well as animals are impelled by nature towards ends advantageous to themselves'.[17] Law, according to Grotius, is known to man through the exercise of discretion and rational judgement. In asserting this law of nature, Grotius did not abandon the theological roots of the law, declaring that there exists 'another source of law besides the source in nature, that is, the free will of God, to which beyond all cavil our reason tells us we must render obedience'.[18] However, Grotius was ultimately able to secularize natural law and, in doing so, according to Sir Hersch Lauterpacht: 'He gave it added authority and dignity by making it an integral part of the exposition of a system of law which became essential to civilized life. By doing this he laid, more truly than any writer before him, the foundations of international law.'[19]

International law, or the law of nations as it is referred to by Grotius, is a necessary aspect of the society of states. Accordingly, international law is not subject to the arbitrary whim of national self-interest. It is necessary for states to have regard to the long-term benefits of the maintenance of law in preference to short-term advantage. Thus, as Grotius notes:

---

14. de Vitoria (1557). See further Hamilton (1963).
15. Gentili (1585).
16. Grotius (1625), p. 40.
17. *Idem*, p. 39.
18. *Idem*, p. 41.
19. Lauterpacht (1946), p. 24.

For since ... the national who in his own country obeys its laws is not foolish, even though, out of regard for that law, he may be obliged to forgo certain things advantageous to himself, so that nation is not foolish which does not press its own advantage to the point of disregarding the laws common to nations. The reason in either case is the same. For just as the national, who violates the law of his country in order to obtain an immediate advantage, breaks down that by which the advantages of himself and his posterity are for all future time assured, so the state which transgresses the laws of nature and of nations cuts away also the bulwarks which safeguard its own future peace. Even if no advantage were to be contemplated from the keeping of the law, it would be a mark of wisdom, not of folly, to allow ourselves to be drawn towards that to which our nature leads.[20]

The work of the classical writers did much to formulate the rules that applied between the independent sovereign nations which characterized the international landscape of the fifteenth and sixteenth centuries. However, the beginning of modern international law can be traced back to the evolution of the modern state-system in Europe and, in particular, the Treaty of Westphalia in 1648 which brought an end to the Thirty Years War and 'marked the acceptance of a new political order in Europe'.[21] Although the role of the classical writers did not disappear, greater and greater emphasis came to be placed on the actual practice of states as the basis for international law. Thus, as one writer has noted: 'Side by side there proceeded naturally a kind of action and reaction between the customary rules and the works of the great writers.'[22]

One of the key developments in this new political structure of Europe was the emergence of the doctrine of sovereignty, a doctrine first formalized by Jean Bodin in *De Republica* in 1576.[23] Bodin's theory of

---

20. *Idem*, pp. 42–3.
21. Brierly (1963), p. 5. The Treaty of Westphalia did not result in the creation of a new system of states. The emergence of states as autonomous entities had been taking place since the fifteenth century. However, the Peace of Westphalia had the effect of 'crystallizing' this development. According to Cassese, the Peace of Westphalia, which in fact consisted of two treaties signed at Munster and Osnabrück, 'constituted a watershed in the evolution of the modern international community', first, by recognizing Protestantism at an international level thereby allowing for the separation of Church and state, second, by upgrading a number of small states to the status of members of the international community and, third, by crystallizing a new political distribution of power in Europe which resulted in the *de facto* disintegration of the Holy Roman Empire. See Cassese (1986), pp. 34–8.
22. Shearer (1994), p. 11.
23. Brierly (1963), p. 7.

sovereignty envisaged the sovereign as a 'constitutional ruler subordinate to the fundamental law of the State'.[24] According to Bodin: 'No one has defined absolute power, or rather power that has been freed from laws. For if we define "freed from all laws" [as absolute power] no prince anywhere possesses sovereignty, since divine law, the law of nature, and the common law of all people, which is established separately from divine and natural law, bind all princes.'[25] However, in practice, the theoretical restraints that constitutional law placed upon sovereigns did not materialize. Thus, J. L. Brierly has noted:

> In the sixteenth century ... the barriers against absolutism were giving way, and the consolidation of strong governments with no effective checks on the powers of rulers was breaking down the medieval idea of law as a customary rule which sets limits to all human authority and was making it natural to think of law as man-made, the manifestation of a ruler's superior will.[26]

The process by which the doctrine of sovereignty came to dominate both international law and international relations was consummated by Thomas Hobbes[27] who declared that 'law neither makes the sovereign, nor limits his authority; it is might that makes the sovereign and law is merely what he commands'.[28] Taking his analysis of the work of Bodin and Hobbes to its logical conclusion, Brierly concludes that, if it is correct that sovereignty means absolute power and states are sovereign, then 'there is no escaping from the conclusion that international law is nothing but a delusion'.[29]

The challenge of illustrating the full extent of that delusion was taken up by a number of legal philosophers, including Jeremy Bentham and, most notably, by John Austin, a nineteenth century English jurist. Austin believed that every law 'properly so called' is 'a rule laid down for the guidance of an intelligent being by an intelligent being having power over him'.[30] Accordingly, for Austin, law is the command of a superior. Such a command is a 'signification of desire' on the part of the superior which can be 'distinguished from other significations of desire by this peculiarity: that the party to whom it is directed is liable to evil from the

---

24. *Idem*, p. 11. See generally *idem*, pp. 7–12, for a discussion of Bodin's theory.
25. Translated by and quoted in Pennington (1993), p. 8.
26. Brierly (1963), p. 12.
27. See, in particular, *Leviathan*, which was first published in 1651.
28. Brierly (1963), p. 12.
29. *Idem*, p. 16.
30. Austin (1995), p. 18.

other, in case he comply not with the desire'.[31] In other words, for Austin, the two fundamental requirements of law 'properly so called' are the command of a superior backed up by sanctions.

Austin's work was generally derivative of the work of Bentham who believed that 'all laws command or prohibit or permit some form of conduct'.[32] While Austin based his approach on a study of the criminal law, Bentham's subtler analysis of law, based on the principle of utilitarianism,[33] was able to include an analysis of other laws such as property law within its scope. However, according to Bentham, property law and other civil laws were not 'complete laws' but only part of laws. Thus, Bentham regarded rights to property as being merely exceptions limiting the scope of prohibitory laws which were complete laws.[34] Accordingly, 'Bentham, like Austin, is rooted to the concepts of sovereignty and the habit of obedience'.[35]

Although Bentham may have provided a more acceptable definition of law in the sense that it could more easily include international law within its scope, albeit as incomplete law, it is Austin's definition of the law that has proved to be the more influential.[36] Indeed it is Austin and the so-called 'Austinian Handicap' which has provided the most direct challenge to students of international law. Thus Austin used his definition of law to deny the legal character of international law, which he saw simply as positive morality.[37] He did not deny the existence of

---

31. *Idem*, pp. 21–2.
32. See Freeman (1994), p. 212.
33. According to Bentham, 'by the principle of utility is meant that principle which approves or disapproves of every action whatsoever, according to the tendency which it has to augment or diminish the happiness of the party whose interest is in question... An action then may be said to [conform to] utility when the tendency it has to augment the happiness of the community is greater than any it has to diminish it.' Bentham (1996), p. 13.
34. In the case of property law, the prohibition was not to 'meddle' with a piece of land. See Freeman, (1994), p. 212.
35. *Idem*, p. 213.
36. According to Lord Lloyd of Hampstead, 'There are few, if any, at the present day, who regard [Austin] as wholly successful in [his] undertaking or as being altogether clear-minded in his basic aims, but, nevertheless, Austin's thought still remains worthy of examination not only on account of his widespread influence, especially in common law countries but also by reason of his penetrating powers of applying analysis to jurisprudence' (*idem*, p. 213).
37. While Austin did recognize the existence of positive rules regulating the conduct of states in their international relations, these could not properly be described as laws insofar as they were not commanded by a sovereign and lacked the necessary enforcement procedure.

international rules, which he defined as 'laws or rules which are imposed upon nations or sovereigns by opinions current amongst nations'. However, according to Austin:

> The body by whose opinion the law is said to be set, does not command, expressly or tacitly that conduct of the given kind shall be forborne or pursued. For, since it is not a body precisely determined or certain, it cannot, *as a body*, express or intimate a wish. As a body, it cannot signify a wish by oral or written words, or by positive or negative deportment. The so-called rule which its opinion is said to impose, is merely the sentiment which it feels, or the opinion which it holds, in regard to a kind of conduct.[38]

Fundamentally for Austin, states, which are themselves sovereign, cannot be *subjected to* the law, they can only agree to limit their own rights through consent. Where states subsequently change their minds and chose to ignore the agreements they have made, they are subject only to a moral obligation not to withdraw their consent rather than a legal obligation which would punish such a change of mind. Such a voluntarist system cannot, according to Austin, be law.

To be fair to Austin much of the international law that existed at the time he was writing did not lend itself to any particular definition of law. If it did exist at all, international law was there simply to recognize 'the delimitation of power among the various members of the international community'.[39] Rules on territorial sovereignty existed alongside rules on the acquisition of title to territory, which included the right to take territory by force. Indeed no general constraint was placed on the threat or use of force. Other rules provided, on the basis of *laissez-faire* philosophy, for the freedom of the high seas and freedom of trade. The basic ordering principle was the so-called balance of power, which was based on great power hegemony and the attempts by those great powers 'not to trespass upon their respective spheres of influence in order to avoid friction and conflict'.[40]

The balance of power system continued essentially until the outbreak of the First World War. Nevertheless, the period covering the end of the nineteenth and beginning of the twentieth century was witness to a number of attempts to strengthen the role of international law. Pre-war efforts to develop more fully the rule of law in international relations saw the enactment of the Hague Conventions for the Pacific Settlement of

---

38.   Austin (1995), p. 124.
39.   Cassesse (1986), p. 46.
40.   *Idem*, p. 45.

International Disputes in 1899 and 1907 which brought about the creation of the Permanent Court of Arbitration. The period had also witnessed the establishment of nascent human rights institutions such as the British and Foreign Anti-Slavery Society and the International Committee of the Red Cross,[41] as well as various proposals for the creation of a system of world law such as that put forward by the Universal Peace Congress in 1908. The process culminated in the creation of the League of Nations and the Permanent Court of International Justice (PCIJ) in 1920. According to Antonio Cassesse the PCIJ 'was intended by its creators (among whom was American President Woodrow Wilson[42]) to exert a powerful influence as an agency for resolving conflict'.[43]

In order to achieve this aim, the drafters of the Court's Statute suggested that, as well as treaties and customary international law,[44] a further category of legal rules should be applied by the Court, that is 'general principles of law recognized by civilized nations'. Cassesse is in no doubt that 'plainly the advocates of this doctrine endeavoured to introduce natural law principles in international relations'.[45] He considered that:

> [T]he supporters of the new source were politically motivated. They intended to go beyond the traditional limitations of the international legal system by broadening the existing legal network through the addition of principles reflecting Western legal philosophy ... However modest the scope of the principles, the attempt was revolutionary, because for the first time an international heteronomous law (that is, rules imposed from outside and not resting on the free will of States) was to be created ... the role of the new law was self-evident: it was meant to restrict State sovereignty as much as possible whenever the absence of treaties or custom left States free to behave as they liked.[46]

It was this apparent resort to natural law coupled with the rhetoric of peace and world law which was seized upon by the emerging realist scholars as the proof that international law was the natural home of utopianism and idealism. Thus, E. H. Carr's condemnation of

---

41. See further Koh (1997), p. 2612.
42. According to Slaughter Burley (1993) at 208, 'From the realist perspective, Woodrow Wilson and his followers were the high priests of the "legalist-moralist" tradition in American foreign policy.'
43. Cassesse (1986), p. 170.
44. For a discussion of treaties and customary international law as sources of international law, see below, Chapter 2.
45. Cassesse (1986), p. 170.
46. *Idem.* On treaties and customs generally, see below.

international law that: 'Since 1919, natural law has resumed its sway, and theories of international law have become more markedly utopian than at any previous time.'[47]

It is worth noting at this stage, however, that the conviction of international law on the basis of its guilt by association with idealism may have been fundamentally misplaced. Whilst there undoubtedly was a resurgence in natural law thinking after the end of the nineteenth century it is clear that the prevailing legal philosophies remained positivist, even realist in character. In other words, international law remained wholly dependent upon the will of states. The idea that states could be constrained by external sources such as the law of nature was consistently rejected by the international lawyers of the time.

For example, the Hague Conventions were the first to introduce into international law the distinction between legal and political disputes. By making such a distinction, the drafters of the Conventions recognized that certain disputes between states were not amenable to legal determination.[48] Secondly, while the League of Nations was created ostensibly 'to prevent the recurrence of world-wide armed conflicts',[49] the League's Covenant did not itself prohibit war or, indeed, the resort to force short of war. Nor did it provide for any system of enforcement of the law against a state breaking the League's system. Crucially, the Covenant was binding only on state parties to it, which did not include the United States, Germany, Japan and the USSR.[50]

The continuing positivist dominance of international law was apparent in the Statute of the PCIJ and in its work. Although the Statute required the Court to have regard to the 'general principles of law recognised by civilised nations' as a source of international law, the PCIJ seldom referred to this category of international law. Indeed, on the rare occasions that the PCIJ and its successor, the International Court of Justice (ICJ), has resorted to general principles, it has only been with respect to matters of procedure rather than matters of substance.[51] Finally, Article 36 of the Statute of the PCIJ made it clear that the jurisdiction of the Court was not compulsory. Each state had separately to consent to the exercise of jurisdiction by the Court in any given case.

---

47. Carr (1939), p. 224. For a full discussion of realist approaches to international law, see below, Chapter 3.
48. Lauterpacht (1933), p. 27.
49. Cassesse (1986), p. 60.
50. See further Cassese (1986), pp. 60–1.
51. See further below, Chapter 2.

Furthermore, Article 36 provided for jurisdiction only in relation to *legal* disputes between state parties. Thus, according to Lauterpacht, 'a Government wishing to promote its interests ... [was] in a position to argue that, although a definite dispute may fall within one of the categories enumerated [in Article 36], it does not come within the purview of the Court on the ground that it is not a "legal" dispute'.[52]

The clearest assertion of continued support for the positivist/realist position came in the form of the decision of the PCIJ in the *Lotus Case*.[53] The case concerned the assertion of criminal jurisdiction by a state outside its territory. The Court held that, while states were not entitled to exercise jurisdiction in the territory of another state, there was nothing to stop a state exercising jurisdiction over persons, property and events outside their territory.[54] In other words, international law permitted states to do whatever they were able to do insofar as it did not interfere directly with the rights of another state. The decision, which was secured by the casting vote of the President, the Court having been split 6 to 6, is evidence that legal positivism continued to hold sway amongst the legal fraternity including the elite of the bench of the World Court. The decision of the PCIJ in the *Lotus Case* was, in fact, much criticized by many at the time as being too positivist.[55] The strongest criticism came from Brierly who noted that: '[The Court's] reasoning was based on the highly contentious metaphysical proposition of the extreme positivist school that law emanates from the free will of sovereign independent states, and from this premise they argued that restrictions on the independence of states cannot be presumed.'[56]

Nevertheless, international law was developing in a way which increasingly qualified the unrestricted freedom of states. One of the factors that led to this development was the increased willingness of states to enter into treaties which did more than simply delimit the extent of their independence. A second factor was to be found in the attempts to place legal restrictions on the use of force by states. Both factors were apparent in the creation of the League of Nations.

The League of Nations is generally regarded as having been a failure. However, the League did lay the foundations for the later development of the United Nations. In particular, the PCIJ, in spite of its apparent

---

52. Lauterpacht (1933), p. 36.
53. (1927) PCIJ Rep. Ser. A, No. 10, at 28.
54. See Dixon (1993), pp. 114–15.
55. See Brownlie (1998), p. 305.
56. Brierly (1928), p. 155.

limitations and the initial scepticism of states, managed during the inter-war period to increase its workload and many of its decisions remain relevant today. The League was also responsible for the first moves away from the unlimited right of states to use force in international relations. Thus, while, as noted above, the League of Nations Covenant did not itself prohibit war nor the resort to force short of war, it did place certain minimal procedural requirements on the resort to war.[57] In 1928, a number of states signed and ratified the General Treaty for the Renunciation of War, otherwise known as the Kellog-Briand Pact. The Pact, which supplemented the Covenant and remains in force today, was the first international instrument to attempt to limit the resort to war as an instrument of foreign policy.[58] The Pact too is generally regarded as a failure, not least because of its application only to war rather than to force in general. However, as one commentator has noted, the Pact was 'a vital development in the law of force, for it demonstrated that a general ban on "war" was politically and legally possible.'[59]

The succession of the League of Nations by the United Nations marked the beginning of a new initiative towards the creation of an international society based on the rule of law. The purposes of the United Nations to maintain international peace and security; to develop friendly relations among states; to achieve international cooperation in solving international problems; and to harmonize the actions of states in the attaining of these common ends,[60] were to be achieved in accordance with seven basic principles. These included recognition of the sovereign equality and internal sovereignty of states, as well as a requirement to fulfil obligations in good faith and to settle international disputes peacefully. Crucially, the Charter required in Article 2(4) that states refrain in their international relations from the threat or use of force.

The Charter provided a framework for the future development of international law. In particular, it further developed the move towards a more coercive system of international law based on collective enforce-ment. The idea of collective action in international law had been first institutionalized in the Covenant of the League of Nations and was consummated in Chapter VII of the UN Charter. As will be shown later, Chapter VII provides for the possibility of enforcement action being taken by the Security Council against state acts which are identified as

---

57. Covenant, Articles 10–16.
58. General Treaty for the Renunciation of War, Article 1.
59. Dixon (1993), p. 250.
60. UN Charter, Article 1.

breaches of the peace, threats to the peace or acts of aggression. The general failings of this system are well documented and will be discussed further in Chapters 4 and 5 below. It is worth noting at this stage, however, that it is the failure of the United Nations system of coercive international law that forms the basis of the realist assertion that international law is irrelevant to the power politics that underlie the international system. On the other hand, the drafters of the UN Charter envisaged the development of international law in a number of ways that moved beyond the coercive paradigm. For example, the Charter of the United Nations envisaged fuller economic and social cooperation among states and specifically called for the promotion of universal respect for, and observance of, human rights. Similarly, the Charter provided the basis for the creation and implementation of the decolonization process. Finally, the Charter envisaged a more formalized structure for the pacific settlement of international disputes, headed by the ICJ.

The last fifty years have witnessed many changes in the international system which have had a profound effect on international law. The Cold War was a dominant factor throughout most of this period. So too was the consummation of the decolonization process, which, coupled with the demise of communism and the break-up, in particular, of the Soviet Union and the former Yugoslavia, has brought about an increase in the number of states from around fifty in 1945 to today's total which numbers in excess of 200 states. New perspectives on international law have emerged during this period, in particular, the Soviet and Third World perspectives which have challenged the Western dominance of international law. Finally, international law has witnessed an enormous development in the number of fields it encompasses. It is this final development which, to a large extent, has been conditioned by the other factors mentioned above, which has provided the greatest impetus for and, at the same time, the greatest challenge to, international law. As Friedmann noted as early as 1964:

> The time has come to attempt at least a partial ordering of this bewildering mass of new developments ... as an aid to our understanding of modern legal problems that have arisen outside the traditional scope and methods of international law ... In particular, we must overcome the traditional distinction ... between diplomacy and political science thinking, on the one side, and 'black-letter law' on the other.[61]

---

61. Friedmann (1964), p. 70.

In order fully to understand the development of and challenges to international law, however, it is necessary first to consider questions relating to the nature of international law and, indeed, whether it is binding on states at all.

THE BINDING NATURE OF INTERNATIONAL LAW

Reference has already been made to the Austinian handicap which posits that international law is not law properly so called because it is not commanded by a sovereign, nor is it centrally enforced. At one level, the controversy over the Austinian handicap is no more than a controversy about the meaning of words. Overcoming the Austinian handicap and the bringing of international law within the accepted definition of the law is therefore seen by many as a primary focus of the international lawyer. International relations scholars, on the other hand, see this focus on the meaning of the word 'law' as missing the point. Thus, according to one commentator: 'The important question for international relations theory is whether a body of rules governing the relations of states can exist in the absence of authoritative central institutions, not whether these rules are "really law".'[62] To assume, however, that lawyers in general, and international lawyers in particular, spend their days arguing about what is and what is not law properly so called is to do them a major disservice.

Lawyers recognize that the very process of defining words is inherently subjective. Indeed, as one commentator has pointed out, 'since a definition is the product of the definer's analysis, it should not be generalised beyond the limits within which it was framed'.[63] Another commentator has been more forthright in his condemnation of Austin's approach, noting that: 'Austin's opponents could ... have challenged him on the simple and unassailable ground that he was assuming a power that no man possessed: the power of dictating to others the meanings in which they should use words.'[64] However, in seeking to answer the question 'What is law?' lawyers are not seeking, or at least should not be seeking, an all-encompassing definition or even concept of law.[65] Rather, they are looking for characteristics common to legal rules

---

62. Nardin (1983), p. 120.
63. Dias (1954), p. 219.
64. Williams (1945), p. 48.
65. Distinctions have been drawn between attempts to define law and attempts to provide a concept of law. However, while there may be some differences between a definition and a concept, the purpose of both is to identify the essential characteristics of the phenomenon of law.

which distinguish them from other rules and which are capable of binding the subjects to which they are addressed. Indeed, one writer believes that the question 'would be more candidly expressed in the form "can such rules as these be meaningfully and truthfully said ever to give rise to obligation?".'[66] In other words, international lawyers and international relations scholars are, in effect, addressing much the same question.

Before moving to consider international relations perspectives on the relevance of international law, it is necessary first to consider the lawyer's response to Austin's challenge. The most commonly cited critique of Austin's definition of law for the purposes of domestic law, at least, is that of H. L. A. Hart. Hart sums up Austin's analysis of law as follows:

> On this simple account of the matter … there must, wherever there is a legal system, be some person or body of persons issuing general orders backed by threats which are generally obeyed, and it must be genuinely believed that these threats are likely to be implemented in the event of disobedience. This person or body must be internally supreme and externally independent. If, following Austin we call such a supreme and independent person or body of persons the sovereign, the laws of any country will be the general orders backed by threats which are issued whether by the sovereign or subordinates in obedience to the sovereign.[67]

However, referring specifically to municipal law, Hart continues: 'If we compare the various different kinds of law to be found in a modern system … with the simple model of coercive orders … a crowd of objections leap to mind'.[68] Hart then examines why the simple model of coercive orders fails to reproduce what he refers to as 'the salient features of a legal system'.[69] He concludes that Austin's definition of law does not even properly explain the archetypal coercive law, that is the criminal statute, far less the great variety of other forms of law which cannot be regarded as coercive. Such other laws include 'those conferring legal power to adjudicate or legislate (public powers) or to create or vary legal relations (private powers)'[70] and may even include international law.

Hart devotes a chapter of his book to dealing specifically with the problem of international law. He identifies two principal sources of doubt

---

66. Hart (1961), p. 212.
67. *Idem*, p. 25.
68. *Idem*, p. 26.
69. *Idem*, p. 77.
70. *Idem*.

concerning the legal character of international law, both of which arise from adverse comparison of international law with municipal law. The first form of doubt is essentially the Austinian handicap, that law is a matter of orders backed by threats. 'The second form of doubt springs from the obscure belief that states are fundamentally incapable of being the subjects of legal obligation.'[71] Hart notes first that the identification of ' "having an obligation" or "being bound" with "likely to suffer the sanction or punishment threatened for disobedience" . . . distorts the role played in all legal thought and discourse of the ideas of obligation and duty'.[72] As to the second source of doubt regarding the nature of the sovereignty of states, Hart notes that: 'Whenever the word "sovereign" appears in jurisprudence, there is a tendency to associate it with the idea of a person above the law whose word is law for his inferiors or subjects.'[73] However, he rejects this notion, stating that:

> The simplest answer to the present objection is that it inverts the order in which questions must be considered. There is no way of knowing what sovereignty states have, till we know what the forms of international law are and whether or not they are mere empty forms.[74]

In other words, Hart argues that sovereignty is itself a legal concept. It is therefore impossible to argue that sovereignty places a state above international law without knowing what limitations international law places on the sovereignty of states. Reference has already been made to the opinion of Brierly that if sovereignty is absolute, international law can be nothing but a delusion. It will be argued in Chapter 2 that international law does in fact limit the external sovereignty of states. How much that sovereignty is limited is dependent on the development of international law. For present purposes, however, it is sufficient to note that it is international law that defines the extent of state sovereignty and, accordingly, any argument that the sovereignty of a state places it above international law must be rejected. Accordingly, for Hart, Austin's definition of law is not, in and of itself, capable of denying the character of international law as a system of law which is binding on its subjects.

Other writers have been similarly dismissive of the Austinian handicap. One of the most straightforward of recent critiques is to be found in the work of Terry Nardin, a political scientist. Nardin identifies

---

71. *Idem*, p. 210–11.
72. *Idem*, p. 212.
73. *Idem*, p. 215.
74. *Idem*, p. 218.

two prerequisites of Austin's definition of law; legislation and enforcement. As to legislation, Nardin notes that the requirement that law can only exist where it is the result of legislative activity is unduly restrictive 'for it excludes laws created by custom, by the courts, or by an act of political founding or constitution-making, and thus denies to customary, common and constitutional law the name "law".'[75] Nor does the existence of legislative institutions make a legal system. As Nardin points out: 'The existence of legislative institutions may be a feature of many legal systems, but the diversity of mankind's legal experience suggests that it is neither a definitive feature nor an indispensable condition of legal order.'[76] As to the requirement of enforcement, Nardin notes quite simply that 'Coercion alone cannot create rights or obligations of any sort, legal or non-legal. On the contrary, enforcement *presupposes* the validity of the law that is enforced.'[77] In other words to make the existence of law dependent upon the existence of enforcement ignores the necessity that enforcement can only occur in situations where a legal obligation already exists.

Is the international legal system, therefore, a system of law? For Hart, a legal system must possess both primary rules, that is the rules that directly regulate the conduct of the members of a society, and secondary rules which state the criteria by which the primary rules are identified, altered and applied.[78] As Hart observes:

> Most systems have, after some delay, seen the advantages of further centralisation of social pressure; and have partially prohibited the use of physical punishments or violent self-help by private individuals. Instead they have supplemented the primary rules of obligation by further secondary rules, specifying or at least limiting the penalties for violation, and have conferred upon judges, where they have ascertained the fact of violation, the exclusive power to direct the application of penalties by other officials. These secondary rules provide the centralised official sanction of the system.[79]

Further, for Hart, a legal system must also contain a basic rule of recognition, that is a general agreement among those to whom the law is addressed that the law is binding on them. To Hart, it is a problem that international law is lacking in secondary rules which will ensure its

---

75. Nardin (1983), p. 122.
76. *Idem*, p. 123.
77. *Idem*, p. 126 (emphasis in original).
78. *Idem*, p. 155.
79. Hart (1961), p. 95.

certainty and ability to change. Crucially, however, the absence of a basic rule of recognition in international law ensures that international law can exist only as a set of rules rather than a legal system. Thus, according to Hart:

> What is the actual character of the rules as they function in the relations between states? Different interpretations of the phenomena to be observed are of course possible; but it is submitted that there is no basic rule providing general criteria of validity for the rules of international law, and that the rules which are in fact operative constitute not a system but a set of rules ...[80]

Hart's analysis of the concept of law has been influential and remains influential even among international lawyers. In particular, Hart's assertion that a system consisting only of primary rules is uncertain, static and inefficient has been responded to by international lawyers who are working within some of the new fields of international law, such as the law concerning the environment, to draft conventions which do not simply state the 'rules' but provide mechanisms for the change and development of those rules within the framework of those conventions. Furthermore, the work of the International Law Commission on the issue of State Responsibility, for example, is directed towards the identification of secondary rules whereby wronged states can assert the breach of a rule of international law and claim compensation in respect of it.

On the matter of the existence of a rule of recognition in international law, various possibilities for such a rule had been asserted before Hart completed his work. International lawyers have, for example, for many years, asserted that the binding principle of international law is the rule of *pacta sunt servanda*, that is the rule that states must fulfil their obligations in good faith. Similarly, Kelsen has asserted that 'the basic norm of international law ... must be a norm which countenances custom as a norm-creating fact, and might be formulated as follows: The state ought to behave in such a manner as the others usually behave (believing that they ought to behave in that way), applied to the mutual behaviour of states.'[81] Put more simply 'states should behave as they have customarily behaved'.

Generally, however, international lawyers have been unconcerned by this search for a rule of recognition. Thus, according to Ian Brownlie, 'in

---

80. *Idem*, p. 231.
81. Kelsen (1966), p. 564.

many societies there is nothing which approximates to a single rule of recognition as a guide to the law-determining agencies'.[82] He continues: 'Law is relative to the social order of things, and the reasons for its effectiveness are not to be referred to a single notion of obedience or of appreciation of the validity of norms according to a central principle'.[83]

Why, then, is international law binding on states? For many international lawyers, the answer is simple – because states accept that it is binding upon them. To others this answer may seem too simplistic. However, to attempt to look beyond this simple answer to find some other overriding, all-encompassing basis for the existence of obligation is a fruitless and never-ending task. Sir Gerald Fitzmaurice manifestly and convincingly explained the essence of the impossibility of such a search in a seminal article in 1956 entitled 'The foundations of the authority of international law and the problem of enforcement'. For Fitzmaurice, the search for the legal authority of international law 'is a sort of will-o'-the-wisp, an *ignis fatuus* that only recedes further into the distance as one approaches it, and that can never actually be reached'.[84]

Fitzmaurice illustrated the problem by reference to the 'comfortable proposition' that international law is binding because states have given their consent to it. However, 'consent could not, in itself, create obligations unless there were already in existence a rule of law according to which consent has just that effect'.[85] It might of course be possible to assert that such a rule exists. For example one could assert as many have done that: 'There is a customary rule of international law that the consent of the states to a rule makes that rule binding upon them.'[86] As will be shown, this may or may not actually provide an explanation as to why states consider themselves to be bound by a particular form of rules, that is the rules arising from treaties. However, it does not provide a satisfactory explanation for the binding nature of international law in general. As Fitzmaurice notes, 'the difficulty is merely removed a stage further back, and the enquirer will have to ask what is the juridical foundation for this customary rule itself, and what is it that makes *that* rule binding'.[87] It may be that the search here is for the elusive 'rule of recognition' required by Hart. However, according to Fitzmaurice, 'here

---

82. Brownlie (1981) p. 7.
83. *Idem*, p. 7.
84. Fitzmaurice (1956), p. 8.
85. *Idem*, p. 9.
86. *Idem*.
87. *Idem* (emphasis in original).

again, a duty is postulated that has itself, in a legal sense, to be accounted for'.[88] He concludes that 'however the matter is put, finality can, in the nature of the case, never be attained'.[89]

The matter is, in mathematical terms, 'an infinite regress – a series in which each proposition is explicable in terms of the previous one, and derives its validity from it; but this antecedent proposition itself requires to be accounted for by a similar process'.[90] It is worth noting that the same problems exist in trying to identify the fundamental basis of legal obligation for all law, not just international law. In terms of domestic law, for example, the question of the binding authority of legislation regresses to a challenge to the authority of the legislature to enact binding law. According to Fitzmaurice, if the ultimate source of the authority of law cannot be identified within the law itself, 'the ultimate source of the validity of ... law must be extra-legal'.[91] Similarly, Brierly had earlier noted that: 'There need be no mystery about the source of obligation to obey international law. The same problem arises in any system of law and it can never be solved by a merely *juridical* explanation. The answer must be sought outside the law.'[92]

Of course, some difficulty will arise in identifying exactly what that extra-legal source of obligation is. For Fitzmaurice it is to be found in the concept of justice. Brierly, on the other hand, identified the 'ultimate explanation of the binding force of all law' as being the need for man 'in so far as he is a reasonable being, to believe that order and not chaos is the governing principle of the world in which he has to live'.[93] Neither of these explanations can be fully accepted. The problem faced by Fitzmaurice is in sustaining the argument that law is inherently just while Brierly must answer the question as to whether order cannot be achieved without law. The answer would appear to be rather more straightforward, as was suggested earlier. That is that the binding nature of international law lies in the *political* acceptance by states that rules of international law do exist and are binding upon them.

International law is a reality. As Brownlie has noted, 'the actual use of rules described as rules of international law by governments is not to be questioned'.[94] He continues:

---

88. *Idem.*
89. *Idem.*
90. *Idem.*
91. *Idem,* p. 12.
92. Brierly (1954), p. 55.
93. *Idem,* p. 57.
94. Brownlie (1981), p. 1.

All normal governments employ experts to provide routine and other advice on matters of international law and constantly define their relations with other states in terms of international law. Governments and their officials routinely use rules which they have for a very long time called the 'law of nations' or 'international law'. It is not the case that the resort to law is propagandist – though it sometimes is. The evidence is that reference to international law has been a normal part of the process of decision-making.[95]

It will be shown later that this view of the binding nature of international law is generally accepted amongst political scientists as well as international lawyers. In particular, the work of E. H. Carr, one of the leading proponents of the realist school of international relations, is fundamentally in agreement with the line of reasoning set out above.[96] However, the assertion of the binding nature of international law is insufficient. If international law is to be taken seriously as a factor in the relations of states, it is necessary to show further that international law is effective.

THE ENFORCEMENT OF INTERNATIONAL LAW

Rosalyn Higgins has argued that: 'The main contemporary interest in the place of sanctions is as a mark of continuing non-communication between international lawyers and some scholars of international relations.'[97] Certainly, as will be shown, realist scholars, while not denying the existence of law as 'law', have argued that it is the lack of centralized sanctions which is the source of the lack of relevance and efficacy of international law. This view, which is regarded by Higgins as lacking in sophistication and being ignorant of the nature and function of international law, has, nevertheless, dominated much thinking and writing about international law. For example, Stephen Ratner, himself an international lawyer, has recently argued that 'without mechanisms to bring transgressors into line, international law will be "law" in name only'.[98] He is critical of the position of international lawyers in this regard noting that: 'This state of affairs, when it occurs, is ignored by too many lawyers who delight in large bodies of rules but often discount patterns

---

95. *Idem*, p. 1.
96. See below, Chapter 3.
97. Higgins (1982) p. 33.
98. Ratner (1998), p. 69.

of noncompliance.'[99]

One reaction to this criticism is simply to deny the need for the enforcement of international law. Hart, for example, raised the idea that international law is a specific form of law in which 'there is neither a similar necessity for sanctions (desirable though it may be that international law should be supported by them) nor a similar prospect of their safe and efficacious use'.[100] He continued:

> This is so because aggression between states is very unlike that between individuals. The use of violence between states must be public, and though there is no international police force, there can be very little certainty that it will remain a matter between aggressor and victim, as a murder or theft, in the absence of a police force, might. To initiate war is, even for the strongest power, to risk much for an outcome which is rarely predictable with reasonable confidence. On the other hand, because of the inequality of states, there can be no standing assurance that the combined strength of those on the side of international order is likely to preponderate over the powers of aggression. Hence the organisation and use of sanctions may involve fearful risks and the threat of them add little to natural deterrents.[101]

More recently, so-called compliance theorists, such as Abram Chayes and Antonia Chayes, have argued that efforts aimed at strengthening enforcement regimes are 'largely a waste of time'.[102] For the Chayeses, the threat of sanctions is irrelevant to the conduct of relations between states. For them, compliance with international agreements is best achieved through 'an iterative process of discourse among the parties [to a treaty], the treaty organisation, and the wider public'.[103] While the Chayeses generally focus on compliance with international agreements, that is formal treaties, Thomas Franck has developed an analysis of compliance which has, at its core, the concepts of fairness and legitimacy. While the work of such theorists is generally to be welcomed and developed, this should not be done at the expense of developing and building upon those enforcement mechanisms that exist in international law. Lori Damrosch has recently made this point in the following terms:

> Without denying the importance of these [compliance] perspectives to our understanding of the theoretical and practical underpinnings of the

---

99. *Idem*, pp. 69–70.
100. Hart (1961), p. 214.
101. *Idem*, p. 214.
102. Chayes and Chayes (1995), p. 2.
103. *Idem*, p. 3.

system as it has existed up to this point, I am convinced that the truly 'misguided' attitude would be to conclude that enforcing international law is unnecessary or unrealistic. It may well be true that compliance is the ultimate goal and enforcement is merely a means to that end; and if non-enforcement strategies are more effective than coercive ones in inducing certain kinds of compliance, then of course it should make sense to favour the policy most likely to yield the desired result. But this does not mean abandoning enforcement as one among various strategies for achieving compliance.[104]

Centralized Enforcement Machinery

The lessons of the two World Wars, which blighted the earlier part of the twentieth century, were undoubtedly hard lessons to learn. As the Second World War reached its climax, statesmen in the leading allied nations sought to devise an international system which would maintain international peace and security. This was to be done principally through the development of a collective security system 'for the prevention and removal of threats to the peace, and for the suppression of acts of aggression or other breaches of the peace'.[105] To that end, one of the fundamental principles declared in Article 2(4) of the UN Charter was that: 'All members shall refrain in their international relations from the threat or use of force against the territorial integrity or political indepen-dence of any state, or in any other manner inconsistent with the purposes of the United Nations.' Having sought to prohibit the individual use of force by states in this way, the drafters of the Charter put in place a system of collective enforcement which was designed to ensure that states did not need to resort to force except in extreme circumstances of self-defence. The collective enforcement system, which is provided for primarily in Chapter VII of the Charter, envisages a central role for the Security Council in the maintenance of international peace and security. It provides in Article 39 that the Security Council 'shall determine the existence of any threat to the peace, breach of the peace or act of aggression'. Having made this determination the Security Council can provide for measures not involving the use of force to be undertaken against a breaching state.[106] Such measures may include the disruption

---

104. Damrosch (1997), p. 23.
105. UN Charter, Article 1(1).
106. UN Charter, Article 41.

of economic relations, most usually by the imposition of economic sanctions, and the severance of diplomatic relations. Finally the Security Council may authorize such use of force as may be necessary in order to restore international peace and security.[107]

As might be imagined, there is a vast array of literature by both international lawyers and international relations scholars relating to the collective enforcement system of the United Nations. It is not intended here to provide an overview of this literature. Nor, indeed, is it intended to provide a detailed analysis of the Chapter VII procedures at this juncture. The second part of this book contains a case study examining the Chapter VII collective security system in detail. For present purposes, brief consideration will be given to the problems of the collective enforcement system and to questioning whether such a system is indeed necessary at all.

The principal problems of the United Nations' collective security system emerged very early on in the post World War Two era. Briefly stated, these include the problem of the veto, the problem of defining a 'threat to the peace, breach of the peace or act of aggression' and the lack of willingness among states to provide military personnel to be placed under the direct control of the United Nations. The second and third of these problems will be considered further in Chapters 4 and 5 below. However, it is undoubtedly the exercise of the veto that has caused greatest damage to the whole conception of the collective security system as envisaged in the United Nations Charter. The Security Council is made up of fifteen member states of the United Nations including the five permanent members (United States, United Kingdom, Russia, China and France). These permanent members are required to concur on all votes of the Security Council except purely procedural matters.[108] Hence, by not concurring in any non-procedural votes, any or all of the permanent members can veto a resolution of the Security Council.

Throughout the Cold War, the exercise of the veto became almost routine. Thus, it would be fair to say, in relation to the determination of a threat to the peace, breach of the peace or act of aggression, at least, that if the United States did not veto a particular resolution, the Soviet Union (Russia) would. This led to an apparent stagnation of the collective security system for over forty years. This did not mean, however, that the Security Council or, indeed the United Nations, was powerless to act against an offending state. As Shaw has pointed out:

---

107. UN Charter, Article 42.
108. UN Charter, Article 27.

In practice, the Security Council has applied all the diplomatic techniques available in various international disputes. This is in addition to open debates and the behind-the-scenes discussions and lobbying that take place. On numerous occasions it has called upon the parties to a dispute to negotiate a settlement and has requested that it be kept informed.[109]

Shaw cites, in particular, Resolution 242 (1967) dealing with the Middle East as an example of such a practice. While the resolution did not seek to impose a settlement through the use of the collective security system, it recommended 'a set of principles to be taken into account in resolving a particular dispute'.[110] Shaw concludes that 'in this instance the Security Council proposed that a dispute be tackled by a combination of prescribed proposals reinforced by mediation'.[111]

Neither has the United Nations itself been rendered obsolete by the over-use of the veto. The United Nations has a central role to play in the enforcement of international law in general. Aside from the issue of the imposition of forcible sanctions, the United Nations is heavily involved in the development and strengthening of non-forcible measures in support of international law. One particular area of development in this regard has been in relation to the enforcement of human rights law. An example of such a development is to be found in the implementation machinery of the 1966 International Covenant on Civil and Political Rights (ICCPR).

Under that system three procedures are set out for the implementation and supervision of the Covenant and the rights set out therein. These require first that state parties submit occasional reports to the Secretary-General of the United Nations 'on the measures they have adopted which give effect to the rights recognised [in the Covenant] and on the progress made in the enjoyment of those rights'.[112] The reports are considered by the Human Rights Committee which has the power not only to involve other specialized agencies of the United Nations in the process, but also to report back directly to the state parties. The reporting procedure is obligatory on state parties to the Covenant. According to P. R. Ghandhi: 'The Committee's comments provide a general evaluation of a State Party's report and of the dialogue with the delegation, and take note of factors and difficulties that affect the implementation of the Covenant, of positive developments that may have occurred during the

---

109. Shaw (1997) p. 843.
110. *Idem*, p. 843.
111. *Idem*, p. 844.
112. ICCPR, Article 40(1).

period under review and of specific issues of concern relating to the application of the provisions of the Covenant.'[113]

A second procedure is envisaged under Article 41(1) of the Covenant and provides for the Human Rights Committee to consider communications from a state party which 'claims that another State Party is not fulfilling its obligations under the ... Covenant'. Here, the procedure is optional and depends upon both states accepting the competence of the Human Rights Committee to hear such complaints. The procedure is further weakened by the ability of the infracting state to accept or reject any conclusions and it is perhaps not surprising to note that the procedure has yet to be invoked by any state. Nevertheless, as Ghandhi has noted, 'it is a substantial step forward to give one state *locus standi* to complain about the treatment by another state of its own nationals'.[114]

The third procedure is the right of individual petition provided for in the Optional Protocol to the Covenant. As its name suggests, this system is not mandatory on state parties to the Covenant unless they have, in addition, signed up to the Optional Protocol. Furthermore, the Human Rights Committee does not sit as a court in relation to such matters but simply forwards its views to the state party concerned and to the individual. While these procedures are undoubtedly limited, not least by the fact that they do not apply as a matter of course to all members of the United Nations, the existence of the procedures and the centrality of the United Nations to them emphasizes the important role played by the United Nations in this regard.

Even in matters relating to international peace and security, the United Nations has a considerable role to play beyond what is provided for in Chapter VII of the UN Charter. In particular, the United Nations has developed for itself a peacekeeping role which exists outside the peace enforcement provisions of Chapter VII. Indeed in his *Agenda for Peace* in 1992, the UN Secretary-General envisaged a five-stage process for United Nations' involvement in securing international peace and security. These are preventive diplomacy, peacemaking, peacekeeping, peace-building and peace-enforcement. It is only the last of these measures which is directly envisaged in Chapter VII of the UN Charter. The peacekeeping role of the United Nations is nowhere mentioned in the UN Charter. However, it is a role which has developed directly out of the stagnation of the Chapter VII enforcement procedures as a result of the over-use of the veto. As early as 1950, already frustrated by

---

113. Ghandhi (1998), p. 24.
114. *Idem*, p. 27.

the use of the veto, the General Assembly passed the so-called Uniting for Peace Resolution.[115] The resolution cited the secondary role of the General Assembly and Secretary-General in the maintenance of international peace and security, declaring that where the Security Council failed to exercise its primary responsibility as a result of the use of the veto, the General Assembly could consider the matter and make recommendations. Such a recommendation could include a recommendation for the use of force.

The constitutionality of the resolution was tested before the ICJ in the *Certain Expenses Case*[116] in which the ICJ agreed that the General Assembly and Secretary-General were entitled to make recommendations insofar as they did not amount to 'enforcement actions' which remained within the exclusive power of the Security Council under Chapter VII. While the General Assembly has invoked these procedures on a number of occasions since 1950, it is the Security Council itself that has invoked the right to deploy peacekeeping forces in situations where agreement could not be reached on the deployment of peace enforcement measures. The essential difference between the two procedures involves the use of force and the consent of the state against which measures are being taken. In relation to peacekeeping measures, the use of force is available only in self-defence and, crucially, any measures must have the consent of the target state.

At the time of writing, a further development of the peacekeeping procedures is occurring in relation to East Timor. In this ongoing situation, the Security Council initially appeared reluctant to deploy a peace-enforcement operation without the consent of Indonesia, the territorial state. However, having received such consent, the Security Council has effectively agreed to the deployment of a peace-enforcement operation which has been authorized to use 'all necessary means' to bring about an end to the conflict. It remains to be seen whether this will set a precedent for peacekeeping/peace-enforcement operations in the future.

The biggest question about such measures, however, concerns the extent to which they actually achieve what they are intended to do. Leaving aside the difficult question about what the objectives of specific operations are, it is questionable whether any enforcement operation involving the use of force is a suitable response to the use of force by a particular state. Even where such operations are able to bring a speedy

---

115. General Assembly Resolution 377 (V).
116. (1962) ICJ Rep. 151.

end to an actual conflict situation, as appeared to be the case in relation to the removal of Iraq from Kuwait in 1991, the end result of such actions may be as problematic as the original conflict. Thus, in relation to the continuing 'punishment' of Iraq, it would seem to be the ordinary citizens of Iraq rather than the regime itself that are suffering the most. The experience of dealing with the situation in the former Yugoslavia makes it clear that quick-fix solutions are no replacement for sustained and lengthy peace-building measures. On the other hand, it can never be known the extent to which the existence of the Chapter VII procedures and the other centralized enforcement mechanisms set out above have, over the years, constituted a deterrent against aggression by states. That having been said, it is worth referring again to Hart's statement that 'the organisation and use of [centralized enforcement] sanctions may involve fearful risks and the threat of them add little to natural deterrents'.[117]

Given that the centralized enforcement machinery of the United Nations has been defeated by the use of the veto, at least during the Cold War period, the question must remain as to why states during this period continued not only to accept the binding authority of international law but also, in the words of Henkin, to 'observe almost all principles of international law and almost all of their obligations almost all of the time'.[118] The answer to this question may well lie once again, outside the realm of international law and within the realm of what Hart describes as 'natural deterrents'. Two of these extra-legal considerations will be considered below before brief consideration is given to measures which are available to individual states as mechanisms for the enforcement of their own rights under international law.

Extra-legal Considerations

Law-habit

The first of these extra-legal considerations is commonly referred to as law-habit and flows from the earlier assertion that the binding nature of international law is to be found in the political acceptance by states that international law exists and is binding on them. The idea that states follow international law out of respect for the law has been strongly asserted by Louis Henkin. He has noted, for example, that:

---

117. Hart (1961), p. 214.
118. Henkin (1979), p. 47.

> in domestic society individuals observe law principally from fear of consequences, and there are 'extra-legal' consequences that are often enough to deter violation, even where official punishment is lacking ... In international society, law observance must depend more heavily on these extra-legal sanctions, which means that law observance will depend more closely on the law's current acceptability and on the community's ... current interest in vindicating it.[119]

The fact is that in areas where there is considerable cooperation between states ranging from the exchange of diplomats to the regulation of international telecommunications, the international community perceives considerable benefit to exist in the observance of the law.

International law is itself created by states. Two consequences flow from this. First, it is more likely that international law will be in accordance with the interests of the international community in general than would perhaps be the case if international law were imposed by a centralized law-making body. Secondly, and perhaps more importantly, in order for the law to change and develop it must be recognized that states may, on occasion, consider it necessary to breach the existing law in order to bring about change. This is particularly the case in relation to the development of customary international law. Where a particular rule has developed over a period of time and is firmly established as a rule of international law, such a breach will be reacted to by other states in a negative way which will serve to confirm the existing rule. However, where other states perceive the breach in more positive terms as an attempt to change an unsatisfactory or outmoded rule of international law, that breach itself, if accepted and acted upon by other states, may well lead to the development of a new rule of international law.[120]

It may well be that in areas of international law where the sense of international community is less well developed, the restraining qualities of law-habit are less visible. In such cases states may well perceive that 'when it really hurts' their interests are better served by violating the law even if the intention is not to try to bring about a change in the law as it stands. Thus, Hans Morgenthau has observed that while 'the great majority of rules of international law are generally unaffected by the weakness of its system of enforcement', there are a minority of 'important and generally spectacular cases' where observance of the law is supplanted by considerations of the 'relative power of the nations concerned'. In such cases, according to Morgenthau, 'considerations of

---

119. *Idem*, p. 97.
120. See further below, Chapter 2.

power rather than of law determine compliance and enforcement'.[121]

The first point to note here is that no system of law, even systems of law which are based entirely upon coercion, can eliminate breach of the law altogether. The prohibition against murder, for example, is common to most if not all legal systems, many of which provide the ultimate sanction of the death penalty as a deterrent. Yet no legal system has entirely eliminated the commission of murder. If Morgenthau's analysis were to be applied to the municipal law of, for example, the United States, where murder is a daily occurrence, one might be tempted to argue that the prohibition against murder, in many areas of the United States at least, is irrelevant and can be disregarded.

Morgenthau's analysis is, of course, more subtle than this analogy portrays. What Morgenthau is particularly concerned about is not the spectacular violation of the law itself but the perception that the more powerful the state, the more easy it is for them simply to ignore the law when it suits them. However, Henkin has observed that:

> if the suggestion is that when it costs too much to observe international law nations will violate it, the charge is no doubt true. But the implications are less devastating than might appear, since a nation's perceptions of 'when it really hurts' to observe law must take into account its interests in law and in its observance and the costs of violation.[122]

Such an assertion does not amount to a denial of the efficacy and relevance of international law, rather it is an acceptance that international law is part of a wider process which recognizes the existence of political, economic and other non-legal factors which must be taken into account by states when determining whether or not to comply with the law. Indeed, as Henkin himself has noted: 'Law is one force – an important one among the forces that govern international relations at any time; the deficiencies of international society make law dependent on other forces to render the advantages of observance high, the costs of violations prohibitive.'[123]

121. Morgenthau (1973), p. 291.
122. Henkin (1979), p. 98.
123. *Idem*, p. 98.

Reciprocity

As an extra-legal concept, reciprocity constitutes a powerful restraining factor on the activities of states. Reciprocity is relatively unimportant in a centralized legal system in which the primary reliance of the subjects of the law is the existence of legal obligation and the rights and duties that flow therefrom. However, in a decentralized legal system such as the international legal system, reciprocity plays an essential role. While reciprocity may be regarded in purely negative terms as a tit-for-tat process which spirals downwards so as to undermine any sense of cooperation existing between states, it is as a positive factor acting to restrain states from engaging in illegal activities that reciprocity is at its most effective. As Michael Byers has recently noted, the 'broad social concept of reciprocity, which states apply on the basis of either short- or long-term considerations of self-interest, may be responsible for a great deal of inter-state co-operation or exchange, outside or in addition to any international legal obligations'.[124] In this context, increased interdependence of states at all levels of interaction strengthens the positive nature of reciprocity. Thus the process of globalization and the development of technology strengthen reciprocity as part of the social process.

Reciprocity has itself been incorporated into the process of international law and may be regarded as an essential principle of international law particularly insofar as international law constitutes a 'multitude of bilateral relationships'[125] between states. Although the concept of bilateralism has been criticized by some lawyers as detracting from the purported universality of international law, that is that international law applies to every state regardless of the relations that exist between any two particular states, an alternative, and perhaps more satisfactory, explanation of the relations between states is that each and every rule of international law consists of a single or series of bilateral relations between states. Thus, according to Byers, 'if a bilateral legal relationship in respect of any particular rule is multiplied so that similar relationships in respect of the same rule exist between all states, the rules would seem to be general in application'.[126] In this context, states may not have particularly close relations with all states but will be concerned about their bilateral relations with individual states. In such cases it is the protection of the relations with the closest state that will determine the

---

124. Byers (1999), p. 89.
125. *Idem*, p. 88.
126. *Idem*, p. 89.

nature of a particular state's dealings with all states in respect of a particular rule. Reciprocity therefore encourages cooperation on the basis of the highest common denominator.

The clearest illustration of this legal conception of reciprocity at work is to be found in relation to the exchange of diplomatic agents. As a sub-system of international law, the law of diplomatic privileges and immunities is relatively well-developed and is strongly adhered to by states on a daily basis, in spite of the lack of any overriding enforcement machinery. The primary reason for this is the inherent reciprocal basis of diplomatic relations. According to Eileen Denza, reciprocity is itself 'a constant and effective sanction for the observance of nearly all the rules of the [Vienna Convention on Diplomatic Relations 1961]'.[127] She continues:

> Every state is both a sending and receiving state. Its own representatives abroad are in some sense always hostages. Even on minor matters of privilege and protocol their treatment may be based on reciprocity. For the most part, failure to accord privileges or immunities to diplomatic missions or to their members is immediately apparent and is likely to be met by appropriate countermeasures.[128]

Clearly not all areas of international relations are as interdependent as are diplomatic relations between states. Nevertheless, the possibility of reciprocal action plays an important role as a non-legal factor which states will take into account in deciding whether or not to breach a particular rule of international law. Where reciprocity is recognized and accepted in the international legal process itself, the positive aspects of reciprocity appear to be increased.

The Enforcement of International Law by Individual States

Decentralized non-forcible measures

International law provides generally for states to utilize self-help measures in order to enforce their rights under international law. For centuries the primary self-help mechanism was the resort to war. However, the use of force in international relations has, for the most part,

127. Denza (1998), p. 2.
128. *Idem.*

been rendered illegal under international law and, accordingly, individual states can no longer legally resort to the use of force except where such force is necessary in self-defence. On the other hand, international law does recognize the right of states to engage in lawful countermeasures ranging from the breaking off of diplomatic relations to the imposition of sanctions. That such measures should not involve the use of force goes without saying.

It cannot be denied that the inherent subjectivity of such self-help measures is problematic. Thus, without the existence of a centralized body capable of determining the existence of a breach of international law and determining a suitable response where such breach occurs, it is left to individual states to determine the existence of the breach and the extent of the countermeasure. To that extent, it may truly be said that international law favours the more politically and economically, if not militarily, powerful state. Nevertheless, the problem is not as stark as it might at first seem.

First, any determination by a state that a breach of international law has occurred must itself be made by reference to the law. A state cannot simply act on a whim and states do, in their practice, consistently refer to international law in justification of the lawfulness of countermeasures. It has been argued that international law is lacking objective criteria for the making of such determinations. Thus, Hart's assertion, referred to above, that international law lacks secondary rules of determination. However, international law is developing such rules of determination through various means. Thus reference can again be made to the work of the International Law Commission on the Law of State Responsibility, which is seeking to provide those very criteria which Hart sees as lacking in the international legal system. While this work is ongoing, many of the proposed rules of state responsibility have already been accepted by states as part of customary international law. Furthermore, in the process of treaty making, states are increasingly accepting the compulsory resort to dispute settlement procedures ranging from the ICJ to special courts, such as the International Law of the Sea Tribunal set up under the auspices of the Law of the Sea Convention 1982, as a means for objective third party determination of breaches of relevant international rules. Similarly, where possible and appropriate, states are utilizing their own domestic judicial structures, rather than political organs in order to make the necessary determination. This form of determination is dependent upon the application of international legal principles within domestic systems and is increasingly relevant, particularly in relation to the enforcement of international human rights obligations against individuals. This aspect will be discussed further below in the case study dealing with the attempts to extradite General Pinochet from the United Kingdom to Spain.

Decentralized forcible measures

As noted above, the only remaining mechanism by which states are legally entitled to use force in their relations with one another is in the exercise of self-defence. The right of self-defence has been recognized as an essential element of international relations for centuries. However, until the right to resort to war as a means of self-help was formally removed by international law, the legal justification of self-defence was rarely invoked. Nevertheless, the traditional definition of the right of self-defence was established in the *Caroline Case* in 1837. Following a dispute between Britain and the United States over the supplying of arms to American nationals who were conducting raids into Canada which was then British territory, officials of both states agreed on the basic criteria of self-defence which required that there existed 'a necessity of self-defence, instant, overwhelming, leaving no choice of means and no moment for deliberation'.[129] While the actual circumstances of this case involved only the United States and Great Britain, the basic principles agreed in the case have been noted with approval on many subsequent occasions both by individual states and by international bodies. Accordingly, it is generally accepted that these criteria are part of customary international law and, as such, are binding on all states.

The criteria have been tested on many occasions since 1837, particularly in the latter part of the twentieth century following the specific reaffirmation of the 'inherent' right of self-defence in Article 51 of the UN Charter. During that period, few, if any states have resorted to the use of force without asserting the legal justification of self-defence. Thus the US quarantine of Cuba, support for the contras in Nicaragua, and attacks in Grenada and Panama, among others, have all been justified on the basis of self-defence. Similarly, interventions by the Soviet Union in Hungary, Czechoslovakia and Afghanistan have been justified on the same basis. Even the invasion by Iraq of Kuwait in 1990 was justified by Iraq as self-defence in support of the claim that Kuwait was part of Iraqi territory. The difficulty here, as with the determination of the legality of lawful countermeasures, is that the determination by a state that it has been threatened to the extent that it is allowed to use

---

129. *Caroline Case*, 29 BFSP 1137–8; 30 BFSP 195–6.

force in self-defence is inherently subjective. Thus, US claims to have been acting in self-defence following their attacks on Tripoli following the terrorist bombing of a discotheque in Berlin and, more recently, US attacks, on Afghan and Sudanese territory following the bombings of US embassies in East Africa in August 1998, can hardly be said fully to have fulfilled the criteria laid down in the *Caroline* incident. Nevertheless, the perception by the United States that in both cases there existed a continuing threat to United States' security interests cannot be directly challenged. The problem may well be exacerbated if, as many writers claim, there exists a right of anticipatory self-defence in the face of an imminent armed attack.[130]

Here again, however, international law sets the standards within which states will seek to place their justification. In this context, the ICJ in its advisory opinion on the *Legality of the Threat or Use of Nuclear Weapons*[131] has recently focused on necessity and proportionality as being the dominant criteria. Accordingly, as Malcolm Shaw has made clear: 'Quite what will be necessary and proportionate will depend on the circumstances of the case. It also appears inevitable that it will be the state contemplating such action that will first have to make that determination.'[132] Nevertheless, such a justification will have to be acceptable to the international community. Thus, Shaw continues: '[the determination] will be subject to consideration by the international community as a whole and more specifically by the Security Council under the terms of Article 51 {of the UN Charter]'.[133]

The issue of self-defence is perhaps one of the most problematic in contemporary international law. Even if third party determination were compulsory as part of international law, the nature of self-defence is such that states will be unwilling to wait for a determination of the existence of a threat to their security before taking what they determine to be in their interests. Furthermore, even where the Security Council is able to overcome the problem of the veto and make a determination that a purported measure of self-defence is in fact an act of aggression, as it did in the case of the Iraqi invasion of Kuwait, the existence of the veto

---

130. For a discussion of anticipatory self-defence see Shaw (1997), pp. 789–91.
131. (1996) ICJ Rep., para. 41.
132. Shaw (1997), p. 791.
133. *Idem.*

ensures that the five permanent members of the Security Council will be able to veto a resolution directed at them or one of their allies. Nevertheless, by delimiting the criteria in which self-defence can lawfully be exercised, international law is setting standards which states will seek to achieve in order to avoid condemnation by other states in the international community.

CHAPTER 2

THE GENERAL PRINCIPLES OF INTERNATIONAL LAW

In considering the nature and development of international law a number of assumptions have already been made about the general principles of international law. In particular, the consideration so far has progressed on the basis that states are sovereign, that states are the primary subjects of international law, and that the principal sources of international law are treaties and customary international law. The purpose of this chapter is to explain further and develop these basic assumptions as well as to introduce readers to some critical analysis, principally developed by international lawyers, regarding these basic assumptions.

STATES AS SOVEREIGN ENTITIES

Mention has already been made of the historical development of the concept of sovereignty, a concept which is at the root of much of the mis-understanding about international law. In particular, the belief in the concept of the 'absolute sovereignty' of states has questioned the possibility of international law not just as law but as a system of binding rules capable of affecting the behaviour of states. Thus, according to Hans Morgenthau, there is an apparent logical incompatibility of two assumptions which are central to international law: 'the assumption that international law imposes legal restraints upon the individual nations and the assumption that these very same nations are sovereign'.[1] Logic would seem to dictate that if sovereignty is absolute then international law and sovereignty are incompatible and international law is 'nothing but a delusion'.[2] However, Morgenthau was unwilling to make this

---

1. Morgenthau (1973), p. 307.
2. Brierly (1963), p. 16.

assertion, noting instead that sovereignty and international law are not incompatible insofar as international law is 'a decentralised, and hence weak and ineffective, international legal order'.[3] Accordingly for Morgenthau, '[international legal] rules are, as a matter of principle, binding only upon those nations which have consented to them'.[4] He continued:

> Only a relatively small number of rules of international law do not owe their existence to the consent of the members of the international community. They are either the logical precondition for the existence of any legal system such as rules of intepretation and rules providing sanctions, or they are the logical precondition of the existence of a multiple-state system, such as the rules delimiting the jurisdiction of individual states. Rules of this kind are binding upon all states, regardless of their consent, and might be called the common or necessary international law, the *jus necessarium* of the modern state system. Indeed, it makes sovereignty as a legal concept possible. For without the mutual respect for the territorial jurisdiction of the individual nation, and without the legal enforcement of that respect, international law and a state system based on it could obviously not exist.[5]

While this may have provided an adequate description of the international law that existed at the turn of the century, it cannot be viewed as accurate in respect of international law as we approach (at the time of writing) the twenty-first century. The question which therefore arises is how has the inherent incompatibility between the concept of the sovereignty of the state and the binding nature of international law been overcome?

What Is a State?

The logical starting point for an inquiry into this question is to define what is meant by the word 'state'. The basic criteria for statehood are to be found in Article 1 of the Montevideo Convention on the Rights and Duties of States 1933 which requires that: 'The state, as a person of international law should possess the following qualifications: (a) a permanent population; (b) a defined territory; (c) government; and (d) capacity to enter into relations with other states.'[6] The Convention itself has been ratified by only a very small number of South American states.

---

3. Morgenthau (1973), p. 307.
4. *Idem.*
5. *Idem.*
6. 28 AJIL, Supp., 75 (1934).

However, it is generally considered to have become the accepted definition of statehood and has evolved into a rule of customary international law. The requirements of population and territory are relatively uncontroversial. Essentially international law imposes no lower limit on the size of a population and recognizes that a population may be nomadic.[7] The question of territory does not require that a state have undisputed boundaries, simply that the territory have 'a sufficient consistency'.[8] Accordingly, Israel is generally considered to be a state in spite of the continuing dispute as to the exact extent of its territory. The requirement of government does not specify any particular type of government. In particular, there is no requirement that a government be democratic in order that the entity in question constitutes a state.

The most controversial of the criteria of statehood set out above is the fourth, that is the capacity to enter into international relations with other states. There is some debate as to whether this criterion requires that an entity be recognized by other states in order for it to exist as a state. If this were the case, recognition of a new state would be constitutive of statehood. However, the question immediately arises as to how many states are required to recognize an entity as a state before it exists as a state. The answer is unclear. If, for example, only one state were to recognize an entity as a state, as is the case in relation to the Turkish recognition of Northern Cyprus, that would surely be enough for an entity to fulfil the necessary criterion. The requirement that an entity be recognized by more than one state requires an arbitrary delimitation of the number of states that are required to recognize an entity before it can properly be called a state. Would recognition by five states be sufficient? Or ten? Or would the majority of states be required to recognize the new state? Or perhaps recognition by the overwhelming majority of states is required. Clearly, while the constitutive theory is superficially attractive as a way of denying statehood to entities and, more particularly, regimes which operate outside the normality of international relations, it has a number of drawbacks. Primarily, the question must be asked as to what is the status of an entity which in fact satisfies all the objective criteria of statehood but is not recognized by a sufficient number of states. Crucially, the question must be asked as to whether or not it is subject to international law?

Given the consequences of the constitutive theory outlined above, the

---

7. *Western Sahara Case* (1975) ICJ Rep. 12.
8. *Per* German-Polish Mixed Arbitral Tribunal in *Deutsche Continental Gas-Gesellschaft v Polish State* 5 A.D. 11 at p. 15 (1929).

majority of international lawyers consider recognition to be merely declarative of the status of an entity as a state under international law. Recognition is, therefore, an essentially political act. This does not mean, however, that recognition is entirely devoid of legal effect. The recognition of an entity as a state is required before a state can enter into bilateral relations with that entity. On the other hand, an express act of recognition is not required and can be implied from the actual creation of bilateral relations. More importantly, with regard to the municipal law of a state, an entity is devoid of the rights and duties of a state within municipal law if it is not recognized, either expressly or impliedly, by the state in question.

What then is meant by the requirement of capacity to enter into relations with other states? According to the US Restatement of the Law:

> An entity is not a state unless it has competence, within its own constitutional system, to conduct international relations with other states, as well as the political, technical and financial capabilities to do so. An entity which has the capacity to conduct foreign relations does not cease to be a state because it voluntarily turns over to another state some or all control of its foreign relations.[9]

It would appear, therefore, that the essence of the criteria of capacity to enter into relations with other states is that an entity be independent. What then is meant by independence? The leading case in this area is the *Austro-German Customs Union Case*.[10] The case involved the proposed creation of a customs union between Germany and Austria in 1933. Article 88 of the Treaty of Saint-Germain 1919 had provided that the independence of Austria was inalienable and a 1922 Protocol to that Treaty had provisions on the economic independence of Austria to the same effect. The PCIJ was asked whether the proposed customs union breached the terms of the Treaty or its Protocol. The Court held by eight votes to seven that the proposed customs union would be incompatible with the 1922 Protocol. Seven of the majority held that it would be incompatible with Article 88 of the Treaty. The opinion of the majority was to the effect that independence required *sole* right of decision in all matters political, financial or other. However, the decision was very much dependent on its facts. In particular, the majority were concerned with the ongoing expansion of Germany which the 1919 Treaty had been intended to suppress. Accordingly, the decision of the majority is not

9. American Law Institute (1986), Vol. I, s. 201, p. 73.
10. (1931) PCIJ Ser. A/B, No. 41.

regarded as providing an acceptable definition of independence. It is the separate opinion of Judge Anzilotti in the case which is now regarded as providing the better view of independence. According to Anzilotti:

> [T]he independence of Austria within the meaning of Article 88 is nothing else but the existence of Austria within the frontiers laid down by the Treaty of Saint-Germain, as a separate State and not subject to the authority of any other State or group of States. Independence as thus understood is nothing more than the normal condition of States according to international law.

This position clearly illustrates that insofar as states normally enter into bilateral and multilateral arrangements which affect their *sole* right of decision in international relations, that does not interfere with their independence and, consequently, their statehood. The classic modern illustration of this point is the existence of the European Union.

The European Economic Community was created in 1957, primarily as an economic institution aimed at improving living standards in Western Europe. The consequent creation of the European Common Market and, eventually, the Single European Market in 1986, brought with it increasing calls for closer political integration of the member states. The creation of the European Union in 1992 resulted in commitments from all member states to work towards a Common Foreign and Security Policy. This began as a separate non-integrated pillar of European cooperation but has more recently been fully integrated into the European institutional structure by the Amsterdam Treaty. The closer cooperation in foreign and defence matters has already been witnessed in the attempts to deal with the break-up of the former Yugoslavia. More recently, in Kosovo, the European Union was seen to speak with one voice on policy matters. There is no reason to doubt that this 'ever closer union' of the member states of the European Union will continue. However, few would argue that the member states of the Union are anything other than independent states. Nevertheless, the impact of the European Union on the issue of state sovereignty remains a hotly debated issue.

State Sovereignty and International Law

The issue of sovereignty has recently come to be regarded as a political hot potato in the debate within the United Kingdom regarding its existing and future commitments with regard to the European Union. In particular, the current debate on whether or not to enter into the Single

European Currency is often painted in stark terms as a choice between the retention of sovereignty and the handing over of British sovereignty to Brussels. Put in such terms, the issue of the maintenance of British sovereignty is shrouded in emotion. The fact of the matter is, however, that the sovereignty argument used in this context is not only misleading, it is fundamentally incorrect. Perhaps surprisingly, the clearest argument on this point is to be found in the work of Morgenthau. According to Morgenthau: 'Sovereignty is not freedom from legal restraint.' He continued:

> The quantity of legal obligations by which the nation limits its freedom of action does not, as such, limit its sovereignty. The oft-heard argument that a certain treaty would impose upon a nation obligations so onerous as to destroy its sovereignty is, therefore, meaningless. It is not the quantity of legal restraints that affects sovereignty, but their quality. A nation can take upon itself any quantity of legal restraint and still remain sovereign, provided those legal restraints do not affect its quality as the supreme law-giving and law-enforcing authority.[11]

One might add, for sake of clarity the words, 'upon its territory'. For if sovereignty is to mean anything in international law, it is with regard to the question of title to territory that it is most closely associated.

Once again, one might turn to UK membership of the European Union to illustrate this point. The fact of the matter is that European legislation is passed on a daily basis. Much of that legislation is directly applicable in the United Kingdom, meaning that it does not have to be enacted separately into UK law to have effect within it. This applies often to legislation to which the United Kingdom has not only not given its direct consent but which, in many cases, it has actually opposed. Furthermore, such legislation is enforceable not only by the UK authorities but also, in many cases, directly by European institutions. Nevertheless, in the same way that the United Kingdom was free to enter into the European Community in 1972, it remains free, subject to the limitations contained in the Treaty of Rome 1957, to leave the Union. Thus, the UK Parliament remains the supreme law-maker in the United Kingdom.

A further crucial point on the relationship between sovereignty and international law was made by Morgenthau when he declared that:

> Sovereignty is not freedom from regulation by international law of all those matters which are traditionally left to the discretion of the

---

11. Morgenthau (1973), pp. 310–11.

individual nations ... The relation between the matters international law regulates and those with which it does not concern itself is fluid. It depends upon the politics pursued by individual nations and upon the development of international law.[12]

A similar point had previously been made by the PCIJ in one of its first cases, the *Nationality Decrees in Tunis and Morocco Case*[13] in 1923 in which it declared that: 'The question whether a certain matter is or is not solely within the jurisdiction of a state is an essentially relative question; it depends upon the development of international law.'

What then is the position of sovereignty in modern international law? Certainly, at the time of the decision in the *Nationality Decrees in Morocco and Tunisia Case*, the idea of what was within the sole competence of states was much broader. Thus, according to Judge Huber, sole arbitrator in the *Islands of Palmas Case*[14] in 1928, anything done on the territory of a state fell within the exclusive competence of that state:

> Sovereignty in the relations between states signifies independence. Independence in regard to a portion of the globe is the right to exercise therein, to the exclusion of any other state, the functions of a state. The development of the national organisation of states during the last few centuries and, as a corollary, the development of international law, have established this principle of the exclusive competence of the state in regard to its own territory in such a way as to make it the point of departure in settling most questions that concern international relations.

This position appears to be reflected in Article 2, paragraph 7 of the UN Charter which states that: 'Nothing contained in the present Charter shall authorise the United Nations to intervene in matters which are essentially within the domestic jurisdiction of any state.' Nevertheless, there are a number of limitations militating against Article 2(7) being read too broadly. First, Article 2(7) is specifically limited by express wording to the effect that the principle of non-intervention 'shall not prejudice the application of enforcement measures under Chapter VII'. Furthermore, use of the words 'essentially within', if given a broad interpretation, gives much more scope for the United Nations to intervene in what might previously have been considered to be within the exclusive competence of a state. This particular point may be illustrated by reference to the development of the international law of human rights during the latter part of the twentieth century. As Michael

---

12. Morgenthau (1973), p. 311.
13. (1923) PCIJ Ser. B, No. 4.
14. (1928) 2 RIAA 829.

Reisman has argued: 'The United Nations Charter replicates the "domestic jurisdiction–international concern" dichotomy, but no serious scholar still supports the contention that internal human rights are "essentially within the domestic jurisdiction of any state" and hence insulated from international law.'[15]

The extent to which states can ever be said to have been endowed with an external sovereignty, which placed them above the law, is certainly debatable. However, in modern day international relations where states interact with one another on a daily basis, not only at governmental level but also at all possible levels of interaction, any claim of absolute sovereignty becomes impossible. As regards the impact of international law on the internal sovereignty of states, this remains a hotly debated issue. However, insofar as international law does exist and states accept that it does exist by continuing to enter into international agreements and by continuing to observe customary international law, the existence of the internal sovereignty of states stands not as an obstacle to international law but as a mechanism providing for the distribution of power in the international relations of states.

STATES AS THE PRIMARY SUBJECTS OF INTERNATIONAL LAW

In order to be considered as a subject of international law, an entity must be capable of possessing rights and duties under international law and have the procedural capacity to enforce those rights and duties. Traditionally only states were considered as fulfilling the necessary requirements. While it will be shown that international law has developed to recognize further categories of subjects, it cannot be denied that states remain the primary subjects of international law.

There are four factors that point towards the primacy of states in international law. First, international law is primarily a system of law between states. It is made by states and is concerned with regulating the interactions of states. Secondly, the ICJ, the principal judicial organ recognized by international law, is open in its contentious jurisdiction only to states.[16] Thirdly, where an individual suffers harm abroad, that individual cannot bring a claim under international law directly against the state in which he/she was harmed. Such a claim must be brought by

---

15. Reisman (1990), p. 869.
16. ICJ Statute, Article 34.

his/her national state. Finally, when a state pursues such a claim, it is not acting as an agent of the individual. It is pursuing its own claim.[17]

More recently, however, in a development considered to be 'one of the more significant features of contemporary international law',[18] the recognized subjects of international law have been expanded to include international organizations and, to a limited degree, individuals. Other putative subjects of international law include insurgents and national liberation movements. However, consideration will be given here only to international organizations and individuals.

International Organizations

Certain international organizations are now commonly regarded as having international legal personality. As international legal persons, international organizations have the capacity to enter into international treaties, convene international conferences, send and receive diplomatic missions, present protests to states and bring international claims.[19] For an international organization to have legal personality it must be distinguishable from its member states and have organs 'capable of exercising such legal capacity and responsibilities on the international plane'.[20]

A fundamental question that arises in this context concerns the extent to which international organizations are dependent on states for their international legal personality. For the early international organizations this was certainly the case and many of the features of these early organizations remain today. For example, all international organizations are created by states by means of a constitutive instrument usually in the form of a treaty. To this extent, international organizations clearly derive their legal personality from states. Nevertheless, two further questions have arisen. First, to what extent is it possible to infer international legal personality from the objects and purposes of an international organization? Secondly, is it possible for international organizations to have objective legal personality?

---

17. See the judgment of the PCIJ in *Mavrommatis Palestine Concessions Case (Jurisdiction)* 1924 PCIJ, Ser. A, No. 2, p. 12, where the court observed that: 'Once a state has taken up a case on behalf of one of its subjects before an international tribunal, in the eyes of the latter the state is sole claimant.'
18. Henkin *et al.* (1987), p. 229.
19. See further Rama-Montaldo (1970), p. 123.
20. Henkin *et al.* (1987), p. 321.

With regard to the first question, the primary focus is on the power of an organization to undertake certain acts. Traditionally, in line with the view that international organizations derive their legal personality only from states, it was considered that the powers of an organization had to be specifically provided for in the constitutive instrument of the organization or implied therefrom on the basis of necessity. The leading case on this question is the *Reparations Case* which was heard by the ICJ in 1949.[21] The case concerned the murder of Count Bernadotte, a Swedish national who was killed while serving for the United Nations in the new city of Jerusalem, which was, at the time, under Israeli control. The Court was asked whether the United Nations could itself bring a claim for reparations against Israel in respect of the death of Count Bernadotte. Judge Hackworth (dissenting) stated what might be regarded as the traditional view of the international legal personality of international organizations when he noted that:

> It is to be presumed that such powers as the Member States desired to confer upon [the United Nations] are stated either in the Charter or in complementary agreements concluded by them. Powers not expressed cannot freely be implied. Implied powers flow from a grant of expressed powers, and are limited to those that are 'necessary' to the exercise of the powers expressly granted.[22]

The majority found, however, that, with regard to the bringing of a claim for reparations, although the Charter did not expressly provide for such a possibility, 'it is necessary that, when an infringement occurs, the organization should be able to call upon the responsible state to remedy its default, and, in particular, to obtain from the state reparation for the damage that the default may have caused to its agent'.[23]

More generally, the decision of the ICJ in the *Reparations Case* suggests that international legal personality can be inferred from the purposes for which the organization was created. Thus, according to the Court: 'It must be acknowledged that its Members, by entrusting certain functions to it, with the attendant duties and responsibilities, have clothed it with the competence required to enable those functions to be effectively discharged.'[24] Louis Henkin *et al.* consider this aspect of international legal personality to be inherent.[25] Accordingly, while the *Reparations Case*

---

21. *Reparations for Injuries Suffered in the Services of the United Nations* (1949) ICJ Rep. 174.
22. *Idem*, p. 198.
23. *Idem*, p. 183.
24. *Idem*, p. 179.
25. Henkin *et al.* (1987), pp. 321–2 and 331–3.

dealt specifically with the powers of the United Nations, which the Court recognized as being 'the supreme type of international organisation', the basic principle can be stated that an international organization will be deemed to have sufficient inherent personality as is required in order to allow it to perform the functions for which it was created. This approach is less concerned with the specific details of the constitutive agreement by which the organization was created and more with ensuring the proper functioning of the organization. Further, it allows for the organization itself to develop through its own practice. As Shaw has noted with respect to the United Nations, 'UN experience demonstrates that the derivative denomination is unsatisfactory. The significance of this relates to [its] ability to extend [its] international rights and duties on the basis of both constituent instruments and subsequent practices and to [its] capacity to affect the creation of further international persons and play a role in the norm-creating process.'[26]

This brings into focus the second supplementary question referred to earlier concerning the objective legal personality of international organizations which would allow international organizations to perform any international act which they are not prohibited from doing by their own internal (constitutional) rules even as against states which are not members of the organization. Here again the *Reparations Case* is the leading authority. In it the Court argued that:

> [F]ifty States, representing the vast majority of the international community, had the power, in conformity with international law, to bring into being an entity possessing objective international personality and not merely personality recognized by them alone, together with the capacity to bring international claims.[27]

Accordingly, in that case, a claim for reparations could be brought against Israel even though at the time of the murder of Count Bernadotte, Israel was not a member of the United Nations.

Henkin *et al.* doubt whether, even if such objective legal personality were available to international organizations, they would have reason to use it. They note that: 'There is little reason to expect that any international organizations will assert a general inherent legal power to perform "sovereign" international acts on grounds of their objective legal personality irrespective of the constitutional definition of their functions and powers.'[28] Nevertheless, it is the ability to conduct relations with any

---

26. Shaw (1997) p. 192.
27. *Reparations Case*, p. 185.
28. Henkin *et al.* (1987), p. 333.

other subject of international law which is at the heart of the attribution of objective legal personality. Thus, Malcolm Shaw has noted: 'The creation of objective legal personality will of necessity be harder to achieve and will require the action in essence of the international community as a whole or a substantial element.'[29] Accordingly, it is unlikely that many international organizations beyond the United Nations will achieve objective legal personality.

For many international relations scholars, this analysis of the international legal personality of international organizations will appear formalistic and rigid. However, the impact of the recognition of the international legal personality of international organizations should not be underestimated. First, international organizations were the first entities other than states to be recognized as possessing rights and duties under international law. Secondly, non-lawyers should welcome the focus on the objects and purpose of international organizations in determining legal personality as opposed to the former more rigorously black-letter-type analysis of the relevant constituent instruments. Similarly, such an approach recognizes the fact that international organizations can and do evolve, particularly as regards their internal rules and procedures.[30] Finally, the recognition of the objective legal personality of certain international institutions comes close to recognizing that these organizations can and do operate as unitary actors on the international stage.

Individuals

The question of the personality of individuals under international law has troubled international lawyers for centuries. It is undisputed that individuals are the primary legal subjects of each and every municipal legal system throughout the world. Accordingly, individuals in different states will be subject to different laws depending on such factors as the level of development, the political persuasion and religious heritage of each state. However, it cannot be denied that even among states with vastly different cultural, social and economic backgrounds, there exist many similar, even identical laws. Thus, for example, murder is recognized as a crime in most, if not all, legal systems of the world. Similarly, most legal systems will have some form of law, however

---

29. Shaw (1997), p. 191.
30. See Krasner (1982), p. 187.

rudimentary, governing the exchange of goods and other property. If international law were simply an amalgamation of these different laws into one general legal system there would be no question as to the legal personality of individuals. However, international law is not such a system. It is a system of law that exists to regulate international relations, primarily between states.

According to the traditional view of international law, where individuals are the subjects of rights and duties under international law, those rights and duties are created not by the individuals themselves but by states. Here again, therefore, as with international organizations, individuals, insofar as they are subjects of international law, are regarded as having only derivative rights and duties. According to Phillip Jessup: 'So long ... as the international community is composed of states, it is only through an exercise of their will, as expressed through treaty or agreement or as laid down by an international authority deriving its power from states, that a rule of law becomes binding upon an individual.'[31]

However, the twentieth century has seen a concerted effort among many international lawyers and international relations specialists to recognize the rights of individuals. The most noticeable development in this process has been in the development of the international law of human rights. It is not intended in this book to consider in depth the issue of the place of international human rights in either international law or international relations. Nevertheless, it cannot be denied that the development of international human rights over the past fifty or so years beginning with the UN Charter has had considerable impact on both of these fields of study. No one today could deny the fact that individuals do have human rights recognized at international law. International instruments such as the Universal Declaration of Human Rights 1948 and the International Covenants on Civil and Political Rights and Economic, Social and Cultural Rights of 1966 have established the basic foundations of international human rights law. By virtue of the fact that these instruments are regarded as having evolved into customary international law, the requirement to recognize basic human rights is binding on all states. The issue here, however, is not whether such instruments are binding on states, rather it is concerned with the question whether individuals, by having rights under international law, can be considered as subjects of that law.

The crucial question in this regard depends upon whether individuals

---

31. Jessup (1949), pp. 17–18.

have the capacity to enforce those rights directly under international law. The answer would appear to be dependent upon the requirements of the particular international agreement on which the right is founded and on the attitude of the individual's national state. The best known right of individual petition recognized by a universal human rights treaty is that provided for in the First Optional Protocol to the International Covenant on Civil and Political Rights, Article 1 of which allows a state party to recognize 'the competence of the [Human Rights] Committee to receive and consider communications from individuals subject to its jurisdiction who claim to be victims of a violation by that State party of any of the rights set forth in the Covenant'. However, as the name suggests, this aspect of the Covenant is optional even for those parties to the Covenant itself and there are a number of state parties to the Covenant which have not in fact signed up to the optional protocol. Various other international agreements provide for a direct right of petition by individuals. These include the European Convention on Human Rights of 1950, the European Communities Treaty 1957 and the Inter-American Convention on Human Rights 1969. Thus, as Higgins has noted, 'there is *no inherent reason* why the individual should not be able directly to invoke international law and to be a beneficiary of international law'.[32] However, as she herself admits, where such rights do exist, they are created on the basis of the consent of states. It will not go unnoticed, particularly by liberal scholars in the international relations field, that the vast majority of state parties to these instruments are liberal democratic states.

As regards the imposition of duties upon individuals under international law, the development of this field of international law in fact began in the eighteenth and nineteenth centuries. Recognizing the limitations of territorial sovereignty in respect of certain international crimes, international law sought to establish the individual criminal liability of individuals under international law in respect of those crimes through the jurisdictional principle known as universality. According to this principle, a state has jurisdiction over a particular crime regardless of the place of commission of the crime. It works essentially on the basis that a state is required to prosecute an individual accused of such crimes or, where it is not willing or able to prosecute, to extradite the accused to a state which is willing or able to prosecute.

The origins of the principle of universality lie in the attempts to deal with the problem of piracy. Pirates were able to escape prosecution by

---

32. Higgins (1994), p. 54 (emphasis in original).

operating on the high seas outside the territorial jurisdiction of any state. Accordingly, it was necessary for states to agree that each and every state should be able to exercise jurisdiction in order for pirates to be brought to justice and, perhaps more importantly, to reduce the opportunity for pirates to interfere with the economic interests of the most powerful maritime nations. Similar developments occurred in relation to slave trading as the economic costs of slavery began to outweigh the benefits. The exercise of jurisdiction over pirates and slave traders rarely interfered with the territorial jurisdiction of other states and the principle of universal jurisdiction in respect of such crimes quickly became part of customary international law.

The principle of universality was extended after the Second World War by the Nuremberg and Tokyo Tribunals to cover war crimes. There is some doubt as to the legality of the Nuremberg and Tokyo Tribunals. However, such doubts have been dispelled by the clear acceptance by the international community of the decisions of these tribunals, most notably in the form of the Affirmation of the Principles of International Law recognized by the Charter of Nuremberg adopted by the UN General Assembly on 11 December 1946. Although the Nuremberg and Tokyo Tribunals did, on some occasions, override the territorial jurisdiction of Germany and Japan, many of the alleged offences were committed outside the territory of these states. Furthermore, where territorial jurisdiction did exist, both states had been defeated in the war and little consideration was given by the allied nations to their sovereign rights. It is worth noting that, while some states have successfully prosecuted war criminals in respect of crimes committed during the Second World War in their domestic courts, the majority of such prosecutions took place before the international tribunals at Nuremberg and Tokyo. Similar international tribunals have been set up in recent years to deal with war crimes in Rwanda and the former Yugoslavia. Accordingly it has not been left to individual states to initiate prosecutions in these cases.

Subsequent attempts to provide for universal jurisdiction in respect of other 'international' crimes have had to overcome the fundamental obstacle of the territorial jurisdiction of the state in which the alleged crime has been committed. In such cases, it would appear imperative for states specifically to consent to the exercise of a jurisdiction which has the effect of overriding its own territorial jurisdiction. Accordingly, the creation of such jurisdiction has only been possible through the creation of international treaty regimes which provide for a form of universal jurisdiction to be exercised on the basis of specific consent of the states involved in the regime, through their ratification of the relevant treaty instrument. In fact, successful treaty regimes have been created in order to deal with such matters as hijacking, terrorism, crimes against internationally protected persons and certain so-called crimes against humanity including torture. Nevertheless, it is apparent, that the imposition of international legal responsibility on individuals in this way is, once again, essentially dependent upon the acceptance of these duties by states. The requirement of state consent in this regard is most clearly illustrated by reference to the attempts to create the recently established International Criminal Court. The Court's jurisdiction is not universal. It is able to try only nationals of the states which have signed and ratified its Statute. To date, very few states have fully committed themselves to the Statute.

Of course it may be possible to argue that as states are made up of individuals, it is individuals and not states who are the ultimate beneficiaries of rights under international law. It is with regard to the imposition of duties under international law, however, that the strongest arguments have been made. As Sir Hersch Lauterpacht has put it: '[T]o limit the operation of the duties prescribed by international law to the impersonal entity of the state as distinguished from the individuals who compose them and who act on their behalf is to open the door wide for the acceptance, in international relations of states, of standards of morality different from those applying amongst individuals.'[33] He continued: '[I]t is difficult to escape the conclusion that unless legal duties are accepted as resting upon an individual being, they do not in practice and, to some extent in law, obligate anyone.'[34] Finally, according to Lauterpacht, the lack of procedural capacity should not stop an entity from being accepted as a subject of international law as long as that entity is capable of possessing rights and duties under international law. Thus:

> The fact that the beneficiary of rights is not authorised to take independent steps in his own name to enforce them does not signify that he is not a subject of the law or that the rights in question are vested exclusively in the agency which possesses the capacity to enforce them. Thus in relation to the current view that the rights of the alien within foreign territory are the rights of his state and not his own, the correct way of stating the legal position is not that the state asserts its own exclusive right but that it enforces, in substance, the right of the individual who, as the law now stands, is incapable of asserting it in the international sphere.[35]

---

33. Lauterpacht (1947), p. 438.
34. *Idem*, p. 438.
35. *Idem*.

A similar view is put forward by the proponents of more policy-oriented perspectives of international law, particularly the adherents of the New Haven School of international law, one of whom has noted that 'the fact remains that the individual is the ultimate beneficiary even of the remedy of diplomatic protection ... the international standard for the treatment of aliens (meaning potentially all human beings) and state responsibility for injuries to aliens constitute a vital part of customary international law, not an exception or aberration'.[36] Scholars sympathetic to the New Haven approach argue that the subject/object dichotomy is 'an intellectual prison of our own choosing'.[37] These scholars argue that international law is a decision-making process in which individuals participate. Accordingly, individuals, as well as states and international organizations and, indeed, multilateral corporations and non-governmental groups, are participants in the international legal system. Rosalyn Higgins has explained the philosophy of this approach:

> In the way our world is organised, it is states which are most interested in, for example, sea space, or boundaries, or treaties; it is thus states which advance claims and counter-claims about these. Individuals' interests lie in other directions: in protection from the physical excesses of others, in their personal treatment abroad, in the protection abroad of their property interests, in fairness and predictability in their international business transactions and in securing some external support for the establishment of a tolerable balance between their rights and duties within their national state. Thus, the topics of minimum standards of treatment of aliens, requirements as to the conduct of hostilities and human rights are not simply exceptions conceded by historical chance within a system of rules that operate between states. Rather, they are simply part and parcel of the fabric of international law, representing the claims that are naturally made by individual participants in contradistinction to state-participants.[38]

These and similar analyses have been highly influential amongst international lawyers who, while generally accepting the continuing pre-eminent role of states as the primary subjects of international law, are more and more willing to emphasize the role of the individual in international legal matters. Thus critical international lawyers will focus on the role of organizations such as the International Red Cross in the creation and enforcement of humanitarian law and that of Amnesty

---

36. Chen (1989), p. 77.
37. Higgins (1994), p. 49.
38. Higgins (1978), p. 5.

International with regard to human rights. The development of transnational law dealing with international relations at and below the level of the state is increasingly referred to as a movement away from the statist paradigm. However, unlike international relations, international law cannot simply turn away from existing models and construct new ones without undermining the whole structure of the legal system as it stands today. Accordingly, such theorists are commonly referred to as deconstructivists and find their analysis sidelined. Nevertheless, as we will see, the potential for interdisciplinary work between international lawyers and international relations specialists have given new impetus to such critical approaches, both in international law and international relations.

The position of individuals under international law is well summed up by Shaw:

> [The] vast array of practice with regard to the international rights and duties of the individual under customary and treaty law clearly demonstrates that individuals are subjects of international law. It remains only to determine the nature and extent of this personality, while recognising that the current structure of international relations militates against anything other than a limited personality for individuals.[39]

THE SOURCES OF INTERNATIONAL LAW

The topic of the sources of international law is, perhaps, the most important of all in international law. It underpins all other topic areas, and constant reference must be made to an analysis of the relative weight to be given to the various sources. Nevertheless, there is considerable debate amongst international lawyers as to what is meant by the words 'sources of international law' and, indeed, whether sources is an appropriate term to use. Thus, according to D. P. O'Connell: 'The expression "source" is unclear, for it is a figurative association that is misleading as to the way in which international rules come about.'[40]

It is intended here to consider the sources question in terms of where one finds international law and what gives particular rules of international law their legal status. In the absence of a centralized law-making

---

39. Shaw (1997), p. 190.
40. O'Connell (1971), p. 5.

authority in international law, the task of identifying the relevant rules of international law is rendered substantially more difficult than is the case in municipal law. However, it is generally accepted that the two primary sources of international law are treaties and customary international law. Customary international law will be dealt with first.

Customary International Law

It is for the sake of clarity that it is necessary to consider first the status of customary international law as a source of international law before moving on to consider treaties. As will be shown, treaties cannot constitute a source of universal international law as such, whereas customary international law does purport to bind all states except those that have specifically objected to the creation of a particular rule. Customary international law is classically defined in Article 38(1) of the Statute of the ICJ as 'evidence of a general practice accepted as law'. However, as Higgins has pointed out, 'it is generally accepted that it is custom that is the source to be applied, and that it is practice which evidences the custom ... Thus Article 38 could more correctly have been phrased to read "international custom as *evidenced* by a general practice accepted as law." In fact, this is the way the clause is interpreted in practice.'[41] However one chooses to read this definition, it is clear that customary international law envisages two elements, first, the objective element of state practice and, secondly, the subjective element known as *opinio juris sive necessitatis* or the belief that a particular practice is accepted as law.

The material element – state practice

The requirement of state practice as an element of customary international law may, at first, seem relatively uncontroversial. After all, in a decentralized system of law the question of what states actually do is central to the identification of whether a particular rule of law exists. However, when one begins to consider questions directed at the identification and relevance of particular state practice, one soon realizes that the task of identifying relevant state practice for the purposes of discerning a particular rule of customary international law is not an easy one.

---

41. Higgins (1994), p. 18.

What is state practice?

Certain writers have asserted that state practice is limited to the physical acts of a state. Thus, Anthony D'Amato asserts that a claim cannot be the act of a state until the state has taken the necessary action to turn a claim into actual practice.[42] For D'Amato, a claim that a particular rule of customary international law exists has to be 'enforced' by the state actually doing something. Other writers have, however, disputed this assertion. According to Michael Akehurst, for example, state practice is to be found in the diplomatic correspondence between states in which arguments are made without examination as to whether claims have ever been enforced.[43] For Akehurst, the danger of D'Amato's approach is the inevitable conflict that will flow from states asserting physical acts against one another.[44] As Michael Byers has observed, D'Amato's approach 'leaves little room for diplomacy and peaceful persuasion, and, perhaps most importantly, marginalises less powerful states in the process of customary international law'.[45] The better view therefore is that state practice includes any act or statement by a state. This view is supported by a number of decisions of the ICJ in which the Court has looked at statements and other non-physical acts of states in order to determine the existence or otherwise of rules of customary international law.[46]

Accordingly, one can look to the statements of state governments or executives in order to discover state practice in a certain area. The executive of a state is not a single entity but is made up of numerous departments, many of whose officials have the authority to determine national policy in areas of international law. It is this policy that constitutes state practice rather than the, occasional, physical acts by which states manifest their policy. State practice is not limited either to executive statements or action. It may exist in a decision of a state's courts, or in a legislative act. Thus, for Akehurst, 'state practice means any act from which views about customary international law can be inferred; it includes physical acts, claims, declarations *in abstracto* (such as

---

42. D'Amato (1971), p. 88.
43. Akehurst (1974–5), p. 2.
44. *Idem*, p. 3.
45. Byers (1999), p. 134.
46. See, in particular, the *Asylum Case* (1950) ICJ Rep. 265; the *Rights of United States Nationals in Morocco Case* (1952) ICJ Rep. 176; the *North Sea Continental Shelf Cases* (1969) ICJ Rep. 3; the *Anglo-Norwegian Fisheries Case* (1951) ICJ Rep. 3 and the *Nicaragua Case (Merits)* (1986) ICJ Rep. 14.

General Assembly resolutions), national laws, national judgments and omissions'.[47] Furthermore, as Shaw points out, 'the evidence of what a state does can be obtained from numerous sources'.[48] These would include newspapers and journals as well as official publications, historical records and speeches of government officials. Of particular relevance in this regard are statements made at international meetings, for example, at the General Assembly or at a negotiating conference or simply in the course of a visit to a foreign state.

Duration of state practice

Traditionally, a number of decades were required to pass before a practice could be considered to have evolved into a rule of customary international law. It is now recognized that the development of custom can take place over a relatively short period. However, the claim by some that custom can be instantaneous[49] is extremely dubious. Even if state practice can be identified in the verbal statements rather than physical acts of a state or its representatives, states should be given time to react to a claim that a new rule of customary international law exists. Nevertheless, it is clear that the traditional requirement of long duration is much less important nowadays and that, in new areas of relations between states, a practice can evolve very quickly indeed into a rule of customary international law.

Two examples of rules of customary international law which have developed relatively quickly are the law of outer space, most of which was developed between 1957 and 1966, and the law governing the exclusive economic zone which developed between 1973 and 1983. In the case of outer space law, the development of customary international law was helped by the fact that there were no pre-existing rules of customary international law relating to the use of outer space which had to be overcome by the new rules. Furthermore, few, if any, states objected to the development of outer space law which was premised on the principle of the Common Heritage of Mankind and provided, in particular, for non-appropriation by states of parts of outer space and for the use of outer space exclusively for peaceful purposes. Such principles were initially formulated in General Assembly resolutions which, while not in themselves legally binding, were indicative of state practice in this

---

47. Akehurst (1974–5), p. 53.
48. Shaw (1997), p. 65.
49. See Cheng (1965).

area. The development of the law in this area was also helped by the fact that the only two states that were able to engage in actual physical practice in this area, the United States and the Soviet Union, acted in compliance with the developing principles of customary international law as laid down in the relevant General Assembly resolutions.

The exclusive economic zone or EEZ is an area of sea extending up to 200 miles from a state's coast in which coastal states have certain exclusive rights including *inter alia* the right to explore, exploit, conserve and manage living and non-living natural resources, including, most importantly, fish stocks. The concept of an exclusive economic zone was first mooted at the Third United Nations Conference on the Law of the Sea (UNCLOS III) in 1973. The intention was to provide a compromise between states seeking a 200-mile territorial sea in which states have exclusive control and those seeking to limit the power of coastal states. The compromise proved popular and before the Conference had reached the stage of agreeing on the terms of a draft Convention, many states were asserting in their practice the right to an EEZ. In this case, this was in direct conflict to the previously existing rule that areas beyond the territorial sea constituted the high seas, which were free to all states. Nevertheless, the number of states claiming an EEZ, coupled with the recognition and acceptance of those claims by other states, ensured that the right to claim an EEZ soon became a right established under customary international law.

Generality of state practice

The key requirement of state practice in relation to customary international law is the generality or uniformity of a practice. The ICJ noted in the *Asylum Case* that a customary rule must be 'in accordance with a constant and uniform usage practised by the states in question'.[50] In the *North Sea Continental Shelf Cases* the Court required that state practice 'including that of states whose interests are specially affected, should be both extensive and virtually uniform in the sense of the provision to be invoked'.[51] In the *Anglo-Norwegian Fisheries Case* the Court stated the position in the reverse holding that where the practice of states is generally conflicting and discordant, it is difficult to say that a rule of customary international law has evolved.[52] Essentially, the

---

50. (1950) ICJ Rep. 265, at pp. 276–7.
51. (1969) ICJ Rep. 3, at p. 43.
52. (1951) ICJ Rep. 116, at p. 131.

number of states following a particular practice is central to the determination of the evolution of a practice into a rule of customary international law. That practice must be virtually uniform, it should include the practice of specially affected states and there should be no general conflicting practice. The position was summarized by the ICJ in the *Nicaragua Case (Merits)*:

> It is not to be expected that in the practice of States the application of the rules in question should have been perfect ... The Court does not consider that for a rule to be established as customary, the corresponding practice must be in absolutely rigorous conformity with the rule. In order to deduce the existence of customary rules, the Court deems it sufficient that the conduct of States should, in general, be consistent with such rules, and that instances of State conduct inconsistent with a given rule should generally have been treated as breaches of that rule, not as indications of the recognition of a new rule. If a State acts in a way *prima facie* incompatible with a recognized rule, but defends its conduct by appealing to exceptions or justifications contained in the rule itself, then whether or not that State's conduct is in fact justifiable on that basis, the significance of that attitude is to confirm rather than weaken the rule.[53]

Finally, it is clear that the reaction of other states to a new practice will be determinative of whether that practice evolves into a rule of customary international law. There are five possible responses a state can have to a new practice in customary international law. First, the state can follow the practice. In so doing, the state places itself under an obligation to continue to follow the practice after the evolution of the rule of customary international law. The same outcome is true of the second example of possible state practice, which is acquiescence. If a state acquiesces in the practice of another state, that former state cannot later protest when such practice becomes custom and it may find itself bound by such custom. The third example of possible state practice (or lack of it), is silence. According to Ian Brownlie, 'silence may denote either tacit agreement or a simple lack of interest in the issue'.[54] It is probable, however, that where there is an interest, silence seems to denote acquiescence. It is possible, however, to read too much into silence in any particular instance. This can be seen from the decision of the PCIJ in the *Lotus Case*[55] in which French silence on the question of extraterritorial jurisdiction was probably incorrectly interpreted as acquiescence.

---

53. (1986) ICJ Rep. 14, at p. 88
54. Brownlie (1998), p. 6.
55. (1927) PCIL Rep. Ser. A, No. 10, at 28.

Fourthly, a state may protest about a particular practice. This would slow down the evolution of a new rule of customary international law. It would also result in the protesting state not being bound by the practice were it to become a rule of customary international law. An example of this is to be found in the *North Sea Continental Shelf Cases*[56] in which Denmark and the Netherlands contended that Article 6 of the Geneva Convention on the Continental Shelf of 1958 had evolved into customary international law and was therefore binding on West Germany, which was not a party to the Convention. However, West Germany had continually protested that they would not be bound by the provisions of Article 6. The Court decided first that there was insufficient generality of practice to allow Article 6 to be regarded as a rule of customary international law and, secondly, that even if the practice had been sufficient, West Germany could not be bound because of its protests. Where a sufficient number of states protest about a particular practice, that will prevent the evolution of the practice into customary international law. The fifth and final example of possible state practice is contrary practice. Once again, this will slow down, or, where a sufficient number of states engage in a contrary practice, stop the evolution of a particular rule and the state(s) engaging in the contrary practice will not be bound if and when a rule of customary international law is developed.

The subjective element – opinio juris sive necessitatis

'The philosopher's stone which transmutes the inert mass of accumulated usage into the gold of binding rules'[57] or simply a fiction to disguise the creative power of the judges? Literally translated, *opinio juris* means the belief that an act is legally necessary and is intended to allow a proper distinction to be made between law and mere usage. The concept is best illustrated by example. As was noted above, it is sometimes said of resolutions of the General Assembly of the United Nations that they create instant custom especially if they are unanimous or a substantial number of states vote for them and they are of a general norm-creating character.[58] As the United Nations is made up of all but four or five states, each of which has a vote in the General Assembly, it is easy to see how a resolution of the General Assembly can be looked upon as

---

56. (1969) ICJ Rep. 3.
57. Thirlway (1972), p. 47.
58. See, in particular, Cheng (1965).

creating instant custom. The difficulty, however, is that resolutions of the General Assembly are not legally binding instruments and so states, when voting for a particular resolution, do not have the intention to be legally bound by the terms of that resolution. In other words, the *opinio juris* necessary for a practice to become custom is lacking. It may be that if the states continue to follow the practice as laid down in the resolution in a manner that shows intention to be bound then that practice will evolve into customary law in what might be a relatively short time. Thus, the General Assembly resolutions on outer space contributed substantially to the development of the customary international law of outer space. However, the passing of the resolution is not in and of itself enough to create customary international law.

The relevance and effect of *opinio juris* as a necessary element of customary international law has been controversial ever since it was first formulated by Geny at the end of the nineteenth century.[59] Some writers believe that *opinio juris* alone is determinative of customary international law. Thus, Bin Cheng, a leading proponent of the idea of instant customary international law, has argued that there need be 'no usage at all in the sense of repeated practice' provided that *opinio juris* can be 'clearly established'.[60] Other writers have played down the subjective element of *opinio juris*, arguing that it is difficult to identify. Hans Kelsen, for example, argued that it was 'almost impossible' to discover the sentiments or thoughts of states as to why they were engaging in a particular practice.[61] Nevertheless, most writers, and, indeed, the ICJ, are agreed that customary international law requires both practice and *opinio juris* as necessary elements. Thus, according to the ICJ in the *North Sea Continental Shelf Cases*, an act must be carried out 'in such a way as to evidence a belief that this practice is rendered obligatory by the existence of a rule of law requiring it'.[62] The Court continued: 'The states concerned must therefore feel that they are conforming to what amounts to a legal obligation. The frequency, or even habitual character of the acts is not in itself enough.'[63]

In the case of established rules of customary international law this does not present any particular problems. Thus, where a practice has evolved over a long period of time, the identification of a specific date at

---

59. Geny (1919), para. 110.
60. Cheng (1965), pp. 35–6.
61. Kelsen (1966), pp. 450–4.
62. (1969) ICJ Rep. 3, at 44.
63. *Idem.*

which time a new rule of customary international law emerged is of minor importance. In that respect, it is possible to look at the development of a practice over a period of time and determine that, at some stage, whenever that may have been, states began to consider themselves as being bound to follow that practice rather than simply choosing to follow that practice. A particular problem does arise, however, with regard to the formation of new customary international law and changes in existing customary international law. This problem has recently been identified by Byers as the 'chronological paradox' which requires that 'states creating new customary rules must believe that those rules already exist, and that their practice, therefore, *is* in accordance with law'.[64] Thus, the requirement that there be a legal obligation to follow a particular rule 'would seem to make it impossible for new rules to develop, since *opinio juris* would only exist in respect of those rules which were *already* in force'.[65]

Many arguments have been put forward as a solution to this paradox.[66] One of the clearest is that of Akehurst who has argued that *opinio juris* constitutes statements not beliefs. He has asserted, further, that there is no requirement that states genuinely believe that any statement as to the legally binding nature of a particular rule is in fact true. However, if other states react by making similar statements, that may well result in the development of new customary international law. Thus, according to Akehurst:

> This is the main way in which customary law changes. States assert that something is already a rule of international law. Maybe the state concerned have made a genuine mistake, maybe they know their statements are false – all that is irrelevant. If other states acquiesce, a new rule of customary law comes into being.[67]

The point is, however, that in the decentralized system of law-making that is international law, one or more states must make the first move in order to bring about a change in the law. Except in circumstances that are entirely unique, such as was the case with the early development of space law, that state or those states will necessarily be breaching the previous

---

64. Byers (1999), p. 131.
65. *Idem.*
66. For a discussion of these approaches, see *idem*, pp. 131–3. Byers himself has used techniques developed by regime theorists in international relations to provide an interdisciplinary analysis of this and other problems of customary international law. His work in this context will be considered more fully below.
67. Akehurst (1974–5), p. 37.

law. Thus, in the case of the previously mentioned exclusive economic zone, the zone previously was considered as high seas. For a state to assert in such conditions that it is acting in conformity with the law is to make a mockery of the law. Any assertion of *opinio juris* in such circumstance cannot be an assertion of what the law is but what the state making the claim wishes the law to be. Thus, according to Thirlway, 'the requirement of *opinio juris* is equivalent merely to the need for the practice in question to have been accompanied by either a sense of conforming with the law, or the view that the practice was potentially law, as suited to the needs of the international community'.[68]

Reference to the needs of the international community in this context appears to see the motivation of the states breaching the existing law as being the development of ideas of justice and social need. This need not be the case, however, and most usually will not be the case. Most usually the state will be acting out of pure self-interest and, perhaps, a desire to see the law changed to benefit that self-interest. Whether or not the state is successful in its desire to change the law will depend upon the reaction of other states. As was noted above, states have the option of reacting in a number of ways to a new practice. If they object to it or engage in contrary practice, they are asserting the view that the acting state has breached international law. If states acquiesce in a practice, they are effectively asserting, along with the acting state, the belief in a developing rule of customary international law. That is, the view that the practice is potentially law.

For customary international law to be a dynamic and flexible system of law, rigid application of the requirement of *opinio juris* must be avoided. This does not mean, however, that the requirement of *opinio juris* is negated or undermined. States do not simply assert that a new rule of international law exists or should exist without some sense as to how other states will react to such an assertion. Thus, customary international law is able to develop more easily in the context of today's sophisticated and technologically advanced telecommunications systems. Equally, the increased involvement of states in international conferences and organizations increases the opportunity for states to get a sense of the views of other states on proposed changes to international law. Accordingly, where states assert the belief that a particular practice should be law or is emerging into law, they can truly be said to be asserting their *opinio juris*, albeit a developing *opinio juris*.

---

68. Thirlway (1972), pp. 53–4.

Treaties as Sources of International Law

The traditional approach to the question of why international treaties are binding on states focuses directly on the consent of states. In signing and ratifying international treaties, states consent to be bound by the rules contained therein as against the other state parties to the relevant treaty. However, many questions have been asked about this explanation. Most recently, John Setear has posed the basic question: 'If consent is the basis of treaties, then how can treaties purport to bind a nation that wishes to withdraw its consent?'[69] The inconsistency is set forth in the following terms:

> [T]o argue that the law of treaties rests upon consent and *not* give effect to withdrawals of consent is to say that obligations at time A stem from valid consent, but remain in force at a later time B despite the withdrawal of the consent that sanctified the obligations in the first place.[70]

Other writers have previously identified this problem and have sought to deal with it in various ways. For example, Thomas Franck has put forward a theory which examines the legitimacy of international law as a basis for obligation generally. According to Franck there are four indicators of the legitimacy of a rule of international law: determinacy,[71] symbolic validation,[72] coherence[73] and adherence.[74] As Franck puts it:

> [T]o the extent a rule, or rule process, exhibits these four properties it will exert a strong pull on states to comply. To the extent that these properties are not present, the institution will be easier to ignore and the rule easier to avoid by a state tempted to pursue its short-term self-interest.[75]

While Franck's analysis has prompted a great deal of discussion about

---

69. Setear (1996), p. 160.
70. *Idem.*
71. Determinacy is 'that which makes [a rule's] message clear' (Franck, 1990, p. 52).
72. Symbolic validation is 'the procedural use of ritual and historical pedigree in connection with the preparation of a substantive rule' (Setear, 1996, p. 163). See also Franck (1990), pp. 90–5.
73. Coherence is 'the degree of connection between rational principles on the one hand, and a rule (and its exceptions) on the other' (Setear, 1996, p. 163). See also Franck (1990), pp. 150–3.
74. Adherence is defined by Franck with reference to Hart's division of primary and secondary rules in the following terms; 'the vertical nexus between a primary rule of obligation, which is the system's workhorse, and a hierarchy of secondary rules identifying the sources of rules and establishing normative standards that define how rules are to be made, interpreted and applied' (Franck, 1990, p. 184).
75. *Idem,* p. 49.

state compliance with international law, international lawyers have not generally adopted it, primarily as a result of the difficulty of identifying the existence in any particular case of the four properties. With particular reference to the law of treaties, Setear has explained that 'the various categorisations and evaluations required by the legitimacy-oriented view are nebulous or contradictory'.[76] Furthermore, 'the legitimacy-oriented view proves in the context of the law of treaties to be only partly distinguishable from the consent-oriented view'.[77]

Setear himself draws upon theoretical analysis developed in the field of international relations, particularly that of the institutionalists, to explain his conception of the law of treaties. For Setear, treaties can best be explained by reference to the Prisoner's Dilemma in which treaties constitute a series of 'plays' in a game. Each 'play' constitutes an 'iteration'. Each treaty is therefore a series of iterations which are, crucially, infinite in number. As Setear explains, where a game consists only of a single iteration, 'the only rational strategy ... is for players to defect'. Similarly, where the number of plays is finite, the possibility for cooperation is increased. However, 'the final round is the logical equivalent of an un-iterated game'. Thus, according to Setear: 'Choosing the "defect" action is therefore the dominant strategy, just as in the one-shot game.'[78] On the other hand, 'increasing the number of iterations from a finite to an infinite number allows for mathematically rigorous demonstrations that cooperation is a rational strategy ... Essentially, when there is no known final iteration ... the way is clear for the *possibility* of rational cooperation.[79]

While not wishing to over-simplify what is an extremely complex and well-developed analysis, it is difficult not to agree with Byers' critique of Setear which highlights that an approach such as Setear's removes the law from the law of treaties.[80] As Byers points out, 'the central point of the consent-based theories of international law is that a state, by consenting, binds itself to behave in a certain manner *even if* it subsequently changes its mind about the desirability of such behaviour'.[81] In other words, states have consented to the rule of *pacta sunt servanda*, the requirement that states fulfil their international obligations

---

76. Setear (1996), p. 162.
77. *Idem.*
78. *Idem*, p. 185.
79. *Idem*, p. 186 (emphasis in original).
80. Byers (1997), p. 201.
81. *Idem*, p. 202.

in good faith. As was highlighted in the previous chapter, the basis of this consent is to be found in the *political* acceptance by states that the rules of international law are generally binding on them. The manifestation of the political acceptance with regard to treaties is witnessed by the willingness of states generally to enter into such agreements and the expectation that other states will comply with the obligations contained therein.

A further difficulty arises, however, in discussing treaties as sources of international law. As early as 1925, P. E. Corbett argued that treaties 'can only occasionally, indeed very rarely in proportion to their number, be correctly described as constituting the origin of rules of international law'.[82] The position is summed up by Fitzmaurice:

> the attempts which have been made to ascribe a law-making character to *all* treaties irrespective of the character of their content or the number of parties to them ... is of extremely dubious validity ... The only 'law' that enters into these is derived, not from the treaty creating them – or from any treaty – but from the principle *pacta sunt servanda* – an antecedent general principle of law. The law is that the obligation must be carried out, but the obligation is not, in itself, law.[83]

It may well be thought that we have entered into another discussion of the meaning of the word 'law'. However, the essential problem here is not with the definition of law itself but with the distinction between obligations that are binding on all states and those that are binding only on particular states. Thus, international treaties cannot be considered as sources of universal international law unless they are entered into by all states. In other words, international treaties are not legislation. Nevertheless, treaties are constitutive of legal relations between state parties and are, accordingly, sources of legal obligation between those states.[84]

Some writers have argued, however, that certain large multilateral treaties, which purport to develop the law in a particular area, are capable of being regarded as general sources of international law. Thus, according to Tunkin:

> The existence of a considerable number of multilateral international treaties to which all or almost all states are parties (i.e. general or universal international treaties) and also extensive efforts in the field of codification of international law have led to a situation when

---

82. Corbett (1925), p. 27.
83. Fitzmaurice (1958), p. 157.
84. Corbett (1925), p. 25.

international treaties become a direct method of changing, developing and creating new norms of general international law.[85]

It is probably correct to say that large multilateral treaties can give rise to general obligations among the state parties to the treaty. Reference can again be made to the idea that multilateral treaties constitute a series of bilateral relations between states which, when multiplied, can be said to be of universal application among the state parties. However, the fundamental difficulty with this approach, as with any approach directed at attempting to create universal obligations out of purely treaty-based obligations, is that treaties cannot in and of themselves bind non-party states.[86]

A much more satisfactory approach explaining the impact of multi-lateral treaties on the development of international law is to regard them as instruments which set standards with which non-parties may comply. There is no obligation on non-parties to comply with such standards but where treaties attract the support of a large number of states, the pressure on non-parties to comply may be overwhelming. Thus, according to Shaw, law-making treaties:

> are intended to have an effect *generally*, not restrictively, and they are to be contrasted with those treaties which merely regulate limited issues between a few states. Law-making treaties are those agreements whereby states elaborate their perception of international law upon any given topic or establish new rules which are to guide them for the future in their international conduct.[87]

Where third parties do adhere to treaty rules, they assist in the development of customary international law which may, as a result, be identical to a treaty rule but will bind states in a different way. In such a way, treaty rules may in themselves constitute state practice. However, it is important to note that the state practice of non-parties to the treaty will be crucial to the determination of whether a parallel rule of customary international law exists. Thus non-states parties may fall directly within the category of 'states whose interests are specially affected' identified by the ICJ in the *North Sea Continental Shelf Cases*,[88] who are required to act in conformity with a putative rule of customary international law before it can properly be said to form such a rule. The

---

85. Tunkin (1958), p. 22.
86. *North Sea Continental Shelf Cases* (1969) ICJ Rep. 3, at 25.
87. Shaw (1997), p. 75 (emphasis added).
88. (1969) ICJ Rep. 3.

danger of relying solely on the practice of state parties to a particular convention is that treaties would thereby take on the form of legislation and become binding on all states regardless of consent. As Shaw has noted: 'This would constitute too radical a departure for the current process of law-formation within the international community.'[89]

While it must not be forgotten that treaties lay down specific obligations which are binding directly on state parties, the role of treaties as sources of international law generally is most clearly summed up by Corbett:

> It remains true that treaties play a very large part in the science of international law, though their provisions do not constitute rules of that law. They are one of the principal means of knowing what the law is, because they frequently record the assent of states to propositions which, when their progress towards general consent is complete, become law ... Treaties, then, are important to the international lawyer chiefly as evidence of consent, and so as marking steps in the process by which principles develop into rules.[90]

Other Sources of International Law

Reference has already been made to the category of 'general principles of law' which is recognized as a source of international law in Article 38(1) of the Statute of the ICJ. Originally conceived as a mechanism for restricting state sovereignty in the absence of treaties or customary international law,[91] the category has, perhaps not surprisingly, given rise primarily to procedural rules aimed at assisting the court in the exercise of its functions. Thus rules relating to the admission of circumstantial evidence,[92] estoppel,[93] *res judicata*,[94] and the obligation to make reparations,[95] have all been applied by the ICJ or its predecessor, the PCIJ, as general principles of international law. Shaw has concluded that 'most writers are prepared to accept that the general principles do constitute a separate source of law but of fairly limited scope'.[96]

---

89. Shaw (1997), p. 76.
90. Corbett (1925), pp. 28–9.
91. Cassese (1986), p. 170.
92. *Corfu Channel Case* (1949) ICJ Rep. 4.
93. *Temple Case* (1962) ICJ Rep. 6.
94. *Administrative Tribunal Case* (1954) ICJ Rep. 53.
95. *Chorzow Factory (Indemnity) Case* (1928) PCIJ Rep. Ser. A, No. 17, at 29.
96. Shaw (1997), p. 78.

It has been suggested by some that resolutions of the UN General Assembly constitute separate sources of international law. As has already been discussed above, these resolutions are not in and of themselves binding and so it is difficult to ascribe them any direct role in the law-creating process. However, as with treaties, resolutions of the General Assembly are capable of indicating the support of states for general propositions which may, if they are adopted into the practice of states, evolve into rules of customary international law.

Finally, Article 38(1) of the Statue of the ICJ highlights a number of subsidiary sources of international law, including judicial decisions, and writings of the most highly qualified publicists. Here again, these categories do not in and of themselves constitute the formal sources of international law but do provide evidence as to what the content of the law might be at a particular time. States are then free to accept this evidence by adopting it into their state practice, if they have not already done so.

CHAPTER 3

INTERNATIONAL RELATIONS PERSPECTIVES ON INTERNATIONAL LAW

THE APPROACH OF INTERNATIONAL RELATIONS THEORIES TO INTERNATIONAL LAW

The discipline of international relations is a relatively recent addition to the academic syllabus.[1] However, many of the 'sub-fields'[2] that make up the discipline have been around for centuries and include Diplomacy and Diplomatic History, Economics, Geography, Sociology, Psychology and, of course, Law. Indeed, international law was seen by the organizers of the earliest courses on international relations as being the 'best integrated root discipline' of international relations.[3] Particularly in the United States, early international relations writing was dominated by legal approaches and indeed 'may be said to have sprung from law'.[4] Yet within a short time of the creation of the discipline, international law had come to be regarded as, at best, a necessary evil, at worst, a 'blind alley'.[5]

Realism

By the late 1930s the emerging school of realists considered that anyone who believed that international law could regulate and restrain the struggle for power on the international scene could properly be called an idealist. Leading realists consistently began to question the relevance of

---

1. Wright (1955), p. 26, notes that 'the discipline as a whole cannot be traced back much before World War I'. See also Olson and Groom (1991), p. 62.
2. See Wright (1955), p. vii.
3. *Idem*, p. 33.
4. Olson and Groom (1991), p. 64.
5. Schuman (1948), p. xii.

international law relying on the same factors that led Austin to deny international law its legal character, that is the lack of a legislature, executive and judiciary.[6] On the other hand, none of the early realists specifically rejected the existence of international law, nor even the binding nature of that law. For example, E. H. Carr, one of the leading early realists, opined that '[the] shortcomings of international law, serious as they are, do not deprive it of the title to be considered as law, of which it has all the essential characteristics'.[7] Interestingly, Carr nowhere specifies what, in fact, those characteristics are.

Carr accepts aspects of both natural law thinking and positivist thinking. As to natural law, Carr recognizes the modern conception of 'natural law with a variable content' as being 'no longer something external, fixed and invariable, but men's innate feeling at any given time or place for what "just law" ought to be'.[8] According to Carr, therefore: 'We are now asked to treat law as binding because it is an emanation not of some external ethical principle, but of the ethical principles of a given time and community.'[9] The trouble with this approach Carr sees not in the possibility of variable content of natural law but in the way in which natural law can be used to justify both legal and illegal behaviour:

> The main crux about natural law is not that people differ from time to time and from place to place about what particular rules it prescribes (for this crux may be surmounted by the variable theory), but that natural law (or reason or 'objective right' or any of its other substitutes) can be just as easily invoked to cite disobedience to the law as to justify obedience to it. Natural law has always had two aspects and two uses. It can be invoked by conservatives to justify the existing order, as when the rights of rulers or the rights to property are alleged to rest on natural law. It can equally be invoked by revolutionaries to justify rebellion against the existing order. There is in natural law an anarchic element which is the direct antithesis of law.[10]

As to positivism, Carr describes this as 'the realist view of law',[11] noting, in Austinian terms, that: 'It is regarded as binding because there is an authority which enforces obedience to it.' However, Carr notes that 'no community could survive if most of its members were law-abiding only

---

6. See generally Carr (1939), Chapter 10, and Morgenthau (1973), Chapter 18.
7. Carr (1939), p. 221.
8. *Idem*, p. 224.
9. *Idem*.
10. *Idem*, p. 225.
11. *Idem*, p. 226.

through an ever-present fear of punishment'. Carr concludes that both natural law and positivism provide part of the answer:

> Law is regarded as binding because it represents the sense of right of the community: it is an instrument of the common good. Law is regarded as binding because it is enforced by the strong arm of authority: it can be, and often is, oppressive. Both these answers are true; both of them are only half truths.[12]

For Carr, the essential requirement of law is the existence of a political society. In answering the question why law is binding, Carr states: 'Law is regarded as binding because, if it were not, political society could not exist and there could be no law.'[13] With regard to international law, Carr notes that it 'can have no existence except in so far as there is an international community which, on the basis of a "minimum common understanding", recognises it as binding'.[14] He continues:

> International law is a function of the political community of nations. Its defects are due, not to any technical shortcomings, but to the embryonic character of the community in which it functions ... Rules, however general in form, will be constantly found to be aimed at a particular state or group of states; and for this reason, if for no other, the power element is more obvious in international than in municipal law, whose subjects are a large body of anonymous individuals. The same consideration makes international law more frankly political than other branches of the law.[15]

Carr reserved his strongest criticism for international lawyers who refused to recognize the political foundations of international law. He highlighted, for example, the analysis of Professor Lauterpacht in his seminal work on *The Function of Law in the International Community* where Lauterpacht distinguished between legal disputes, which are suitable for judicial settlement, and political disputes, which are not, concluding that: 'It is not the nature of an individual dispute which makes it unfit for judicial settlement but the unwillingness of a state to have it settled by application of the law.'[16] Of this analysis Carr notes:

> It is a pity that Professor Lauterpacht, having brilliantly conducted his analysis up to the point where the unwillingness of states is recognised

---

12. *Idem*, p. 227.
13. *Idem*.
14. *Idem*, p. 228.
15. *Idem*, pp. 228–9.
16. Lauterpacht (1933), p. 369.

as the limiting factor in the justiciability of international disputes should have been content to leave it there, treating this 'unwillingness', in true utopian fashion, as perverse and undeserving of the attention of an international lawyer.[17]

While Carr may be said to have formulated the early examples of realist theory, it is Hans Morgenthau who is generally recognized as the leading realist thinker of his era. As has been noted in the first two chapters of this book, Morgenthau undoubtedly saw a role for international law in the international relations of states. However, Morganthau's perception of international law was strongly positivist. He saw international law as being based on the specific consent of states and the convergence of national self-interest around specific, deliberately vague and ambiguous treaty provisions.[18] Thus, he was able to conclude: 'The great majority of the rules of international law are generally observed by all nations without actual compulsion, for it is generally in the interests of all nations concerned to honour their obligations under international law.'[19] According to Morgenthau, where international law is complied with it is because '[m]ost rules of international law formulate in legal terms such identical or complementary interests. It is for this reason that they generally enforce themselves, as it were, and there is generally no need for specific enforcement action.'[20] For Morgenthau, therefore, international law involved no specific 'obligation'. It was simply something states complied with where their interests so demanded. Where national self-interest demanded action contrary to perceived rules of international law, the only obligation on states was to act in their own self-interest.

It was perhaps this aspect of Morgenthau's work which led later writers on classical realism to reject the notion of international law entirely. George Kennan, for example, was scathing of the 'legalistic-moralistic approach to international problems'.[21] For Kennan, the idea that law and, in particular, the Charter of the United Nations could be used to 'suppress the chaotic and dangerous aspirations of governments in the international field',[22] was fanciful. In particular, Kennan saw three fundamental difficulties with a legalistic approach. First, states could not be subordinated to an international judicial regime because not all states

---

17. Carr (1939), p. 249.
18. Morgenthau (1973), p. 277.
19. *Idem*, p. 291.
20. *Idem*.
21. Kennan (1984), p. 95.
22. *Idem*.

were 'reasonably content with their international borders and status, at least to the extent that they would be willing to refrain from pressing for change without international agreement'. Secondly, international law 'envisages a world composed exclusively of sovereign states with a full equality and status'. Finally, international law assumes that sanctions will constrain the 'bad behaviour of states'. What is particularly interesting about Kennan's criticisms of international law is that most international lawyers would have little difficulty in agreeing with this criticism of what is effectively a vision of an Austininan model of international law relying primarily on the subjection of states to the law and the enforcement of the law against them. Whether or not this is the model of international law perceived by the drafters of the UN Charter remains a moot point. As has been shown, it is certainly not the model of international law subscribed to by the vast majority of today's international lawyers.

Nevertheless, the work of Kennan and the earlier classical realists fundamentally influenced the views of international relations scholars on the role of international law. In particular, the realist challenge to international lawyers was to establish the relevance of international law. According to Anne-Marie Slaughter Burley:

> International legal theorists had long grappled with the theoretical conundrum of the sources of international legal obligation – of law being simultaneously 'of' and 'above' the state. Yet endless debates on this question nevertheless assumed that international law rules, however derived, had some effect on state behaviour, that law and power *interacted* in some way rather than marking opposite ends of the domestic-international spectrum.[23]

A further blow to international law from the perspective of international relations was dealt by the emergence of the neo-realists and structural realists. A detailed analysis of the views of neo-realists on the role of international law is impossible because neo-realists simply did not discuss law as such.[24] While the lack of reference to international law may be taken to indicate a general lack of interest, it is clear that the lack of interest was deliberate. Similarly structural realists, while attempting to provide a more broadly-based theory of international relations than neo-realism, rarely consider the existence of international law, let alone its relevance to the relations of states. Accordingly, the structural realist vision of the international order has recently been summarized thus:

---

23. Slaughter Burley (1993), p. 208.
24. Arend (1998), p. 114.

[S]tructural realists believe that the international system lacks a common power and is thus anarchic. As a consequence states are insecure. A state can never be certain that a fellow state will not use military force against it. Accordingly, states must engage in self-help measures to attempt to survive in the international system. They do this by attempting to enhance their power within the system.[25]

If international law is, as has been asserted, more than simply a coercive order, it is, at the very least, a cooperative enterprise aimed at identifying issues of common interest and developing norms and principles in order to advance those common aims.[26] Cooperation is possible within an anarchic system but only where it is directed at 'maintaining or even increasing [a state's] share of world power'.[27] Clearly, therefore, states will enter into treaties which maximize their respective power base. However, states would not be bound by such agreements were they to begin to compromise their position as against the other states party to the agreement or even as against other states generally. Further, the idea that a state would, or even could, consent to be bound by a treaty which reduced its share of world power would be anathema. Accordingly, neo-realists and structural realists, as the realists before them, did not deny the existence of international law;[28] they simply regarded it as epiphenomenal and lacking any independent causal force.[29]

Reference has already been made to the attempts by international lawyers to address the realist challenge. In particular, the work of the New Haven scholars attempted to confront realist criticism head on by focusing on the political or policy aspects of the legal relations between states. Some political scientists, including Stanley Hoffmann[30] and Morton Kaplan,[31] took up the challenge of realism by attempting to

---

25. *Idem*. Arend's analysis draws heavily on the work of John Mearsheimer (1994/5).
26. Law may, of course, exist simply to set the parameters of a particular system without seeking to influence the way in which that system works. Thus, with regard to the anarchic international system, the law may exist, indeed it may even be necessary, to define the state and the limits of state jurisdiction but need not have any involvement in the working of that system. Such an extremely positivist vision of international law, if it ever existed, has long since been rejected.
27. Mearsheimer (1995), p. 82.
28. The realists, both classical and new, have been portrayed as denying the existence of international law. See, for example, Starr (1995), p. 303. However, as has been shown, realists were not particularly concerned with whether or not international law could properly be called law.
29. Slaughter Burley (1993), p. 217.
30. See, in particular, Hoffmann (1968).
31. Kaplan and Katzenbach (1961).

devise a role for international law through an analysis of international systems. On the whole, however, the work of these individuals served only to reinforce realist conclusions about the prospects for international law. Hoffmann was particularly pessimistic, noting that:

> Only when the international system will be less heterogeneous than it is now, when there will be more 'poles' of power, fewer ideological passions, less unevenness in development, greater internal stability in the new states, will one be able to turn the *ad hoc* management of conflicts – kept moderate only by the fear of holocaust – into a legal restraint.[32]

Nevertheless, more recent analysis of the role of international law in international relations by political scientists has revealed increased willingness amongst such scholars to consider more directly the role of international law. The first move in this direction was undertaken by scholars of the institutionalist school.

Institutionalism

Proponents of institutionalism did not deliberately set out to assert the relevance of international law. Indeed, as Slaughter Burley notes, many of the early institutionalists 'had been explicitly distancing themselves from anything called "law" for twenty years'.[33] Furthermore, while much of the early analysis was directed at the relevance of formal institutions, later analysis progressed from 'an emphasis on institutional processes' to 'a more general enquiry into how international organisations work in a larger process'.[34] As Slaughter Burley notes: 'The last step in this progression was the reconceptualization of the entire field of international organization as the study of "international regimes"'.[35] For international lawyers the definition of regimes as 'sets of principles, norms, rules and decision-making procedures around which actor expectations converge in a given issue-area'[36] may be strikingly familiar. For lawyers, regimes may indeed be 'international law under another

---

32. Hoffmann (1968), p. 46.
33. Slaughter Burley (1993), p. 217.
34. *Idem*, p. 218.
35. *Idem*.
36. Krasner (1982), p. 186.

name'.[37] Institutionalists, however, have avoided the 'l' word like the proverbial plague. For institutionalists, regimes may lead to formal agreements but regimes and agreements are not the same thing. Thus, according to Oran Young:

> Some writers have fallen into the habit of equating regimes with the agreements in terms of which regimes are often expressed or codified. In practice, however, international regimes vary greatly in the extent to which they are expressed in formal agreements, treaties or conventions ... Though it may be helpful, formalization is clearly not a necessary condition for the effective operation of international regimes.[38]

It is, of course, possible to argue that international law is not simply about formal agreements either and that the development of so-called 'soft' law as an inherent part of the structure of international law is a recognition of the fact that formalization may be neither possible nor, indeed, desirable.

The lack of willingness among institutionalists to discuss international law may be because international law continues to be viewed as peripheral, if not inconsequential. Thus, Stephen Krasner has drawn a fundamental distinction between the principles and norms of a regime which are 'the basic defining characteristics of a regime'[39] and the rules and decision-making procedures which, if changed, are changes within regimes which do not alter the regime itself. Although not expressly making the point, Krasner's illustrations make it clear that if international law is relevant to international regimes it is only so at the level of rules and decision-making procedures rather than at the level of principles and norms.[40] Nevertheless, Young's earlier conclusion that 'it would be ... difficult to achieve a real grasp of the character of [international] regimes

---

37. Byers (1999), p. 25. It is worth noting that many of the criticisms of regime theory developed by realists could apply equally to international law. Thus, when Young concludes of the realist critique of international regimes that they 'regard international regimes as epiphenomena whose dictates are apt to be ignored whenever actors find it difficult or inconvenient or costly to comply with them, and whose substantive components are readily changeable whenever powerful members of the community find them cumbersome or otherwise outmoded' (Young, 1986–7, p. 116), the focus of the criticism could equally well be international law.
38. Young (1989), p. 24. Young distinguished between formal agreements and informal understandings.
39. Krasner (1982), p. 187.
40. Krasner's main example relates to the revisions of the Articles of Agreement of the General Agreement on Tariffs and Trade (GATT) providing for special and differential treatment for less developed countries (Krasner, 1982, p. 188).

without thinking systematically about questions of international law and organisation'[41] has not been ignored. Thus Andrew Hurrell has pointed out the trend amongst regime theorists to focus less on the 'rather generalised definitions of regimes' and more on 'the need to focus on specific sets of rules'.[42] Hurrell illustrates his point by contrasting Krasner's 1982 definition of a regime set out above with that of Robert Keohane who in 1989 defined regimes as being 'institutions with specific rules, agreed upon by governments, which pertain to particular sets of issues in international relations'.[43] This has led Slaughter Burley to conclude that even if they are unwilling to talk about it, 'political scientists have rediscovered international law'.[44] Furthermore, as Michael Byers has more recently noted:

> [Regime theorists and institutionalists] clearly sense that normal state behaviour does give rise to legal obligation, that some regimes and institutions represent a transformation of power of the kind that they have traditionally studied, into another kind of power – and that this other kind of power, 'the power of rules', subsequently affects what states say and do.[45]

Equally, however, primarily through interaction with regime theorists, international lawyers have rediscovered international relations. Indeed, in an attempt to develop an interdisciplinary framework for international law and international relations, lawyers have been quick to realize the potential of regimes as a tool for advancing the cause of international legal analysis.[46] Indeed, a recent attempt to rationalize the nature of customary international law using regime theory has been proposed by Byers.[47] This attempt to develop the theory of international law will be considered more fully later in this chapter. On a practical level, however, it is clear that, in some areas at least, international lawyers are already drawing on institutionalist approaches. Thus, according to Hurrell:

> [M]any international lawyers have come to view international treaties and conventions over such matters as the environment, not as a

41. Young (1986–7), p. 122.
42. Hurrell (1993), p. 209.
43. Keohane (1989), p. 4.
44. Slaughter Burley (1993), p. 220.
45. Byers (1999), p. 31.
46. Slaughter, Tulumello and Wood (1998) present a bibliography of interdisciplinary works in international law and international relations, many of which draw upon regime analysis.
47. Byers (1999).

definitive and unchanging set of rules, but rather as a means of creating law-making frameworks. Their purpose is to provide a framework for negotiation in which the techniques and general principles of international law can be employed, first to negotiate and formalise accepted but very general principles, and second to create means of facilitating ongoing negotiations from which more specific, 'harder' rules may subsequently emerge.[48]

While institutionalism and regime theory may have provided the most immediate results in terms of interdisciplinary analysis of international law, two further theories developed by international relations scholars have begun to provide a basis for further interdisciplinary collaboration in this area. These are liberalism and constructivism.

Liberalism

For Slaughter Burley liberalism constitutes 'a new paradigm'[49] which will serve to inform both international relations and international law. She highlights three fundamental assumptions of liberal theory, identified by Andrew Moravcsik in 1992, as being first that: 'The fundamental actors in politics are members of domestic society, understood as individuals and privately constituted groups seeking to promote their independent interests.'[50] Slaughter Burley notes that liberal theory in this sense challenges the state-centred account common both to realism and institutionalism[51] and, one might add, traditional approaches to international law. Secondly: 'All governments represent some segment of domestic society, whose interests are reflected in state policy.'[52] Finally, 'the behaviour of states – and hence levels of international conflict and co-operation – reflects the nature and configuration of state preferences'.[53]

For international law, liberal theory presents both opportunities and challenges. Slaughter Burley notes that 'liberal theory provides a powerful theoretical framework for the analysis of transnational law'[54] which she defines as including 'all municipal law and a subset of

---

48. Hurrell (1993), p. 209.
49. Slaughter Burley (1993), p. 226.
50. Moravcsik (1992), quoted in Slaughter Burley (1993), p. 227.
51. Slaughter Burley (1993), p. 227.
52. *Idem*, p. 228.
53. *Idem*. See further Moravcsik (1997), pp. 516–21.
54. Slaughter Burley (1993), p. 230.

intergovernmental agreements that directly regulate transnational activity between individuals and state and governments'.[55] However, as Slaughter Burley herself notes: 'Although this area of law is growing apace, it remains a definition and a category without a theory. The result is a seemingly random hodgepodge of doctrines and topics connected as a field only by a common "international" or "foreign" element.'[56]

One of the main problems with this category of transnational law is that it is often regarded as being outside the mainstream of public international law. The subject of private international law, for example, which deals with the 'international' or 'foreign' aspects of legal transactions among individuals is regarded as separate to and distinct from public international law. Similarly, the law on international trade is seldom, if ever, dealt with in mainstream texts on public international law, except insofar as such transactions are regulated by international agreements among states. Even in the field of international human rights, the primary focus of public international lawyers is to analyse the obligations on states rather than individuals. The public international law conceptualization of human rights recognizes that individuals have rights and remedies under international law only insofar as states have provided for such rights and remedies, for example, through the creation of an international human rights tribunal or through the right of individual petition.[57] It is perhaps only in the field of international criminal law that individuals are recognized as having direct obligations under international law. However, as the recent attempt to extradite General Pinochet from the United Kingdom to stand trial in Spain on accusations of violations of international criminal law, and the attempts to create an International Criminal Court, have shown, the direct criminal responsibility of individuals under international law remains subject to the creation of such responsibility by states either through treaty or by customary international law.[58] This public/private distinction has been criticized by, among others,[59] feminist scholars as being 'a culturally constructed ideology'.[60] These scholars, however, admit that the distinction 'continues to have a strong grip on legal thinking'.[61] It is perhaps ironic that the distinction which feminists have attacked as being

---

55. *Idem.*
56. *Idem.*
57. See above, Chapter 2.
58. See further below, Chapter 6.
59. See also the work of Third World legal scholars such as Bedjaoui (1979).
60. See generally Charlesworth, Chinkin and Wright (1991).
61. *Idem.*

central to liberal theory[62] is, in terms of public international law at least, under attack from liberal scholars.

One further problem with liberal theory for international lawyers relates to the centrality of the liberal democratic state in the liberal research agenda. While international lawyers may find some strengths in the assertions that liberal democratic states maintain a commitment to the rule of law and that such a commitment can be used to show why such states comply with international law, such an assertion cannot explain why international law is binding on all states regardless of their political orientation. For international lawyers, international law is a universal system and any explanation of why states obey international law needs to address both liberal and non-liberal states.

The problem is highlighted by Slaughter Burley's 'archetype' liberal institution, the European Union. For Slaughter Burley the key to the success of European Union law 'lies in the receptivity of the national courts of the [Union's] member states to accepting the possibility of supranational law as *law*, as a body of rules interpreted and applied by a non-political entity'.[63] The point is, however, that for international lawyers, European Union law is not international law. Certainly, the Union is constructed on the basis of an international treaty, which finds its existence and validity in international law. However, the body of European Union law which has developed since the enactment of the Treaty of Rome in 1957 has developed on the basis that the Treaty created a new type of law, European Union law, which can be directly applicable in Member States and, in many cases, directly effective and so capable of enforcement by individuals within their own national legal systems. European Union law is undoubtedly an example of where international law can lead given the relevant liberal conditions. However, it is misleading to regard it as the archetype of the international law of the future.

In an effort perhaps to address some of these difficulties, Slaughter Burley has put forward a dual agenda of liberal institutionalism as the basis of future interdisciplinary research in international law and international relations. According to Slaughter Burley:

[A]lthough much of the debate will be conducted between Institutionalists and Liberals, in the end both approaches will continue to recognise
the complementarity of the other. Institutionalists will continue to
believe that systemic explanations provide the most powerful and

62. *Idem.*
63. Slaughter Burley (1993), p. 234.

parsimonious starting point but that explanations focusing on domestic politics and individual action will be important residual tools. Liberals, on the other hand, will claim that Liberal theories will be necessary to explain the formation of state interests, but that Institutionalist theories are critical at the bargaining stage. In either case, legal adherents of both schools will find a bridge to each other, as well as to travelling political scientists.

Certainly, in this context, Slaughter Burley has accurately predicted the basis of much recent work in international law, particularly in relation to the question of why states obey international law.

Constructivism

Although regarded essentially as a 'critical' branch of international relations theory, constructivism is perhaps the theory which offers most to mainstream international lawyers. Constructivists share with structural realists the central beliefs that states are the primary actors in the international system; that states behave as unitary actors; that the structure of the international system is anarchic (that is, it has no central authority); and that theorizing about the system is critical for an understanding of international relations.[64] Most international lawyers would have little difficulty with subscribing to these central tenets. However, according to Wendt, while structural realists believe that the international system is made only of a distribution of material capabilities such as military might, economic resources, natural and physical resources and the like, constructivists believe that the system is also made of social relationships.[65] With regard to this last, critical, tenet, international lawyers would generally be in agreement with the constructivist philosophy.

The belief that the international system is a social system is pervasive amongst international lawyers. Grotius based his philosophy of natural law on the existence of man's impelling desire for society. He opined that '[the] maintenance of social order ... is the source of law properly so-called'.[66] Similarly, Westlake, one of the leading positivist philosophers in international law, was of the view that 'the cause why any rules of international law exist is the social nature of man and his material and

---

64. Arend (1998), p. 126.
65. Wendt (1995/6), p. 73.
66. Grotius (1625), p. 40.

moral surroundings'.[67] Comparable views have been provided by leading international lawyers of different schools ever since. Indeed, the existence of law as 'a social process' formed the basis of the highly influential work of the New Haven scholars.

For constructivists the basic elements of the social construct are the existence of first, shared understandings, expectations or knowledge; secondly, material resources; and thirdly, practices. With regard to the third element, constructivists believe that through their practices states generate certain norms of behaviour (shared expectations) and these norms are as much a part of the structure as material elements. In these insights, constructivists find themselves very closely tied to the so-called 'British School' of international relations scholars. Hedley Bull, the leading proponent of this school, has argued that the maintenance of order in any society presupposes the existence of common interests which are guided by rules.[68] Consequently, the British School envisaged a central role for international law in the maintenance of international society. Thus, according to Bull:

> A *society of states* (or international society) exists when a group of states, conscious of certain common interests and common values, forms a society in the sense that they conceive themselves to be bound by a common set of rules in their relations with one another, and share in the working of common institutions.[69]

Specifically on international law, Bull concludes:

> The international law to which, in some measure, all states in the global international system give their formal assent still serves to carry out its traditional functions of identifying the idea of a society of states as the operational principle of world politics, stating the basic rules of coexistence and facilitating compliance with those and other rules.[70]

Hurrell, who is variously described as a constructivist, reflectivist and member of the British School, is even more categorical. Having noted 'the role of international law as constructive of the structure of the state system itself',[71] he later continues:

> Being a political system, states will seek to interpret obligations to their own advantage. But being a legal system that is built on the consent of

---

67. Westlake (1894), p. 80.
68. Bull (1995), p. 2.
69. *Idem*, p. 13.
70. Bull (1995), pp. 154–5.
71. Hurrell (1993), p. 59.

other parties they will be constrained by the necessity of justifying their actions in legal terms.[72]

The views of other constructivists on the role of international law is not as clear. Nevertheless, Anthony Arend considers that it 'has a great deal to contribute to the understanding of the role played by legal rules in international politics'.[73] Indeed, Arend asserts that there are two conclusions relevant to the impact of constructivism on international law. First, international rules are part of the international system and, secondly, international legal rules help create state identity and interest.

RECENT INTERDISCIPLINARY WORK ON THE ROLE OF INTERNATIONAL LAW

As international relations scholars have begun to reject the realist paradigm that places international law on the periphery of the relations of states, the potential for interdisciplinary scholarship between the two disciplines has flourished. Slaughter, Tulumello and Wood have presented a bibliography of interdisciplinary scholarship in this area which details almost 100 works, most of which have been published in the last decade. It is not intended here to provide an overview of this work, a task more expertly undertaken by Slaughter and her associates. Rather, having focused in the preceding pages on the development of international relations approaches which appear to recognize a distinct role for international law in the relations of states, the following section will focus on three recent attempts by international lawyers directly to utilize these approaches in explanation of some of the general principles of international law highlighted earlier in this book. Thus, Michael Byers has drawn on regime theory in examining the role of customary international law. Harold Koh has relied on liberal and constructivist theories in an examination of why states obey international law. Finally, Anthony Arend has focused on constructivism in explanation of why international rules matter.

---

72. *Idem*, p. 61.
73. Arend (1998), p. 129.

Byers: Custom, Power and the Power of Rules

One of the leading international lawyers focusing on the relationship between international law and international relations is Michael Byers. In a recently published book entitled *Custom, Power and the Power of Rules: International Relations and Customary International Law*, Byers has sought to tackle head on a factor in international relations which international lawyers have 'seemed reluctant to investigate',[74] that is power. For Byers, power includes primarily military and economic power but may also include 'moral authority, which could be defined as the ability to appeal to general principles of justice'.[75] Crucially for Byers, power also includes the 'power of rules'. Thus, while states are capable of exercising raw, unsystematized rules, most usually in pursuit of short term gains, states generally realize that 'the application of raw power through the direct application of military power or economic coercion tends to promote instability and escalation'.[76] Thus, according to Byers:

> More frequently, states will apply power within the framework of an institution or legal system. States seem to be interested in institutions and legal systems because these structures create expectations of behaviour which reduce the risks of escalation and facilitate efficiency of action ... However, a legal system such as the international legal system does more than simply create expectations and promote stability. It also fulfils the essentially social function of transforming applications of power into legal obligation, of turning 'is' into 'ought' ... Legal obligation represents a society's concerted effort to control both present and future behaviour. International society uses obligation to confer a legal specificity on rules of international law, thus distinguishing them from the arbitrary commands of powerful states and ensuring they remain relevant to how states behave.[77]

For Byers, four principles of international law provide a framework for the development of specific rules of customary international law and,

---

74. Byers (1999), p. 15.
75. *Idem*, p. 5. According to Byers: 'In the human rights field it is possible that the existence of a high degree of moral authority in support of some customary rules has discouraged states which might otherwise have opposed those rules from so doing. It might also have discouraged them from openly engaging in violations of those rules, and from admitting to concealed violations. Power devolved from moral authority and an associated shift in international society's perceptions of justice, may also have played a role in the process of decolonisation' (*idem*, pp. 5–6).
76. *Idem*, p. 6.
77. *Idem*.

indeed, international law in general. These principles are jurisdiction, personality, reciprocity and legitimate expectation. Each principle, according to Byers, affects 'the application of power by states as they seek to develop, maintain or change rules of customary international law'.[78]

The principle of jurisdiction is defined as a state's 'authority to make, apply and enforce rules within a certain geographic area'.[79] Byers continues: 'the principle of jurisdiction qualifies the applications of power within the process of customary international law by giving each state the right to control, and therefore to limit, the legally relevant practice of other states within its own territory'.[80] Similarly, the principle of personality is deemed to apply equally to all states, which are together regarded as the only holders of full legal personality. The effect of this principle on the power of states is apparent 'because the supporting and opposing practice of less powerful states is considered together with that of more powerful states when determining the existence and content of individual customary rules'.[81]

Reference has already been made to the centrality of the principle of reciprocity to international law. For Byers, reciprocity requires that 'any state claiming a right under [customary international] law has to accord to all other states the same right'.[82] Thus Byers concludes:

> By ensuring that any state claiming a right under general customary international law accords that same right to all other states, the principle of reciprocity qualifies the application of power in at least three ways: first, in respect of what states claim, and, how they go about making such claims; secondly in respect of how states respond to the claims of other states; and, thirdly, in respect of how states go about persistently objecting to emerging or newly developed customary rules with which they disagree.[83]

Finally, for Byers, all rules of international law involve legitimate expectation. In relation to customary international law, 'any change from a voluntary pattern to a customary rule involves the transformation and legitimisation of patterns of behaviour, around which expectations of a legal character necessarily develop'.[84] Furthermore, treaty rules are

---

78. *Idem*, p. 10.
79. *Idem*, p. 54.
80. *Idem*, p. 55.
81. *Idem*, p. 76.
82. *Idem*, p. 89.
83. *Idem*, p. 90.
84. *Idem*, p. 107.

dependent on legitimate expectation 'because they are based on the general customary rule of *pacta sunt servanda* which requires that treaty obligations be upheld in good faith'.[85] Byers concludes generally that 'the principle of legitimate expectation means that states are legally justified in relying on each other to behave consistently with previous assurances or patterns of behaviour – if those assurances or that behaviour is of a type, and takes place within a context, such that it is considered relevant by most if not all states'.[86]

Legitimate expectation would appear to be the cornerstone principle for Byers' understanding of the international legal system and, to that extent, Byers' exposition comes close to echoing Kelsen's analysis of the *grundnorm* of international law as being the expectation that states should behave as they have customarily behaved. However, Byers extends his analysis to argue that legitimate expectation is also important to international regimes and institutions, and, in particular, the persistence of regimes and institutions in international society. Thus, he develops Keohane's analysis of the 'sunk costs' inherent in regimes and institutions, that is 'the irretrievable investment of an actor's time and power in creating a regime or institution'.[87] For Byers, the ultimate 'sunk cost' is legitimate expectation and, accordingly, it is the existence of international law which is able to account, in a large part, for the persistence of international regimes and institutions. Thus Byers explains:

> The principle of legitimate expectation, in particular, may be as important as the non-legal factors put forward by Keohane and others, in terms of its ability to explain the persistence of international regimes and institutions. Moreover, it would seem that an explanation for the persistence of regimes and institutions that was based on the principle of legitimate expectation could be compatible with an understanding of the international system as largely responsive to applications of power in the furtherance of state interests. In short, the principle of legitimate expectation, unlike other non-legal factors, is largely external to short-term interest calculations and applications of power precisely because it is a principle of international law.[88]

Having analysed some of the problems of customary international law highlighted above, including the chronological paradox and the epistemological circle,[89] Byers seeks to draw directly on institutionalism

---

85. *Idem*.
86. *Idem*.
87. *Idem*, p. 108.
88. *Idem*, p. 109.
89. See, in particular, Chapter 2 of his book.

in explanation, primarily, of the character of *opinio juris* and its relevance to customary international law. Thus, Byers notes that 'the process of customary international law is clearly an institution'.[90] He highlights the definitions of institutions and regimes provided by Keohane,[91] Young,[92] and Krasner,[93] all of which could be applied to customary international law, before focusing on Wendt's definition which frames institutions primarily in terms of 'collective knowledge'.[94] Byers suggests that 'if the customary process is understood as involving a "collective knowledge" or set of shared understandings, *opinio juris* may then be understood as being those shared understandings which enable states to distinguish between legally relevant and legally irrelevant state practice'.[95]

Byers' approach can be criticized in a number of ways. From the perspective of the international lawyer the description of *opinio juris* in these terms may add little to their understanding of the concept. Thus, the belief that a practice is legally binding has little relevance if it is held only by one or a small number of states. It is, accordingly, self-evident that *opinio juris* must exist as a set of shared beliefs in the legal relevance of a particular practice. Furthermore, Byers does little to assist the practitioner whose job it is to discover in a particular case whether there is sufficient generality of practice coupled with *opinio juris* in order for a rule of customary international law to exist. Similarly, judges are concerned not with generalities about the nature of customary international law but rather with the existence of specific rules binding on states.

Nevertheless, Byers' analysis is to be welcomed for a number of reasons. First, it focuses directly on the relationship between power and law in international relations. In doing so, Byers highlights the important role played by law in qualifying the application of power. Secondly, by directly utilizing leading scholarship from the field of international relations, Byers is able, more than mainstream lawyers, to enter into an interdisciplinary dialogue with international relations scholars and assist those scholars in understanding aspects of the international legal system. Finally, Byers' work does directly address certain of the fundamental problems of customary international law, in particular, and international

---

90. *Idem*, p. 147.
91. Keohane (1989).
92. Young (1989).
93. Krasner (1983).
94. Wendt (1992), p. 399.
95. Byers (1999), p. 148.

law, in general, and will certainly be the catalyst for future debate within
the international legal fraternity.

Koh: Why Nations Obey

In a leading review published in the *Yale Law Journal* in 1997, Harold Koh
asks the question 'Why do nations obey international law?'. The focus of
the review is the work of compliance theorists Abram Chayes and
Antonia Chayes, and Thomas Franck, both of which are works focusing
on states' compliance with international norms. Having critiqued both
works, Koh concludes that both 'reach the same intuitive answer to why
nations obey', that is 'that voluntary obedience, not coerced compliance,
must be the preferred enforcement mechanism'.[96] He continues:

> If nations internally 'perceive' a rule to be fair, says Franck, they are more
> likely to obey it. If nations regularly justify their actions to treaty partners
> in terms of treaty norms, suggest the Chayeses, it is more likely that
> those nations will 'voluntarily' comply with those norms. Both analyses
> suggest the key to better compliance is more *internalized* compliance.[97]

For Koh, international law is best described as a transnational legal
process which involves three phases:

> One or more transnational actors provokes an *interaction* (or series of
> interactions) with another, which forces an *interpretation* or enunciation
> of the global norm applicable to the situation. By so doing, the moving
> party seeks not simply to coerce the other party, but to *internalize* the new
> interpretation of the international norm into the other party's internal
> normative system. The aim is to bind that other party to obey the
> interpretation as part of its internal value set. Such a transnational legal
> process is normative, dynamic and constitutive. The transaction
> generates a legal rule which will guide future transnational interactions
> between the parties; future transactions will further internalize those
> norms; and eventually, repeated participation in the process will help
> reconstitute the interests and even the identities of the participants in the
> process.[98]

As can be seen in the above quotation, Koh utilizes analysis from each of
institutional, liberal and constructivist international relations theory in
his explanation of why nations obey international law. For Koh, it is

---

96. Koh (1997), p. 2645.
97. *Idem*, pp. 2645–6 (emphasis in original).
98. *Idem*, p. 2646 (emphasis in original).

important to look beyond the state so as not to miss what he refers to as 'the transnational revolution.'[99] Thus he criticizes institutionalist interest theories as showing 'relatively little explanatory power in such areas as human rights, environmental law, debt restructuring, international commercial transactions, where non-state actors abound, pursue multiple goals in complex nonzero-sum games, and interact repeatedly within informal regimes'.[100]

On the other hand, Koh criticizes 'liberal' identity theory which seeks 'to explain compliance at the level of domestic political structure'.[101] Such an approach fails to accept that states may be 'neither permanently liberal nor illiberal, but make transitions back and forth from dictatorship to democracy, prodded by norms and regimes of international law'. Thus, according to Koh: 'Identity analysis leaves unanswered the critical constructivist question: To what extent does compliance with international law itself help *constitute the identity* of a state as a law-abiding state, and hence as a 'liberal' state?'[102]

Finally, Koh notes that a constructivist, international society approach 'recognizes the positive transformational effects of repeated participation in the legal process'.[103] However, such an approach 'does not isolate, much less fully account for, the importance of process factors that arise not merely from the *existence* of international community, but from countless iterated transactions within it'.[104] Thus, according to Koh:

> As governmental and non-governmental actors repeatedly interact within the transnational legal process, they generate and interpret international norms and then seek to internalize those norms domestically. To the extent that these norms are successfully internalized, they become future determinants of why nations obey. The international society theorists seem to recognize that this process occurs, but have given little close study to the 'transmission belt,' whereby norms created by international society infiltrate into *domestic* society.[105]

Accordingly, Koh rejects all three theories as sufficient explanations in themselves for why nations obey international law. He argues, however, that: 'These explanations can be used together as complementary

---

99. *Idem*, p. 2649.
100. *Idem*, pp. 2649–50.
101. *Idem*, p. 2650.
102. *Idem* (emphasis in original).
103. *Idem*.
104. *Idem*, p. 2651 (emphasis in original).
105. *Idem* (emphasis in original).

conceptual lenses to give a richer explanation of why compliance with international law does or does not occur in particular cases.'[106] To this extent, Koh's analysis highlights the fact that international lawyers need not subscribe exclusively to one or other of the theories advanced above. Indeed, Koh's combination of the three theories into a theory of transnational legal process apparently places law at the forefront of international relations. Thus, according to Koh:

> In tracing the move from the external to the internal, from one-time grudging compliance with an external norm to habitual internalized obedience, the key factor is repeated participation in the international legal process. That participation helps to reconstitute national interests, to establish the identity of actors, and to develop the norms that become part of the fabric of emerging international society.[107]

On the other hand, it has to be said that Koh's conception of the role of international law is dependent on the internalization of international legal norms into domestic law. While Koh recognizes that internalization can be social, political and legal, his focus is primarily on legislative internalization which 'embeds international law norms into binding domestic legislation or even constitutional law which officials of a non-complying government must then obey as part of the domestic legal fabric'.[108] As such, Koh's analysis is most directly relevant to states whose international legal obligations are capable of such internalization, that is liberal states. Furthermore, the focus on the internalization of international law fails to take account of the fact that many provisions of international law are neither capable of being, nor intended to be, made part of the domestic legal system.

Finally, while the internalization of rules of international law may indeed assist the compliance of states with international law, states are clearly capable of complying with laws which have not been internalized. Thus, Koh's reference to the political internalization movement that is working to bring about the internalization of the European Convention into UK law[109] fails to take account of the fact that the Convention has, on numerous occasions, been enforced against the United Kingdom since the 1950s. On each occasion the UK has accepted the relevant decision of the European Court of Human Rights, even where such decision has been highly critical of the United Kingdom's position. The

---

106. *Idem.*
107. *Idem*, p. 2655.
108. *Idem*, p. 2657.
109. *Idem.*

internalization of the Convention, which has now occurred by virtue of the Human Rights Act 1998, will not directly affect the United Kingdom's compliance with the Convention. Rather it will put in place new mechanisms by which UK citizens are able directly to pursue their rights under the Convention before the UK courts rather than having to pursue them before the European Court of Human Rights in Strasbourg.

Koh's analysis is undoubtedly open to criticism along the lines set out above. In particular, Koh's analysis seems overly optimistic about the role of international law. Nevertheless, Koh's use of analysis developed in the field of international relations again highlights the opportunities for interdisciplinary analysis in this area.

Arend: Do International Rules Matter?

A final example of such interdisciplinary work focusing on the role of international law in general is to be found in Anthony Arend's article entitled 'Do legal rules matter?' published in the *Virginia Journal of International Law* in 1998. Arend focuses directly on constructivism in order 'to present a series of specific conclusions about the relationship of international legal rules to international politics'.[110]

For Arend, international rules are socially constructed. They are created by authoritative state practice. Arend focuses on the concept of *opinio juris* to argue that 'rules take on their significance as legal rules as states come to believe them to be law and act according to that belief'.[111] Secondly, for Arend, international legal rules have intersubjective meaning. In other words, there is common shared understandings of international rules. In an analysis very close to that of Byers, Arend argues that: 'Legal rules cannot exist without shared expectations of authority.' He notes, however, that 'this conclusion does not mean that every conceivable putative rule reflects shared meaning ... But unless one argues that there is no international law at all, there must be shared understandings about most of the vast corpus of international legal rules.'[112]

Arend's third conclusion is that international legal rules constitute the structure of the international system. Thus, as Hurrell has pointed out, 'rationalist models of co-operation miss the crucial link between the

---

110. Arend (1998), p. 141.
111. *Idem*, p. 142.
112. *Idem*.

costs and benefits of specific legal rules and the role of international law as constitutive of the structure of the state system itself'.[113] Similarly, Kocs, on whom Arend relies heavily, has noted that the legal rules that structure the international system 'exist ... as a set of underlying implicit rules which create a framework that allows for formal agreements between states to be meaningful'.[114] In a way which is again reminiscent of the work of Byers, Ahrend identifies five of these basic principles as being the principles of sovereignty, personality (described by Arend as 'the criteria for membership of the international system' and which also determine 'when non-state actors will be endowed with rights and duties'[115]), rules on the binding nature of international law such as good faith and the provision of a language for diplomacy. Finally, on this point, according to Arend, 'international law gives normative value to actions and claims made by international lawyers'.[116] Thus, 'when states of other international actors contemplate a particular action, legal rules provide guidance about what procedure to follow for the act to be considered legitimate'.[117] For Arend, the prime example of such an occurrence was in relation to the Gulf War in which the United States and her allies used international law in order to provide the greatest degree of legitimacy for their actions.[118] Crucially, however, it is the reaction of other states, based on international law, that determines the ultimate legitimacy of such actions.

Fourthly, for Arend, the effect of legal rules on the identity and interests of states is subject to empirical testing. While constructivist approaches can be criticized generally for their inherent circularity as a result of the mutually-constitutive relationship between agent and structure, Arend sees legal rules as being less susceptible to superficial and whimsical change because they are 'identifiable parts of the structure of the international system'.[119] Thus, with respect to legal rules, although they can change through state practice, 'there are relatively clear criteria to determine when the rule itself has changed'.[120] Therefore, according to Arend, 'legal rules themselves provide an excellent yardstick for examining the effect of an important element of the structure of the

---

113. Hurrell (1993), pp. 214–15.
114. Kocs (1994), p. 538.
115. Arend (1998), p. 143.
116. *Idem*, p. 145.
117. *Idem*.
118. On the legality of the allied actions in the Gulf War, see below, Chapter 4.
119. Arend (1998), p. 146.
120. *Idem*, p. 147.

international system upon the identities and interests of states'.[121]

Finally, and perhaps most crucially for Arend, international legal rules change the identity and interests of states. Arend cites examples of identity and interest changes to different groups of states, including the Group of 77, archipelagic states and geographically disadvantaged states, brought about during the negotiation of the 1982 Law of the Sea Convention. One has to wonder whether indeed it was the resulting legal principles or simply a by-product of the process of negotiation that was the ultimate catalyst towards the changes in identity and interests of the states involved. Nevertheless, it is clear that the resulting legal rules supported and strengthened those identity and interest changes.

Arend concludes that 'the constructivist approach enhances our understanding of the role legal rules play in international relations ... constructivism demonstrates the significance of international rules in the international political arena'.[122] As such, Arend's analysis is to be welcomed. In the light of the historical links between international lawyers and leading scholars in the constructivist school referred to above, it is perhaps not surprising that constructivist scholarship of the type referred to by Arend is at the forefront of the interdisciplinary efforts to explain the role of international law.

CONCLUSIONS

The preceding analysis has highlighted the opportunities for interdisciplinary scholarship between international lawyers and international relations scholars. It has to be said that much of the reason for the failure in the past properly to develop such scholarship was the continued adherence of international relations scholars to realist perspectives which played down the role of international law in the relations of states. Nevertheless, international lawyers should not go uncriticized for their failure to address key insights of international relations scholars on matters such as the relative power of states, both militarily and economically. Crucially, international lawyers have perhaps been too quick to over-emphasize the potential of international law and its ability to restrain states in the exercise of their power. Equally, however, international relations scholars should recognize that international lawyers are not, in general, idealists. They are not seeking to impose

---

121. *Idem.*
122. *Idem*, pp. 152–3.

on states a system of international law akin to municipal law. What they are seeking to do is to develop rules on which states can agree which provide a framework within which states are able to cooperate.

For the time being, much interdisciplinary scholarship is originating in the legal world, with international lawyers drawing on international relations scholarship to provide new ways of looking at international law and its relevance to international relations. However, such work could not have begun without key developments in international relations theory, highlighted in this chapter, which have allowed international relations scholars once again to consider the relevance of international law. At best, this new-found willingness for international lawyers and international relations scholars to work together will deepen our understanding of the causes of, and potential legal responses to, international problems. It will also sharpen our understanding of what particular institutional arrangements are able to do. At worst, however, interdisciplinary work simply restates what has already been done, misinterprets core presumptions of international relations or international legal scholarship or identifies vague similarities between international relations and international law.

It is possible to see the overall framework of interdisciplinary scholarship by identifying four approaches. First, there is mere dabbling. This is not truly representative of interdisciplinary collaboration, as there need be no conscious attempt to challenge, supplement or develop ideas and techniques on questions of common concern to both disciplines. Such dabblers should not be overtly criticized. Where two disciplines have developed in the way international law and international relations have, it may be that, at an early stage of combined scholarship, all that can be hoped for is for a degree of dabbling which may result in more properly interdisciplinary scholarship emerging at some time in the future. Dabbling shows awareness of the other discipline and the challenges or similarities it offers to their own work. It must be made clear at this point that one of the purposes, if not the primary purpose, of this book is to provide students of both international law and international relations with information on one another's discipline such as to allow the dabbling to start.

Secondly, some international lawyers have realigned international law with politics and have crafted new conceptions of international law, as traditionally perceived. In this way international lawyers have opened up the possibility for international relations scholars to make substantial contributions to international law. Included among these approaches should be the New Haven School and the works of Byers, Koh and Ahrend highlighted above. Thirdly, some international relations scholars have developed theories which have come to recognize a role for international law in international relations. These approaches have been highlighted above and include institutionalism, liberalism and constructivism.

The next stage along the road to truly interdisciplinary scholarship is through the fourth approach, the development of a collaborative research agenda. This fourth stage is at a very early stage of development and, as such, it is beyond the scope of this book. However, Slaughter, Tulumello and Wood have recently highlighted the areas in which such a collaborative research agenda may be developing. They identify three areas around which international lawyers and international relations scholars are converging: 'international governance, social construction and liberal agency'. They continue:

> This focus on substantive themes cross-cuts established paradigms and self-directed disciplinary boundaries and leads us to six clusters of research questions on which a collaborative research agenda might be built. These six clusters fall under the headings of regime design, process design, discourse on the basis of shared norms, transformation of the constructive structures of international affairs, government networks and embedded institutionalism.[123]

For present purposes it is sufficient to note that the prospects for interdisciplinary scholarship between international relations and international law have improved greatly in recent years. The future of such scholarship is dependent on students of each discipline having an understanding of the other. Hopefully the first part of this book has gone some way to providing the necessary introduction.

---

123. Slaughter, Tulumello and Wood (1998), p. 369.

CHAPTER 4

PREVENTING THE USE OF FORCE BY STATES: KOREA, THE GULF CONFLICT AND BEYOND

INTRODUCTION

Much has already been made about the relevance of centralized sanctions to the existence and efficacy of international law. For Austin, the absence of centralized sanctions was one of the factors, along with the absence of a sovereign commanding the law, which pointed towards the non-existence of international law as law properly so called.[1] Similarly, the realist critique of the efficacy of international law is premised, to a considerable degree, on the lack of centralized enforcement machinery.[2] It is possible to argue that this focus on the need for centralized enforcement of international law is misplaced and fails to take account of the special characteristics of international law. Indeed, it was argued in Chapter 1 of this book that the decentralized enforcement mechanisms which dominate the enforcement of international law are able to overcome Morgenthau's accusation that international law 'delivers the enforcement of law to the vicissitudes of the distribution of power between the violator of the law and the victim of the violation'.[3]

Nevertheless, while the absence of a decentralized enforcement system does not render international law ineffective, it is accepted by many that a centralized enforcement machinery would strengthen the cause of international law. Such thoughts must have been going through

---

1. See above, Chapter 1.
2. See above, Chapter 3.
3. Morgenthau (1973), p. 290.

the minds of the drafters of the original collective enforcement system, the League of Nations Covenant. Similar ideas were undoubtedly present in the minds of the drafters of the UN Charter who saw the failure of the League of Nations as deriving from sources other than the collective enforcement system itself. Indeed, where the drafters of the UN Charter sought to remedy certain of the deficiencies of the League system, it was, in particular, by providing for greater centralization.

The collective enforcement system envisaged by the UN Charter is, on paper at least, surprisingly straightforward. First, it should be recalled that the UN Charter *prima facie* prohibits in Article 2(4) the 'threat or use of force against the territorial integrity or political independence of any state or in any other manner inconsistent with the purposes of the United Nations'. By removing from states the right to resort to war in order to enforce a legal right – the primary mechanism of the self-enforcement of international law that had existed up to that point – the aim was to avoid prolonged armed conflict between individual states and to remove the potential for such conflicts to escalate into more widespread hostilities. However, the prohibition on resort to force by individual states, except in the case of self-defence,[4] created a vacuum in the enforcement of international law. This vacuum was to be filled by providing, in effect, for a UN army, capable of mobilizing on short notice, which would be able to enter into any conflict situation and deal quickly and decisively with the aggressor state.

It will be recalled that the basis of this system is to be found in Chapter VII of the UN Charter, comprising Articles 39–51. According to Article 39:

> The Security Council shall determine the existence of any threat to the peace, breach of the peace or act of aggression, and shall make recommendations, or decide what measures shall be taken in accordance with Articles 41 and 42 in order to maintain or restore international peace and security.

Article 39 is the key to the unlocking of the Chapter VII enforcement system. Without the determination that there exists a threat to the peace, a breach of the peace or an act of aggression, the United Nations would not have the authority to take action in any given situation. However, where such a determination is made, the effect is to override any claim by a state that a matter is entirely within its domestic jurisdiction.[5]

---

4. See above, Chapter 1.
5. UN Charter, Article 2(7).

Accordingly, the power bestowed on the Security Council in this context is considerable and one would not expect it to be used without due consideration.

Article 40 allows the Security Council to recommend the taking of provisional measures in order to contain a situation. However, the real power of the Security Council is to be found in Articles 41 and 42 of the Charter. In terms of Article 41, the Security Council is authorized to impose measures not involving the use of force against an aggressor state. These include economic sanctions, the severance of communications and the breaking off of diplomatic relations.[6] Ultimately, the Security Council has the power, in terms of Article 42, to authorize the use of force. The precise wording of Article 42 is as follows:

> Should the Security Council consider that measures provided for in Article 41 would be inadequate or have proved to be inadequate, it may take such action as may be necessary to maintain or restore international peace and security. Such action may include demonstrations, blockade, and other operations by air, sea or land forces of Members of the United Nations.

The original conception of the framers of the Charter was that the Security Council would have its own standing military force under its direct control. Thus Article 43 provides that Member States are to enter into agreements with the Security Council to make forces available to the Council on demand. Furthermore, Article 47 provides for the establishment of a Military Staff Committee 'to advise and assist the Security Council on all questions relating to the Security Council's military requirements for the maintenance of international peace and security . . .'[7] Finally, the right of individual and collective self-defence is affirmed in Article 51 of the Charter which provides that states which are the subject of an armed attack are entitled to use force in self-defence, but only until the Security Council has taken measures in order to restore international peace and security.

As a theoretical framework, Chapter VII of the UN Charter has been described as 'a perfect representative of a collective security system'.[8]

---

6. Article 41 provides that: 'The Security Council may decide what measures not involving the use of armed force are to be employed to give effect to its decisions, and it may call upon the Members of the United Nations to apply such measures. These may include complete or partial interruption of economic relations and of rail, sea, air, postal, telegraphic, radio and other means of communication, and the severance of diplomatic relations.'
7. UN Charter, Article 47.
8. Arend and Beck (1993), p. 51.

However, the reality falls far short of the vision. First, the problem of the veto has already been highlighted.[9] This problem is particularly acute in relation to the operation of the collective security system of the Charter because it places the permanent members of the Council above the system, ensuring that they can never properly be regarded as aggressor states under that system. Thus as Anthony Arend and Robert Beck have noted: 'at best, the Charter established only a "modified" or "limited" form of collective security'.[10] In practice, the effect of the veto has been far more damaging. Even where permanent members have not been directly involved in a use of force, they have consistently vetoed draft resolutions directed against allied states. Thus, the United States has repeatedly blocked resolutions aimed at identifying the situation in the Middle East as a threat to international peace and security, particularly where those resolutions have directly condemned the actions of Israel. Similarly, the Soviet Union vetoed 121 resolutions in the period 1946–86.[11] In many cases the exercise of the veto had little to do with the protection of any vital interest of the Soviet Union.[12]

Even if the difficulty of the veto were to be overcome, a second major stumbling block becomes apparent. That is, the failure to establish a standing military force under the direct control of the UN Security Council on the advice of the Military Staff Committee. A strict reading of the Charter indicates that the establishment of such a force is a prerequisite of any military action being taken under Chapter VII. Undoubtedly, the drafters of the Charter were extremely optimistic in believing that such a military body could be established. On the other hand, they were entitled to believe that, having signed up to the Charter, states would attempt to comply with Article 43 of the Charter. However, it is clear from the wording of Article 43 that member states did not, in fact, commit themselves to the creation of a standing UN army. Rather they committed themselves, at some time in the future, to enter into agreements with the UN Security Council to provide forces for UN enforcement actions. Once it became apparent that the five permanent members of the Security Council were unwilling or, indeed, unable to enter into such agreements, the expectation that other states would enter

---

9. See above, Chapter 1.
10. Arend and Beck (1993), p. 52.
11. White (1995), p. 12.
12. White cites as an example the Soviet Union's veto of a proposed resolution that would have condemned the Indian invasion of Goa in 1961. For White this was 'an example of the veto being used not for any vital protective purpose but, in this case, to express support for India, the Third World and anti-colonialism' (White, 1995, p. 11).

into such agreements disappeared.

Having examined the terms of the UN Charter on collective security and highlighted some of the fundamental difficulties with the Chapter VII regime, it is now possible to focus on the situations in which the Chapter VII procedure has been used and to highlight some of the legal issues arising therefrom. Between 1945 and 1990, the Security Council authorized the use of force in terms of the Chapter VII procedures only twice: in Korea in 1950 and against Rhodesia in 1965. Since 1990, the Chapter VII procedures have been used in relation to the Gulf Conflict (1990–1), Somalia (1992), Bosnia (1993) and Haiti (1993). Most recently, the procedures have been used in respect of the situation in East Timor (1999). Notably, there was no direct Chapter VII authorization given for the US led intervention in Iraq in response to their non-compliance with earlier Security Council resolutions (1998) nor, indeed, in relation to the NATO intervention in Kosovo (1999). These situations will be discussed further below.

Undoubtedly the Security Council has been more willing to use the Chapter VII procedure in the 1990s. This must be due in a large part to the break-up of the former Soviet Union and the ending of the Cold War. This in turn has resulted in a perceived reluctance among the permanent members of the Security Council to rely on the veto, particularly between 1990 and 1995.[13] However, the increased use of the Chapter VII procedure during the 1990s has been due also to the development of a functional approach to the interpretation of the requirements of Chapter VII. This aspect of the legal issues surrounding the operation of Chapter VII will be examined after a brief analysis of the UN involvement in the Korean War in 1950.

KOREA (1950)

The first real test of the Chapter VII procedure of the UN Charter came in June 1950 when North Korean forces moved over the 38th parallel into South Korean territory. Korea had been divided at the end of the Second World War as a result of the defeat of Japan, which had, for some time, been in control of the territory of Korea. The territory north of the 38th parallel had been surrendered by the Japanese to the Soviet Union and

---

13. White notes: 'With the end of the Cold War in the late 1980s the number of vetoes has decreased dramatically, for instance in 1991 no vetoes were cast by the permanent members' (White,1995, p. 12).

the territory below that line was surrendered to the United States. At the time of the invasion the Soviet Union was boycotting meetings of the Security Council in protest at the representation on the Security Council of the Republic of China (Nationalist China) instead of the People's Republic of China.

Immediately following the invasion of South Korea on 20 June 1950, the United States complained to the Security Council. On 25 June, the Security Council passed Resolution 82 in which the Council 'noted with grave concern the armed attack upon the Republic of Korea by forces from North Korea'. The Resolution declared the action to be a breach of the peace and called upon 'all Members to render every assistance to the United Nations ... and to refrain from giving assistance to the North Korean authorities'. Two days later on 27 June 1950, the Security Council passed Resolution 83 which 'recommended that the Members of the United Nations furnish such assistance to the Republic of Korea as may be necessary to repel the armed attack and to restore peace and security in the area'. On 7 July 1950, under considerable pressure from the United States, the Security Council passed Resolution 84 establishing a Unified Military Command under the leadership of the United States. This Resolution recommended that states should make military forces and other assistance available to the United States. The Soviet representative resumed his seat on 1 August 1950 and effectively blocked all further Security Council resolutions in relation to the situation in Korea.

With regard to the operation of Chapter VII, the first question to arise from the Korean situation is what was the effect of the Soviet Union's absence from the Security Council when the relevant resolutions were passed? A strict reading of the provisions of the UN Charter would indicate that all the permanent members of the Security Council are required to vote in favour of a resolution before it can be passed. However, clear practice of the Security Council, supported by a decision of the ICJ,[14] is in favour of regarding the abstention of a permanent member as being something less than a veto. The question which then arises is whether the Soviet Union's absence from the Security Council could be regarded as an abstention. The Soviet Union itself disputes this assertion and has consistently argued that its absence from the vote on the relevant resolutions rendered them invalid. Indeed, it cannot be denied that the Soviet Union, as soon as it resumed its seat, proceeded to veto subsequent resolutions in this matter. On the other hand, the Soviet Union was itself in breach of Article 28 of the Charter by absenting itself

---

14. *Legal Consequences Case* (1971) ICJ Rep., p. 22.

from the meetings of the Security Council.

A further question concerns the lack of operation of Article 43 of the Charter. The difficulties faced by the United Nations in this respect were made clear by the UK representative to the Security Council, Sir Gladwyn Jebb, when proposing the Resolution of 7 July 1950, establishing the Unified Military Command under US control. Having noted that 'it is clear to all concerned that unified command is essential if confusion is to be avoided', Jebb continued:

> Had the Charter come fully into force and had the agreement provided for in Article 43 of the Charter been concluded we should, of course, have proceeded differently, and the action to be taken by the Security Council to repel the armed attack would no doubt have been founded on Article 42. As it is, however, the Security Council can naturally act only under Article 39, which enables the Security Council to recommend what measures should be taken to restore international peace and security.[15]

The commonly held position in 1950 would appear to be that Article 42 was dependent upon Article 43 and so enforcement action could not be undertaken directly by the United Nations. However, it was argued that the Security Council was entitled to make recommendations for military action under Article 39 of the Charter. As recommendations, the Security Council resolutions were not binding on Member States who could simply have ignored them. In fact many states chose to render assistance to the US forces. Such assistance included the sending of armed forces to the region by fifteen other states as well as the United States. This degree of support for the resolutions led Derek Bowett to conclude that: 'There can be no doubt that, in practice, the overwhelming majority of states involved in the Korean action were fully prepared to regard it as a United Nations action involving United Nations Forces.'[16] Thus, while there is some doubt as to the constitutionality of the measures taken against North Korea, a functionalist analysis of the provisions of the UN Charter allows the broader considerations of the aims and objectives of the United Nations, in terms of combating aggression, to be taken into account. Clearly, had the Soviet Union directly vetoed the action in Korea, no question of a broad interpretation of the terms of Chapter VII could have arisen. However, Article 1(1) of the UN Charter declares its basic function as being to 'maintain international peace and security'. The action taken against North Korea ultimately achieved that purpose.

---

15. SC 477 mtg., 5 UN SCOR (1950).
16. Bowett (1964), p. 47.

Therefore, the argument goes, the action was justified. On the other hand, the delegation of power over the UN action to the United States, which ultimately contributed 90 per cent of the force, has been questioned. Thus, Nigel White has noted that a recommendation of the Security Council in this way 'cannot involve a total delegation of authority to a single state without adequate safeguards that prevent the obvious national interests motivating the state to volunteer its forces outstripping the collective security interests of the Security Council'.[17]

An alternative legal justification has been put forward in support of the legality of the US intervention in the Korean conflict. That is, that the operation by the United States, with the assistance of other states, constituted a collective self-defence action undertaken at the request of South Korea in terms of Article 51 of the UN Charter. The primary benefit of this justification is that it avoids any consideration of the constitutionality of the UN resolutions which can simply be ignored. Undoubtedly, the initial operations by the United States immediately after the North Korean invasion were actions of collective self-defence. However, given the direct involvement of the Security Council in calling upon states to assist in the operation against North Korea, it is doubtful whether the action was intended as merely a collective self-defence action, even if it can be justified as such.

One might wonder, therefore, at the justification of the United States in seeking to implement Chapter VII of the Charter by calling a meeting of the Security Council. The primary justification must lie within the inherent limitations of the doctrine of self-defence. As was made clear in the first chapter of this book, self-defence is limited by considerations of necessity and proportionality. In particular, self-defence can be no more than what it implies. It cannot allow for punitive action to be taken against an aggressor state after the successful completion of defensive action. Accordingly, if any enforcement or punitive action were to be legitimately taken against the North Koreans, it could only have been justified in terms of the Chapter VII enforcement procedures.

Perhaps the best legal analysis of the UN action in Korea falls somewhere between the two positions stated above. White, for example, has argued that there may be a middle ground between collective enforcement actions and collective self-defence actions:

Presumably the Security Council can authorise action going beyond simply the defensive. There appears no restriction on the Security

---

17.   White (1995), p. 106.

Council authorising offensive action if that is what is required to maintain or restore international peace and security. However, if the Council is going to authorise offensive force then the resolution, or subsequent resolutions, should clearly state as such. If there are doubts, then the response should be limited to a defensive action. In this respect the UN action is akin to an action in collective self-defence, although its legal basis remains distinct, deriving from Article 39 (and possibly Article 42) rather than Article 51 of the Charter.[18]

The possibility of developing this interpretation of Chapter VII of the Charter was effectively suspended for the following 40 years. As outlined above, repeated use of the veto, particularly by the US and the Soviet Union, during this period effectively denied any further implementation, let alone development, of the Chapter VII procedures. The only exception to this arose in the context of the Unilateral Declaration of Independence by Southern Rhodesia in 1965. As a result of its declared apartheid policies, the UN called upon states not to recognize Southern Rhodesia and imposed a series of economic sanctions against it. By Resolution 221 (1966) the United Kingdom was authorized to use force against shipping seeking to break the UN imposed economic embargo on Southern Rhodesia. In fact, UK forces did not undertake any military action under the authority of the Resolution. It was, accordingly, not until a short time after the end of the Cold War that the opportunity again arose to test the Chapter VII procedures.[19] This opportunity came as a result of the invasion by Iraq of Kuwait on 2 August 1990.

THE GULF CONFLICT (1990–1)

The international reaction to the Iraqi invasion of Kuwait, as with the situation in Korea, began as a textbook UN enforcement action. Thus, within hours of the initial invasion, the Security Council passed Resolution 660 which determined that there existed a breach of international peace and security. The Resolution further demanded Iraq's immediate and unconditional withdrawal from Kuwait. The next

---

18. *Idem*, pp. 107–8.
19. White notes that even in December 1989, after the ending of the Cold War, the US continued to use the veto in order to ensure it was not condemned for its intervention in Panama. White concludes of this action that: 'The end of the Cold War unfortunately does not signify the end of geopolitical limitations as the Panamanian vetoes illustrate, although it is true to say that those limitations are much reduced' (*idem*, p. 13).

step in the implementation of Chapter VII was to impose sanctions on Iraq. This was done by virtue of Resolution 661. Notably, however, Resolution 661 also affirmed 'the inherent right of individual or collective self-defence in response to the armed attack by Iraq against Kuwait in accordance with Article 51 of the Charter'.

The next major development was Resolution 665 which:

> called upon member states co-operating with the government of Kuwait which are deploying maritime forces in the area to use such measures commensurate to the specific circumstances as may be necessary under the authority of the Security Council to halt all inward and outward maritime shipping in order to inspect and verify their cargoes and destinations and to ensure strict implementation of the provisions related to such shipping laid down in Resolution 661.

Resolution 665 brought to a head the debate over the limitations of self-defence apparently imposed by the UN Charter. Article 51 of the Charter, which affirms 'the inherent right of individual or collective self-defence', purports to limit the exercise of that right until such time as 'the Security Council has taken measures necessary to maintain international peace and security'. The full extent of this limitation has always been disputed. In particular, the question has been asked as to what is meant by the words 'measures necessary to maintain international peace and security'. Do they refer to measures which are actually effective to bring about the stated objective? Or is the effect of the words such as to suspend the operation of individual or collective self-defence at the point at which the Security Council becomes involved in the situation? In the context of the Gulf Conflict, the issue arose as to whether the effect of Resolution 665 was to suspend the right of self-defence.[20] The majority of academic opinion appears to favour the view that UN enforcement action and self-defence measures can continue alongside one another. Thus, according to Eugene Rostow:

> The practice of subordinating the right of self-defence to a requirement of prior Security Council permission would be fatal to the right of states to defend themselves. What the Charter prescribes is precisely the opposite rule: that the aggrieved state and its friends and allies may decide for themselves when to exercise their rights of individual and collective self-defence until peace is restored or the Security Council, by its own affirmative vote, decides that self-defence has gone too far and become a threat to the peace.[21]

---

20. See, for example, Greig (1991), p. 398.
21. Rostow (1991), p. 510.

Had the Security Council subsequently been able to rely directly on Chapter VII of the UN Charter as a basis for continuing the action against Iraq, the issue of the true limitation of the right of self-defence, as declared in Article 51, might well have been clarified. However, the failure to implement the agreements envisaged in Article 43 again became crucial. As the allied build-up in the Gulf continued, the Security Council enacted, in November 1990, Resolution 678. Paragraph 2 of Resolution 678 authorized 'member states co-operating with the government of Kuwait, unless Iraq on or before 15 January 1991 fully implements ... the foregoing resolutions [of the Security Council], to use all necessary means to uphold and implement Security Council Resolution 660 and all subsequent resolutions and to restore international peace and security in the area'.

The ambiguity of both the wording and the legitimacy of Resolution 678 are immediately apparent. First, was the Resolution intended to authorize an enforcement action under Chapter VII of the Charter. If so, was the authority to use force given under Article 39, as a recommendation, or under Article 42? If the Resolution was an Article 42 resolution what was the effect of the non-implementation of Article 43? Alternatively, did the Resolution simply affirm the right of the states seeking to liberate Kuwait to act in collective self-defence? If so, why did the Resolution not simply say that? Finally, and perhaps most crucially, what was meant by the words 'all necessary means'?

In one of the most wide-ranging criticisms of the actions of both the United Nations and the United States in the Gulf Conflict, Burns Weston has argued that Resolution 678 lacked legitimacy. He argues that in adopting Resolution 678, 'the United Nations Security Council made light of fundamental UN precepts and thereby flirted precariously with "generally accepted principles of right process"'.[22] He continues:

> [The Security Council] eschewed direct UN responsibility *and* accountability for the military force that ultimately was deployed, favouring instead, a delegated, essentially unilateralist determination and orchestration of world policy, co-ordinated and controlled almost exclusively by the United States ... As a consequence it sets a dubious precedent both for the United Nations as it stands today and for the 'new world order' that is claimed for tomorrow.[23]

The details of Weston's analysis are worthy of further consideration, not

22. Weston (1991), p. 516.
23. *Idem*, p. 517.

least because his strict, black-letter approach stands in direct opposition to the functionalist approach adopted by the majority of commentators in response to the intervention in Korea. For Weston, the action undertaken under the authority of Resolution 678 was not a Chapter VII operation. In particular, for Weston, Article 42 of the Charter is a dead letter because of its 'dependent relationship with Article 43'.[24] Accordingly: 'Whatever military action the Security Council might take to ensure international peace and security, it had to be premised otherwise.'[25] Perhaps that authority is to be found in terms of Article 51 or Article 39.

With regard to Article 51, Weston is unable to find any authority therein for Resolution 678. Having noted that Resolution 678 did not expressly cite Article 51, he continues:

> [E]ven if Resolution 678 can be said to have been rooted in Article 51 and thus to have constituted a delegation of authority relative to the forceful exercise of collective self-defence, the adoption of Resolution 678 on these grounds would have constituted an unprecedented interpretation of Chapter VII. It would appear unsupported by what the Charter drafters had principally in mind for Article 51 which was to safeguard mutual defence and collective security pacts and arrangements, none of which were present in the instant case.[26]

Weston further notes that the customary international law restrictions on self-defence such as the requirement of necessity leaving no time for deliberation were not in existence in the Iraqi case, particularly when Operation Desert Storm began.

Weston considers the direct comparison between the Korean intervention and the situation in the Gulf. He notes the right of the Security Council to make 'recommendations' to maintain or restore international peace and security under Article 39 of the Charter. He accepts that Article 39 had been directly invoked in Korea but argues that 'this was scarcely the kind of recommendation the Charter drafters had in mind when they adopted Article 39'.[27] Weston continues:

> In any event, as if to reject the Korean comparison expressly, the Security Council, in Resolution 678, made an *authorisation* (or *decision*), not a *recommendation*. Also, at the behest of the United States and to secure exclusive US command and control over Persian Gulf operations, it turned down a Soviet proposal to activate the Military Staff Committee

---

24. *Idem*, p. 519.
25. *Idem*.
26. *Idem*, p. 520.
27. *Idem*, p. 521.

provided for in Charter Articles 45–47 to unify the strategic direction of Security Council police actions. In the case of Korea, the Security Council attempted at least the pretence of fielding a unified command under the UN flag.[28]

The idea that Resolution 678 could be justified on the basis of fulfilling the purposes of Chapter VII while not complying directly with its provisions is also considered by Weston. He does not reject outright this so-called 'Article 42½ authorisation'. However, he is of the opinion that 'when human life, (especially innocent human life) and other fundamental values are being put greatly and severely at risk, as surely they were when Resolution 678 was adopted, it seems not inappropriate to insist upon unambiguously articulated war-making authority as a *de minimis* requirement of "right process" '.[29]

While such an approach is clearly preferable to one which ignores the requirements of right process altogether, it is important when dealing with rules in any legal system to be aware of the need for flexibility. Were Weston's approach to be adopted there would, quite simply, be nothing which the international community could have done to deal with Iraq's aggression against Kuwait. Weston himself accepts that the development of a functionalist interpretation of Chapter VII may, in the long term, be a good thing. It is unclear, however, how Weston expects such an approach to arise. If it does not arise through the Security Council itself adopting a functionalist interpretation of Chapter VII and receiving the support, or otherwise, of states, then such a development could never arise. In such cases, the legitimacy of the action will be determined by the level of support shown for the action by the international community. In the present case, the actions of the Security Council and, indeed the allied force which moved against Iraq, received overwhelming international support, not only from Western-oriented states but also from the majority of Arab states.

An alternative analysis of the allied actions in the Gulf in early 1991 is to categorize those actions as measures of collective self-defence. The argument in support of this analysis is essentially the same as was put forward in relation to Korea. It has already been noted that this approach was specifically rejected by Weston. Other writers, however, have asserted that this was the true nature of the action taken against Iraq.[30] However, this approach too denies the current possibility of the United

---

28. *Idem*, pp. 521–2 (emphasis in original).
29. *Idem*, p. 522.
30. See, for example, Rostow (1991).

Nations taking enforcement action under a strict reading of Chapter VII of the Charter. Thus, according to Rostow: 'The coercive powers conferred on the Security Council have not yet become a working part of the process for managing the state system.'[31] Of Resolution 678, Rostow notes that 'except for the word "authorizes", the resolution is clearly one designed to encourage and support a campaign of collective self-defence, and therefore not a Security Council enforcement action'.[32] Similarly, according to Glennon, Resolution 678, like Resolution 83 in respect of the Korean conflict, 'merely exhorts, authorizes or recommends'.[33] In other words, the Resolution was not obligatory. If that is the case, what was the purpose of the Security Council in passing the Resolution and why did it not specifically refer to the right of collective self-defence? Thus, while the description of the action as one of collective self-defence gets round the difficulty of explaining away the inherent problems of Chapter VII of the Charter, it gives rise to other problems, not least the role of the United Nations in such a conflict.

The classification of the action as a measure of self-defence, if accepted, would have considerable consequences with regard to the traditional view of self-defence. As noted in Chapter 1 of this book, the customary international law of self-defence restricts the exercise of that right to situations where there is an overwhelming necessity leaving no choice of means and no moment for deliberation. Such was undoubtedly not the case in relation to the massive preparations for Desert Storm. Furthermore, Resolution 678 gave Iraq a time limit in which to withdraw from Kuwait. Again this is not something that is contemplated by the traditional restrictions on the right of self-defence. Certainly, it might be possible to argue that traditional approaches to the right of self-defence have, or should have, changed. The danger with such an approach is that it effectively undermines the role of the United Nations and does in fact, as predicted by Morgenthau, leave the question of international peace and security wholly to the vicissitudes of the most powerful states.

It cannot be denied that direct UN control over the allied forces in the Gulf Conflict was extremely limited. Indeed, the Security Council did not meet formally between the adoption of Resolution 678 in November 1990 and the end of the conflict in March 1991. The allied forces were required during this period only to provide regular reports to the Security Council as to what measures had already been carried out. Undoubtedly,

---

31. *Idem*, p. 508.
32. *Idem*, pp. 508–9.
33. Glennon (1991), p. 81.

a less ambiguous resolution, particularly one which was able to specify the aims of the action being taken against Iraq, would have been preferable. If the development of a more purposive interpretation of Chapter VII was what was intended then that should have been spelled out in the Resolution itself. Nevertheless, it is probable that this was the effect of the actions against Iraq in early 1991. Thus, according to White:

> The need for greater UN control of the operation does not necessarily signify that the operation was contrary to the UN Charter. The use of force needs to be assessed to see if it achieved those aims set out in Resolution 678 ... The Coalition forces operating under the umbrella of the UN, but not on this occasion using its flag ... did adopt a reasonable interpretation of Resolution 678 limiting the military action to the enforcement of Resolution 660 and other resolutions of the Security Council aimed at securing the withdrawal of Iraq from Kuwait.[34]

THE LEGALITY OF SUBSEQUENT 'ENFORCEMENT' ACTIONS

In the years immediately following the Gulf Conflict, the UN Security Council began increasingly to use its powers under Chapter VII of the Charter. Thus, resolutions declaring the existence of a threat to the peace were passed in relation to Somalia, Bosnia and Haiti. This must have been due in part to the realization that states appeared willing to accept the functional, as opposed to the literal, interpretation of the provisions contained in Chapter VII. It is not surprising, therefore, that Secretary-General Boutros Boutros-Ghali's call in 1992 for governments to conclude agreements with the Security Council under Article 43 fell on deaf ears.[35] If Chapter VII could function without a standing UN army then what need was there for states to enter into those agreements?

On the other hand, disquiet was quickly expressed about potential great power hegemony, particularly in relation to the apparent dominance by the United States of the political agenda in the Security Council. This is manifestly illustrated by the situation in relation to Haiti. The Haitian situation had begun with the overthrow of the democratically-elected President Aristide. The Security Council passed a resolution in June 1993 determining that there existed a threat to international peace and security. Sanctions were imposed then lifted, then replaced by stronger sanctions. The use of force was authorized by

34. White (1995), p. 110.
35. Boutros-Ghali (1992), para. 43.

the Security Council in Resolution 875 in order to enforce the sanctions. This action by the Security Council has been described as 'the greatest extension of UN power' into a situation of civil unrest with the purpose of restoring democratic rule.[36] Questions of whether the Security Council has the power to recognize such situations as threats to the peace have followed, along with more general calls for the power of the Security Council to be reviewable by the ICJ.

Such questions, however, appear to have been overtaken by events, most notably the increased tendency of Russia in the late 1990s to threaten to veto Security Council resolutions in relation to Iraq and the Federal Republic of Yugoslavia. As a result, the attention of international lawyers has now turned to consideration of the legality of the recent interventions in those states by US and UK forces in December 1998 and by NATO forces in April 1999 respectively. In both cases, direct Security Council authorization for the use of force was lacking. However, in both cases, the participating states have relied on a generally functional interpretation of Chapter VII in support of the legality of their operations.

Iraq (1998)

The situation in Iraq between 1991 and 1998 and, in particular, the threat of force used against Iraq in February 1998, will be discussed in depth in the following chapter. What is of primary concern in this context is the question of the legality of the use of force against Iraq in December 1998. The circumstances of the attack on Iraq existed as a direct result of the 1990/1 Gulf Conflict. At the end of that conflict the Security Council had enacted Resolution 687 which imposed on Iraq, *inter alia*, a duty to allow weapons inspections to take place in order to verify Iraqi compliance with their ceasefire obligations. On the other hand, as was noted in 1994 by Christine Gray, Resolution 687 was silent on the matter of 'whether the Security Council may formally or informally authorise the use of force to secure the implementation of [that resolution] and, more controversially, whether individual states may unilaterally use force against Iraq'.[37] A later resolution, Resolution 773, noted the UN's guarantee of the inviolability of the Iraq/Kuwait boundary and noted the willingness of the Security Council to take all necessary measures to secure such inviolability. However, according to Gray, 'neither Resolution 687 nor

---

36. See Hillier (1998), p. 618.
37. Gray (1994), p. 137.

Resolution 773 would justify *UNILATERAL* resort to force by members of the coalition. Nor can the Security Council's warning of grave consequences of any breach be taken as authority to use force.'[38]

Had Iraq carried out another armed attack against Kuwait in the period following the ceasefire, there is little doubt that the coalition forces could have taken immediate action against Iraq in the exercise of collective self-defence. The same could not be said in respect of breaches by Iraq of the disarmament and weapons inspection requirements of Resolution 687. Such an offence would not constitute an armed attack and it would be stretching the limits of anticipatory self-defence too far to claim the right of self-defence in such circumstances. On the other hand, it is clear that Iraq did systematically breach the relevant provisions of Resolution 687 by consistently denying access to IAEA and UNSCOM weapons inspectors. This intransigence elicited responses from the Security Council on two separate occasions in the form of Resolutions 707 and 715 which condemned the actions of the Iraqi authorities but which did not authorize the use of force against Iraq.

Nevertheless continued intransigence was cited by the United States as justification for an attack by US aircraft on a nuclear weapons facility on the outskirts of Baghdad on 17/18 January 1993. In particular, the United States argued that its response was proportionate and, therefore, justified. The UK Government supported the United States' action and argued that 'in light of Iraq's continued breaches of Security Council Resolution 687 and thus of the ceasefire terms, and of the repeated warnings given by the Security Council and members of the coalition, [US] forces were entitled to take necessary and proportionate action in order to ensure Iraqi compliance with those terms'.[39] However, as Gray notes, 'there does not seem to be anything in Resolution 687 that allows such an interpretation ... [it] is not legally convincing'.[40] Gray wonders also 'whether the actual use of force was indeed necessary and appropriate'. She concludes that: 'In whatever light the cruise missile attack is viewed – whether as a response to Iraq's non co-operation, or whether as a measure designed to ensure future co-operation – there must be considerable doubt whether the US attack was proportionate.'[41]

Nevertheless when in January and February 1998 weapons inspectors were again prevented from carrying out their tasks, the United States,

---

38. *Idem*, p. 149 (emphasis in original).
39. HC Debates, Vol. 217, Col. 514, 23 January 1993.
40. Gray (1994) p. 155.
41. *Idem*, p. 156.

together with other states, threatened to use force against Iraq.[42] Perhaps because of these threats, Iraq backed down and agreed to a Memorandum of Understanding which was endorsed by the Security Council in Resolution 1154. Again, no mention of the possible use of force against Iraq was made in that Resolution. As a result of the Memorandum, UN officials were able to resume their inspections. However, by November 1998, Iraq had again challenged the rights of the weapons inspectors to examine various sites in Iraq, most notably the compound surrounding the Presidential Palace. On 18 December 1998 US and UK aircraft began attacking targets throughout Iraq.

On this occasion, the United States and the United Kingdom relied not only on Resolution 1154 but also on Resolution 678 of 1990 and Resolution 687 (1991). As noted previously, Resolution 678 had authorized states acting with the Government of Kuwait to use 'all necessary measures' in order to bring about the removal of Iraqi forces from Kuwait. Thus, according to Lobel and Ratner, 'US and British officials argued that Resolution 678 of 1990, which empowered the United States and other states to use force against Iraq, still governed and continued to provide authority to punish Iraq for cease-fire violations'.[43] This broad interpretation of the continuing effect of Resolution 678 can be challenged on a number of grounds, two of which will be dealt with here. First, the clear intention of the Security Council in passing Resolution 678 was to secure the removal of Iraq from Kuwait. Although allied forces did enter into Iraqi territory towards the end of Operation Desert Storm, they chose not to continue their intervention as far as Baghdad. As has already been noted above, the two primary reasons for this are (1) that if the action was defensive, the legal justification of self-defence would not have permitted the continuation of an attack against Iraq; and (2) the general opinion amongst both academics and, more importantly, politicians was that Resolution 678 did not provide the necessary authority to 'bring Iraq to its knees'. Thus, Douglas Hurd, the British Foreign Minister in 1991, has subsequently written that: 'The coalition ... was formed and sustained for a particular purpose, namely the rescue of Kuwait.' Having noted that: 'No doubt after some days and further casualties we should have been able to overthrow the Government of Saddam Hussein', Hurd concludes that 'when the [US] President and his advisers came to the conclusion that the victory was completed and the war should end at once ... there was no suggestion

---

42. On the legality of the threat of force in these circumstances, see Chapter 5.
43. Lobel and Ratner (1999), p. 124.

that the objective of Desert Storm could or should at that last minute be changed.'[44]

A second objection to the attempted extension of the effect of Resolution 678 in 1998 was the objection of the other permanent members of the Security Council. A legitimate course of action for the United States and the United Kingdom to have followed in response to the Iraqi intransigence on weapons inspection issues would have been directly to seek a mandate from the Security Council for the use of force. However, no such mandate was sought and there can be no doubt that a mandate would not have been forthcoming. Accordingly, one is forced to conclude that the US and UK attacks on Iraq at the end of 1998 constituted an illegal use of force.

Kosovo (1999)

A similar conclusion must be reached in relation to the NATO attacks on the Federal Republic of Yugoslavia in April 1999. However, while a great deal of concern has been expressed about the use of armed force in response to the Iraqi refusal of weapons inspections, the situation in Kosovo was more clearly a breach of general international law and the existence of a major humanitarian disaster in Kosovo could not be denied by anybody except the most hardened observers. As Bruno Simma has stated: 'Contemporary international law establishes beyond any doubt that serious violations of human rights are matters of international concern.'[45] The question is, however, what should the legal response to such a violation be? Undoubtedly peaceful countermeasures are permitted. Equally clear, however, is that the prohibition on the use of force contained in Article 2(4) of the UN Charter severely limits countermeasures involving the use of force.

The possibility of states acting in self-defence has been highlighted above. Such a right is, of course, confirmed in Article 51 of the Charter. However, the prerequisite of such action is the existence of an armed attack. Thus, according to Simma:

> Article 51 has become the subject of certain gross (mis-)interpretations, most of them put forward during the Cold War when the Security Council regularly found itself in a state of paralysis. Against such attempts to turn a clearly defined exception to the comprehensive

44. Hurd (1997), pp. 125–6.
45. Simma (1999), p. 1.

Charter ban on the threat or use of force into a convenient basis for all sorts of military activities, it should be emphasised once again that Article 51 unequivocally limits whatever farther-reaching right of self-defence might have existed in pre-Charter customary international law to the case of an 'armed attack'.[46]

The only other alternative involving the threat or use of force is to be found in Chapter VII of the Charter. The development of the role of the Security Council in the cases referred to above including Somalia, Bosnia and Haiti have confirmed the right of the UN to take enforcement action even in matters which are 'essentially within the domestic jurisdiction of states'. However, there is no entitlement for states unilaterally to take such measures even against states which are accused of gross violations of human rights. The point is once again very clearly made by Simma:

> [I]f the Security Council determines that massive violations of human rights occurring within a country constitute a threat to the peace, and then calls for or authorizes an enforcement action to put an end to these violations, a 'humanitarian intervention' by military means is permissible. In the absence of such authorization, military coercion employed to have the target state return to a respect for human rights constitutes a breach of Article 2(4) of the Charter. Further, as long as humanitarian crises do not transcend borders, as it were, and lead to armed attacks against other states, recourse to Article 51 is not available. For instance, a mass exodus of refugees does not qualify as an armed attack.

It is clear, once again, that the primary stumbling block to the authorization of the use of force in Kosovo was Russian objection to that action. Furthermore, in this case, perhaps in contrast to the US and UK action against Iraq, there did appear to be considerable political support for the attacks against the Federal Republic of Yugoslavia and, indeed, Russian troops were involved in the land offensive. The question might therefore be asked by those not concerned with the legal niceties set out above whether these legal questions matter at all. The answer to this question must surely be that they do.

One of the most illustrative recent analyses of international law and the use of force is that provided by Arend and Beck. These two authors consider there to have been a shift in paradigms in respect of the continued use of force by states in the post-Charter world. Building on arguments originally put forward by Thomas Franck in 1970 in which he

46. *Idem*, p. 3.

detailed the death of Article 2(4) of the UN Charter,[47] Arend and Beck have distinguished between the 'legalistic', 'core interpretist' and 'rejectionist' approaches. Arend and Beck are highly critical of the legalist approach which contends that 'despite violations of the norm, it has *for the most part* exerted a restraining influence on state behaviour'.[48] For Arend and Beck this approach attempts to minimize the fact that 'the norm has been violated frequently and with impunity in some of the most important cases of state interaction. Even though legal scholars may disagree as to the precise list of such violations of Article 2(4) there is broad agreement that such violations have taken place.'[49] While described as the 'legalistic' approach, it is contended that few international lawyers would adopt such a strict approach.

'Core interpretists', according to Arend and Beck, 'contend that the basic prohibition contained in Article 2(4) is still valid, except as modified by authoritative interpretations confirmed in states' practice. Thus, every unilateral use of force is prohibited unless it can be demonstrated that the accepted interpretation of the Charter allows for an exception.'[50] Many international lawyers would fall into this category. Thus, they would recognize the ability of international law to develop practice around what might seem to be fairly rigorous prohibition. Such practice, however, must be based on the acceptance of interpretations by states in general. For Arend and Beck, this approach can be criticized on the basis that any attempt 'to use Article 2(4) in any way to describe the law relating to the recourse to force may simply be perpetrating a legal fiction that interferes with an accurate assessment of state practice'.[51]

Arend and Beck's clear preference is for the 'rejectionist' approach which denies the existence of Article 2(4) altogether. Having noted that 'apart from Professor Franck, no other major international legal scholar has *explicitly* taken this approach, although several have come close', Arend and Beck conclude that:

> Based on what states have been saying and what they have been doing, there simply does not seem to be a *legal* prohibition on the use of force against the political independence and territorial integrity of states as provided in even a modified version of Article 2(4). The rule creating process, authoritative state practice has rejected that norm.[52]

---

47. Franck (1970).
48. Arend and Beck (1993), p. 180 (emphasis in original).
49. *Idem*, p. 181.
50. *Idem*, p. 182.
51. *Idem*, p. 183.
52. *Idem*, p. 185.

In a way, Arend and Beck are entirely correct in their assertion. What they are saying is that state practice does not support an absolute prohibition on the threat or use of force. The point is, however, that Arend and Beck, having rejected Article 2(4), then set out in search of the new post-Charter paradigm for the use of force. In this search, they identify various lawful uses of force including the right of self-defence, the promotion of self-determination and the correction of past injustices and they then identify one unlawful use of force, that is, territorial annexation. In each case they assert legal criteria for the various categories of forceful measures which they discuss. While these lawful and unlawful uses of force may constitute the new paradigm, the question nevertheless arises as to the legality of the use of force in situations which do not easily fall into any of these categories. It is asserted therefore, that the only difference between the position of the 'core interpretists' and that of the 'rejectionists' concerns the starting point of the analysis. For the 'core interpretists', the starting point is Article 2(4) itself; for the 'rejectionists', the starting point is the assumption that states are unrestricted in relation to the use of force.

Crucially both 'core interpretists' and 'rejectionists' recognize that international law can and does change to take account of variations in state practice. The reason few international lawyers favour the rejectionist approach is because they regard the prohibition on the use of force as a binding rule of international law by virtue of both treaty law, in the form of Article 2(4) itself, and customary international law. The fact that certain states choose to breach Article 2(4) should not in itself undermine that rule. Nor should the fact that certain states can apparently breach the rule with impunity undermine the basic rule itself. The rule will only cease to be a rule of international law if the state parties to the UN Charter amend the rule or if there is sufficient state practice and *opinio juris* in favour of an alternative rule. The fact of the matter is that when states use force they seek to justify their actions by reference to an exception to the prohibition. By doing so, states, through their practice, affirm the prohibition rather than undermine it.

The idea that once a rule is written down and agreed upon, it is static and immutable should be rejected. International legal rules like all legal rules are subject to interpretation. The process of interpretation of international legal rules occurs through claims and counterclaims by states. The test of the legality of such claims rests upon the reactions of other states to those claims. The fact that the abuse of the veto system in the Security Council during the past 50 or so years has resulted in the development of more exceptions to the prohibition on the use of force than might have been envisaged by the original drafters of the Charter cannot be denied. Nevertheless, the same process is now being used to test the legality of centralized and unilateral interventions against states accused of breaching international law. It is by virtue of this process that most international lawyers are willing to accept the legality of the action taken against Iraq in 1991. Ten years ago, any talk of the Security Council authorizing a forcible 'humanitarian intervention' in a situation involving human rights abuses occurring wholly within the territory of a single state would have been considered fanciful. Yet with the passing of Resolution 1272 on 25 October 1999 setting up the UN Transitional Administration in East Timor and authorizing it to use all measures necessary to bring about a solution to the crisis in East Timor, albeit with the direct agreement of the Indonesian Government, the United Nations has taken another step towards the realization of its creators.

In this way, the assertion of the *prima facie* illegality of the NATO intervention of Kosovo in March/April 1999 should not be an end to the matter. A number of international lawyers have asserted that the intervention by NATO should be welcomed as an assertion of a developing international law right of humanitarian intervention. Antonio Cassesse has put forward a very strong argument in support of this assertion. Having accepted that the NATO intervention was a breach of the UN Charter, Cassesse highlights the concern of many that 'this dramatic departure from UN standards' will not remain an exception. He notes that:

> Once a group of powerful states has realized that it can freely escape the strictures of the UN Charter and resort to force without any censure, except for that of public opinion, a Pandora's box may be opened. What will restrain those states or other groups of states from behaving likewise when faced with a similar situation or, at any event, with a situation that in their opinion warrants resort to armed force.[53]

However, he continues:

> [A]s legal scholars we must stretch our minds further and ask ourselves two questions. First was the NATO armed intervention at least rooted and partially justified by contemporary trends of the international community? Second, were some parameters set, in this particular instance of use of force, that might lead to a gradual legitimation of forcible humanitarian countermeasures by a group of states outside any authorization by the Security Council.

Cassesse goes on to suggest certain strict conditions under which resort

---

53. Cassesse (1999), p. 25.

to armed force in support of humanitarian protection might be permissible, even in the absence of authorization by the Security Council. These include the existence of 'gross and egregious breaches of human rights' in situations of 'anarchy in a sovereign state' where the 'Security Council is unable to take any coercive action' and 'all peaceful measures have been explored'. Such actions should, according to Cassesse, be taken only by 'a group of states' and should be used 'exclusively for the purpose of stopping the atrocities and restoring respect for human rights'.[54]

It is too early to say whether such developments will result from the NATO intervention in Kosovo. There is no inherent reason to deny the possibility of such a change taking place. However, the crystallization of such a development will require an amendment of the UN Charter or general support for the change in the practice of states coupled with the general belief that such a change is legally necessary. While recognizing the difficulty of the situation, Simma is doubtful as to the desirability of such a development. Thus he notes:

> The lesson which can be drawn from this [crisis] is that unfortunately there do exist 'hard cases' in which terrible dilemmas must be faced and imperative political and moral considerations may appear to leave no choice but to act outside the law. The more isolated these instances remain, the smaller will be their potential to erode the precepts of international law ... a potential boomerang effect of such breaches can never be excluded, but this danger can at least be reduced by indicating the concrete circumstances that led to a decision *ad hoc* being destined to remain singular. In this regard NATO has done a convincing job ... But should the Alliance now set out to include breaches of the UN Charter as part of its strategic programme for the future, this would have an immeasurably more destructive impact on the universal system of collective security embodied in the Charter. To resort to illegality as an explicit *ultima ratio* for reasons as convincing as those put forward in the Kosovo case is one thing. To turn such an exception into a general policy is quite another.[55]

However, the issue here is not whether such developments are desirable or, indeed, likely. The purpose of citing this analysis is to illustrate the way in which lawyers, and, indeed, states are able to approach the interpretation of existing rules and the development of new rules. The key to whether or not a wider right of humanitarian intervention will

---

54. *Idem*, p. 27.
55. Simma (1999), p. 22.

ensue is the reaction of other states and indeed the participating states to the NATO intervention.

CONCLUSIONS

The use of force by individual states remains illegal under international law, subject to certain exceptions. These exceptions are developing through state practice and definitely include the right of self-defence and may in the future include humanitarian intervention. The ultimate exception to the prohibition on the use of force remains collective enforcement under the authority of the UN Security Council. Since 1990, this system has been reactivated and is itself subject to legal developments which focus, ultimately, on the primary function of the Security Council as the principal UN organ for the maintenance of international peace and security. It remains to be seen how well the Security Council will be able to develop in the future given the fact that the veto remains a major stumbling block to its effectiveness. In the meantime states may continue to resort to the use of force where in their determination their self-interest demands such action. However, insofar as states continue to seek to justify their actions by reference to international law, the *prima facie* prohibition on the use of force by states will remain a relevant factor which states will take into account in deciding whether or not to resort to the use of force.

CHAPTER 5

DIPLOMACY AND THE THREAT OF FORCE

You can do a lot with diplomacy, but with diplomacy backed up by force you can get a lot more done.

Kofi Annan

INTRODUCTION

So declared Kofi Annan, Secretary-General of the United Nations, on two separate occasions following the successful negotiation of the Memorandum of Understanding between the United Nations and the Republic of Iraq on 23 February 1998 which brought an end to the stand-off on the question of weapons inspections in Iraq.[1] Put into its context, the statement was undoubtedly a skilful response to questions designed to illicit the views of the Secretary-General about the effect of the military build-up in the Gulf led by the United States and backed by the United Kingdom, among others,[2] in the lead-up to the successful negotiation of the Memorandum of Understanding.[3] Given the history of Iraq's flouting of UN Security Council Resolutions and, in particular Resolution 687, it is hard not to agree with the Secretary-General's implicit assertion that the

---

1. The statement was first made by the Secretary-General at a Press Conference on the morning of 23 February 1998, shortly after the signing of the Memorandum in Baghdad. He repeated it at a Press Conference at the Headquarters of the United Nations in New York after briefing the members of the Security Council on 24 February 1998.
2. At the time of the signing of the Memorandum of Understanding forces had either been offered or committed by the Netherlands, Australia, Canada and Poland. Others, including New Zealand, were considering sending forces to the Gulf region.
3. When the statement was made for the second time on 24 February, the question posed was specifically related to the continued presence of the US and UK forces in the Gulf.

Memorandum of Understanding could not have been achieved without the threat of force. Given the fact that the threat of military action by the United States and the United Kingdom had not been authorized by the UN Security Council, however, it is suggested that the Secretary-General's statement may, of itself, have set a rather dubious precedent for the enforcement of international law.

Much concern was expressed during the lead-up to the signing of the Memorandum of Understanding about the legality of the proposed unilateral military action against Iraq by the United States and the United Kingdom. Similar concerns had been expressed in relation to the allied action in the Gulf Conflict of 1990–1,[4] the cessation of which had led to the passing of Resolution 687 by the UN Security Council; the legality of this resolution was challenged, not surprisingly, by Iraq.[5] It would appear, however, that the majority of commentators were of the view that the allied action in the Gulf in 1990–1 was legal, either as a legitimate exercise of collective self-defence,[6] or, more generally, as a legitimate exercise of collective enforcement under Chapter VII of the UN Charter.[7]

In the present circumstances it would appear that the argument of self-defence would not have been available to the United States and the United Kingdom because of the lack of an armed attack against the sovereignty of another state by Iraq. Furthermore, the justification of collective enforcement would have required a prior authorization of military action by the Security Council, which seemed unlikely given the strong stance against military action being put forward by the other permanent members of the Security Council, particularly France and Russia. Thus, as has been asserted in the previous chapter, when the United States and the United Kingdom resorted to the use of force against Iraq in December 1998, that use of force was illegal. The purpose of this chapter is not to discuss further the legality of the actual use of force in those circumstances, but rather to consider the legality of the threat of force, particularly in relation to the clear linkage between the threat of force against Iraq and the signing of the Memorandum of Understanding in February 1998.

---

4. See, for example, Weston (1991).
5. See Gray (1994), p. 145.
6. See, for example, Rostow (1991).
7. See, for example, Schachter (1991). See generally, Chapter 4 above.

THE THREAT OF FORCE AS A TOOL OF INTERNATIONAL DIPLOMACY

History is replete with examples of states threatening force in order to further their diplomatic objectives, be they legitimate or illegitimate. In fact, the threat of force does form part of the process of UN diplomacy. Perhaps the most important example of the linkage between diplomacy and the threat of force is to be found in Chapter VII of the UN Charter which clearly envisages the threat of force as a key element of the pursuit of peaceful settlements to international disputes by the UN Security Council.[8] Thus, it cannot be doubted that the mounting of Operation Desert Shield against Saddam Hussein in 1990–1 was intended not only to prepare for possible military intervention, but also to bolster the various diplomatic manoeuvres which were being attempted in order to bring a peaceful end to the Iraqi invasion of Kuwait.[9]

The evidence of state practice in this area has led writers on the practice of diplomacy to assert that the threat of force is a legitimate weapon in the diplomat's armoury. Thus, according to Hans Morgenthau, the threat of force is one of three means at the disposal of diplomacy, the other two being persuasion and compromise.[10] He notes that: 'No diplomacy relying only upon the threat of force can claim to be both intelligent and peaceful.' However, he continues:

> No diplomacy that would stake everything on persuasion and compromise deserves to be called intelligent. Rarely, if ever, in the conduct of the foreign policy of a great power is there justification for using only one method to the exclusion of the others. Generally, the diplomatic representative of a great power, in order to be able to serve the interests of his country and the interests of peace, must at the same time use persuasion, hold out the advantages of a compromise, and impress the other side with the military strength of his country.[11]

Another leading commentator on international relations, Thomas Schelling, puts it more bluntly: 'The power to hurt is bargaining power. To exploit it is diplomacy – vicious diplomacy, but diplomacy.'[12] On the

---

8. It can be argued that the mere existence of Chapter VII constitutes a threat of force designed to persuade states to settle their disputes by peaceful means in accordance with the UN Charter.
9. See generally Kemp (1990); Cooley (1991); Dannreuther (1992).
10. Morgenthau (1973), p. 519.
11. *Idem.*
12. Schelling (1966), p. 2.

other hand, Schelling sees the dangers in too much reliance on what he calls brute force by noting that: 'With enough military force a country may not need to bargain.'[13] Schelling argues that there is a distinction between brute force and coercion. In making this distinction, Schelling clearly sees coercion as a legitimate function of diplomacy, something which international lawyers may find difficult to accept.[14]

Schelling initially relates the difference between brute force and coercion to the difference between action and threat. He declares, 'brute force succeeds where it is used, whereas the power to hurt is most successful when it is held in reserve. It is the *threat* of damage, or of more damage to come, that can make someone yield or comply.'[15] He then goes on to note, however, that: 'The difference cannot quite be expressed as one between the *use* of force and the *threat* of force.'[16] He continues: 'sometimes the most effective direct action inflicts enough cost or pain on the enemy to serve as a threat'.[17] On the other hand, Schelling's analysis would appear to suggest that whether or not a use of force or a threat of force constitutes brute force or coercion depends upon whether it is 'undiplomatic' recourse to strength or, alternatively, undertaken in the pursuit of the power to hurt.[18] To a considerable extent, whether the threat or, indeed, the use of force is 'diplomatic' or 'undiplomatic' depends upon the degree of force threatened or used but, much more importantly, it depends upon the intention of the party making the threat. Thus, according to Schelling, whether violence itself is diplomatic or not depends upon: 'Whether it is sheer terroristic violence to induce an irrational response, or cool premeditated violence to persuade somebody that you mean it and may do it again ... ' However, he notes also that in order to be diplomatic, 'violence has to be . . . avoidable by accommodation'.[19] Crucially, therefore, violence or indeed the threat of it has to be in pursuit of a diplomatic objective.

It was noted above that international law has some difficulty accepting the assertion that coercion in and of itself is a legitimate diplomatic

---

13. *Idem*, p. 1.
14. See, for example, Schachter (1984), who denies the right of states to threaten force in support of coercion. Other international lawyers, however, are willing to draw a distinction between permissible coercion and impermissible coercion. See, for example, Higgins (1963), p. 178. For a discussion of Higgins' analysis see below.
15. Schelling (1966), p. 2 (emphasis in original).
16. *Idem*, p. 7.
17. *Idem*.
18. *Idem*, p. 3.
19. *Idem*, p. 2.

activity. On the other hand, there is clearly a role for international law in setting the standards and limits between 'diplomatic' and 'undiplomatic' behaviour. This may be the point at which coercion becomes brute force but, more clearly, it is the point at which diplomacy becomes force.[20]

THE LEGALITY OF THE THREAT OF FORCE

Given the practice of states and the views of the international relations specialists cited above it may seem problematic for international law to seek to outlaw the threat of force. It is clear, however, that such an attempt has been made. Customary international law before the early twentieth century did not prohibit the use of force, let alone the threat of it.[21] Likewise, there is no such prohibition in the Covenant of the League of Nations.[22] The first apparent restriction in international law on the threat of force is to be found in the General Treaty on the Renunciation of War 1928.[23] Having provided that 'the High Contracting Parties should not resort to war for the solution of international controversies', Article 1 also renounced war as an instrument of national policy in states' relations with one another.[24] It is suggested that this reference to national policy cannot be limited purely to the resort to war but encompasses also the threat of resort to war as a means of coercion.

Although still nominally in force, the 1928 Treaty was effectively replaced by Article 2(4) of the UN Charter. Both the threat and the use of force are *prima facie* illegal in terms of Article 2(4). However, while much has been made of the prohibition on the use of force in Article 2(4),[25] little specific attention has been paid in legal literature to the prohibition on the threat of force which has not generally been treated as a separate

---

20. See Walzer (1992), p. 79, where he notes that those in favour of preventive war 'radically underestimate the shift from diplomacy to force'.
21. See Hall (1924), p. 82.
22. Shaw (1997), p. 780.
23. U.K.T.S. 29 (1929), Cmnd. 3410; 94 L.N.T.S. 57.
24. Whether the Treaty prohibited the use of force generally or simply resort to war is a matter of some dispute. See, further, Bowett (1958), p. 87.
25. Key considerations in this context include determination of what is meant by 'force' and what is meant by the phrase 'against the territorial integrity or political independence of any State'. See generally Harris (1998), Chapter 11.

prohibition.[26] Rather the concept of the 'threat or use of force' has been treated as a single prohibition against the use of force in general.[27]

The precise meaning of Article 2(4) has been developed by a number of subsequent Resolutions of the General Assembly of the United Nations, including, in particular, the Declaration on the Inadmissibility of Intervention in the Domestic Affairs of States and the Protection of their Independence and Sovereignty 1965[28] and the 1970 Declaration on Principles of International Law concerning Friendly Relations and Co-operation among States in accordance with the Charter of the United Nations.[29] In both cases, the threat of force is specifically condemned.[30] In the later Resolution, in particular, the threat or use of force is required 'never to be employed as a means of settling international issues'. It also specifically calls upon state parties to an international dispute to 'refrain from any action which may aggravate the situation so as to endanger the maintenance of international peace and security . . . ' and later condemns the 'use of economic, political or any other type of measure to coerce another state in order to obtain from it the subordination of the exercise of its sovereign rights and to secure from it advantages of any kind . . . '[31] Notably, however, a further Resolution on the Definition of Aggression of 1974 defines aggression as 'the use of armed force by a State against the territorial integrity or political independence of another State' but does not within the definition refer to the 'threat' of force.[32] In spite of this clear, and one would consider deliberate, omission from the 1974 Resolution, it would appear from the analysis of the other sources cited

---

26. One exception to this is Sadurska (1988). Sadurska explains the lack of separate legal analysis of the threat of force on the basis that 'either it precedes actual violence and therefore is eclipsed in legal appraisals by the latter, or it is not followed by the use of force and thus ceases to demand prompt legal consideration' (at p. 239).

27. See, for example, Higgins (1963), p. 177, who includes as an illegal use of force, the threat of force, citing the examples of the Czechoslovakian question and the Berlin blockade, among others. See also the ICJ in its advisory opinion to the General Assembly of the United Nations in the *Legality of the Threat or Use of Nuclear Weapons* (1996), para. 47, where it declared that: 'The notions of "threat" and "use" of force under Article 2, paragraph 4, of the Charter stand together in the sense that if the use of force in a given case is illegal . . . the threat to use force will likewise be illegal.'

28. G.A. Resol'n 2131 (XX).

29. G.A. Resol'n 2625 (XXV).

30. Paragraph 1 of Resol'n 2131 declares that ' . . . attempted threats against the personality of the State or against its political, economic and cultural elements, are condemned'.

31. G.A. Resol'n 2625 (XXV), paragraph 1.

32. G.A. Resol'n 3314 (XXIX), paragraph 1.

above, that the threat of force in international relations is *prima facie* prohibited both by international convention and by customary international law.[33]

On the other hand, as has been noted above, in spite of this *prima facie* prohibition, states continue to use the threat of force as a mechanism for the conduct of international relations and, in particular, as a tool of international diplomacy. It would appear, therefore, that there exists, in the practice of states, a distinction between permissible threats of force and impermissible threats of force. To some extent, it may be possible to argue that this practice has resulted in the creation of a new rule of customary international law which is at variance with, or at least exists alongside, the prohibition on the threat of force.[34] On the contrary, however, it is suggested that there exists alongside the state practice insufficient *opinio juris* to assert that a new rule of customary international law exists. As was noted above, customary international law clearly prohibits the threat or use of force. As the ICJ has noted, the *opinio juris* of states in favour of the threat of force being illegal in international law 'may ... be deduced from, *inter alia* ... the attitude of States toward certain General Assembly resolutions, and particularly resolution 2625 (XXV)'.[35]

It is suggested, however, that in spite of this *prima facie* illegality, there are circumstances in which international law will tolerate the threat of force. In the same way that municipal law generally recognizes that in appropriate circumstances, such as provocation, self-defence and the like, coercion of the state is necessary, so international law must recognize that there are circumstances in which the coercion of a state, through the threat of force, or through its use, is legitimate. International law undoubtedly recognizes the 'inherent right of individual or collective self-defence'. It is submitted that international law also recognizes the right to threaten force, where appropriate. Insofar as international law is capable of regulating such a right, the assertion of the right does not undermine the prohibition on the threat of force in the same way that the existence of the right of self-defence does not undermine the prohibition

---

33. The General Assembly resolutions are not themselves capable of forming customary international law but can form the basis for the subsequent development of customary international law. The ICJ has declared in the *Case Concerning Military and Paramilitary Activities in and against Nicaragua* (1986) ICJ Rep., p. 14, that both Article 2(4) and the 1970 Declaration are rules of customary international law. See, in particular, paragraphs 188–90 of the judgment.

34. See generally Sadurska (1988).

35. *Case Concerning Military and Paramilitary Activities in and Against Nicaragua*, para. 188.

contained in Article 2(4). Fundamentally, however, as with municipal law, the sole arbiter of what is a permissible threat of force and what is impermissible is international law itself.

PERMISSIBLE THREATS OF FORCE

Much controversy surrounds the word 'force' in relation to Article 2(4). In particular, the question has arisen as to whether or not it includes economic force and other forms of political pressure not involving the use of military force.[36] What is clear, however, is that the word force does include, and may in fact be limited to, military force. It might be possible simply to conclude that international law dictates that *any* threat of military action against the territorial integrity or political independence of a state is illegal in terms of Article 2(4) of the UN Charter.[37] To do so, however, may be somewhat premature.

In defining the threat and use of force, a key concept for international lawyers, as with specialists in international relations, is the concept of coercion.[38] According to Oscar Schachter, 'a threat to use military action to coerce a state to make concessions is forbidden'.[39] On the other hand, Rosalyn Higgins prefers to talk of permissible and impermissible coercion. In making this distinction, Higgins is aware of the various types of aggression that a state can employ, be they military, economic, diplomatic or ideological. She notes that having determined the *method* of coercion the key factor in determining the permissibility of the coercion is the *degree* of coercion involved.[40]

---

36. See, for example, Goodrich, Hambro and Simons (1969), who conclude that: 'It seems reasonable to conclude that while various forms of economic and political coercion may be treated as threats to the peace, as contrary to certain of the declared purposes and principles of the Organisation, or as violating agreements entered into or recognised principles of international law, they are not to be regarded as coming necessarily under the prohibition of Article 2(4), which is to be understood as directed against the use of armed force.' A similar point is made by Higgins (1963), p. 177, who does, however, include within the definition of the use of force 'ideological and diplomatic methods when these are employed in very high degree and aimed at impairing the territorial integrity or political independence of a state'.
37. This was the conclusion reached by the ICJ in its advisory opinion to the General Assembly in the *Legality of the Threat or Use of Nuclear Weapons*.
38. See, for example, G.A. Resol'n 2625 (XXV) referred to above which talked of measures being used by one state to coerce the other.
39. Schachter (1991), p. 111.
40. Higgins (1963), p. 178.

Higgins accepts that not all of the methods of coercion are by definition force but notes that 'no matter how minimally the military instrument is employed, there is a situation of force' but she continues by noting that 'how the degree employed affects the classification of the use of force as permissible or impermissible is another question'. According to Higgins, therefore, the threat of force is always a use of force but such a threat may not constitute an impermissible use of force, depending on the degree of coercion involved.[41]

A similar approach was adopted by the ICJ in the *Case Concerning Military and Paramilitary Activities in and Against Nicaragua*. In that case, the ICJ, when discussing the principle of non-intervention impliedly distinguished between permitted interventions and prohibited interventions by referring to both the method and degree of coercion used. Thus, according to the Court:

> A prohibited intervention must accordingly be one bearing on matters in which each State is permitted by the principle of State sovereignty, to decide freely . . . Intervention is wrongful when it uses methods of coercion in regard to such choices, which must remain free ones. The element of coercion which defines, and indeed forms the very essence of, prohibited intervention, is particularly obvious in the case of an intervention which uses force, either in the direct form of military action, or in the indirect form of support for subversive or terrorist armed activities within another State.[42]

While the Court makes it clear that all use of force to intervene in the internal or external affairs of another state is impermissible coercion, this will only be the case where the state has the right freely to decide relevant matters. Arguably, therefore, the Court is of the opinion that where the threat is made in pursuance of a legal right on which the state does not have the right freely to decide, it is, at least, permissible.

In relation to the present discussion, it is worth noting that the Court did not specifically include in its definition of forceful interventions the threat of force. That the Court did not regard threats of force as being included in the degree of coercion that would make an intervention impermissible is perhaps arguable from the Court's later finding that

---

41. On legal attitudes to coercion see further, Sadurska (1988), pp. 241–7.
42. *Nicaragua Case*, para. 205.

military manoeuvres held by the United States near the Nicaraguan borders did not constitute a threat of force.[43]

Romana Sadurska has attempted to put forward criteria for the legal appraisal of threats of force which takes account of the practice of states in this area. She identifies three trends 'that appear to form a pattern of shared expectations about the acceptability of this function of threats of force'.[44] These are 'Considerations of Security'; 'Vindication of a Denied Right'; and 'Prudence and Economy'.

In support of the first expectation, Sadurska cites the examples of the US blockade of Cuba in 1962, the United Kingdom's establishment of a 150-nautical-mile exclusion zone around the Falkland Islands in 1982 and the Swedish threat to sink foreign submarines in its territorial waters in 1983 as examples of states threatening force in relation to matters deemed 'vital to their security'. In respect of the two latter examples, it is clear that there was a sufficient linkage with territorial security to deem them matters of internal security, in the case of Sweden, and self-defence, in the case of the Falklands. In respect of the Cuban Quarantine, Sadurska suggests that this was supported or at least tolerated by other international actors.[45] However, whether or not these examples are sufficient to create a new rule of customary international law allowing for the threat of force in such circumstances is extremely doubtful.[46]

With regard to the vindication of a denied right, Sadurska asserts that 'International actors seem to tolerate a threat of force for the vindication of a denied right, provided the right is well established in customary international law or in an agreement'.[47] In support of this argument she relies heavily on the *Corfu Channel Case*,[48] concluding of the decision that 'the Court affirmed that the threat of force applied as a measure of enforcement of a right that had been unlawfully denied (in this case the right of innocent passage through an international waterway in

---

43. *Idem*, para. 227. It is accepted, however, that the Court did consider the circumstances of the specific manoeuvres question and may not have been intending to reach a general conclusion about whether military manoeuvres on a state's border constitutes a threat of force.

44. Sadurska (1988), pp. 260–6.

45. *Idem*, p. 260.

46. Support and tolerance of a particular state practice can both be used to support the development of a new rule of customary international law. However, in the case of the threat of force, the *opinio juris* of states would appear to be clearly in favour of its prohibition.

47. Sadurska (1988), p. 262.

48. (1949) ICJ Rep. 4.

peacetime) was licit'.[49] This reading of the decision of the ICJ is somewhat controversial given the fact that the Court specifically found in that case that the United Kingdom had been in violation of Albania's sovereignty during its mine-sweeping operations of 13 November 1946.[50] Even if this reading is correct, it cannot be said to have resulted in a new rule of customary international law given the explicit requirements of Articles 2(3) and 2(4) of the UN Charter.[51] On the other hand, Sadurska's, analysis when read alongside the decision of the ICJ in the *Nicaragua Case* referred to earlier, does support the view that international law is capable of recognizing the possibility that where the threat of force is made in pursuit of a legal right, such a threat may be permissible.

Finally, Sadurska asserts that: 'The international community seems to approve, or at least tolerate, the actions of a threatener that proceeds with prudence, carefully balancing individual and community values, and strives to achieve the results in the most economical way.' Little evidence is given for this assertion which seems to imply that the 'incremental' build-up of pressure on a state is somehow more acceptable than a 'massive display of military strength'. On the other hand, if the aim is to bring a dispute to a speedy and economic end, the latter option may be the more prudent.

Perhaps the suggestion is that where the threat of force is sufficiently prudent and economic, it will not result in escalation of a crisis into a military conflict. In other words the threat of force can be justified *ex post facto*. It is submitted that this analysis of the legality of the threat of force may well be the most satisfactory and may well be the analysis which ties in most clearly with state practice. On the other hand, if the threat of force is to be regarded as a permitted tool of international diplomacy, the future of world order requires that international law is capable of monitoring the prudence and economy of a threat of force before it results in the outbreak of military conflict.

International law cannot easily set the limits of a right to threaten

---

49. Sadurska (1988), p. 263.
50. The Court noted that 'It can only regard the alleged right of intervention as the manifestation of a policy of force, such as has, in the past given rise to most serious abuses and such as cannot, whatever be the present defects in international organisation, find a place in international law' (*Corfu Channel Case*).
51. Sadurska also refers to the Swedish threat to sink submarines in its territorial sea. Such an action, although perhaps foolhardy, would not constitute a breach of international law as it is not directed against the territorial integrity or political independence of another state.

force in the pursuit of a diplomatic objective. According to Higgins, the right depends upon the degree of the threat of force. The question remains, however, as to who is able to determine that a threat has gone too far. If the resolution of the most recent conflict in the Gulf is properly to be called a victory for the United Nations, the answer is quite clear. That is that the decision lies with the United Nations either in the form of the Security Council or, where occasion arises, the ICJ.

The Security Council is undoubtedly an inherently political organ which is arguably incapable of making legal determinations of this manner. On the other hand, it is suggested that not only is the Security Council the only body in international law which *is* capable of making such a determination, given the jurisdictional problems inherent in the ICJ, but the Security Council already has the power to make such determinations. It can consider any matter which it considers to be a threat to the peace, a breach of the peace or an act of aggression. It is clearly within its powers to determine, therefore, whether a threat of force is permissible given the circumstances in which the issue is being played out.

It is suggested that the willingness of the Security Council to develop its functions in this way would bring many benefits. First, the opportunity would exist for the Security Council to be appraised of threats to international peace and security at an earlier stage than is perhaps the case under normal conditions. In such circumstances, the Security Council would be in a position to monitor the developing situation and in a position to act more quickly and, perhaps, more decisively, were the situation to escalate into a threat to the peace, breach of the peace or act of aggression. Ultimately, the increased willingness of the Security Council to monitor the actions of states in this way would increase the involvement of the United Nations generally in the search for peaceful settlements of such disputes which is surely within the interests not only of the United Nations itself but also of the international community in general.

Secondly, in making the decision whether or not to condemn the threat of force, the Security Council would be required to assess the competing claims of the states involved in the dispute. Were a threat of force to be implicitly authorized, the result would be to strengthen the hand of the party making the request. The opposite would be true where the threat was condemned. It is suggested that such a role for the Security Council would be a positive, rather than a negative, factor in the search for international peace and security. Whereas at the moment, a state which threatens force does so on the basis of its own national interests, a legitimate claim to be acting more generally in the interests of the international community would follow from the Security Council failing to condemn the action, while the states against whom the threat was made would be placed in a more difficult position having been implicitly, or indeed, explicitly, warned by the Security Council that they were being viewed as an aggressor state. On the other hand, were the Security Council to condemn the threat of force, the state making the threat would be under notice that should they choose to proceed to threaten the use of force regardless, the possibility of Security Council action against them would not only be an increased possibility, but may, in fact, make a Security Council condemnation of such action probable, given that the continued threat of force would itself be a clear breach of a prior Security Council Resolution against such action, particularly if the situation were to escalate into violence.

THE LEGALITY OF THE THREAT OF FORCE IN THE GULF CONFLICT

It was asserted in the previous chapter that the use of force by the United States and the United Kingdom against Iraq in 1998 was an illegal use of force. This begs the question whether the threat of force was illegal in the circumstances prevailing in the lead-up to the signing of the Memorandum of Understanding. If one accepts the position of the ICJ in the *Nuclear Weapons Case* cited above then the threat of force in circumstances where the use of force would be illegal, is itself illegal. Therefore, any unilateral threat of force by the US/UK coalition was illegal regardless of the circumstances leading up to the threat of force. On the other hand, perhaps the threat of force would have been a more proportionate response to the continued intransigence of Iraq in relation to Resolution 687 than the actual use of force and therefore should be considered at least permissible.

If one accepts the above analysis that the threat of force is permissible in pursuit of a legal right, it is clear that the legal right to enforce Resolution 687 was not a right belonging to the United States and the United Kingdom. Rather it was a right belonging to the international community at large which therefore could only be enforced by the international community through the auspices of the UN Security Council. Given the fact that three of the permanent members of the Security Council were opposed to the position being maintained by the United States, it would be difficult to argue with the assertion that the action of the United States was a unilateral action not authorized by the UN Security Council.

Clearly, however, although concerned primarily with national self-interest, the US/UK coalition may have a legitimate claim to have been generally acting in the interests of the international community as a whole. It would particularly be legitimate for the United States to claim, as it has done, that it was acting in furtherance of Security Council Resolution 687, a legally binding document under international law. Given the analysis outlined above, it may be possible to assert, therefore, that the threat of force by the US/UK coalition was a permissible threat of force insofar as it was proportionate and in pursuit of a legal right belonging to the international community. Further, if one were to adopt the Sadurska analysis of the legality of the threat of force, the action of the US/UK coalition could be justified on a *ex post facto* basis and commended for its prudence and economy. Indeed it would appear that such a commendation was provided by the Secretary-General whose positive view of the influence of the threat of force on the stand-off in the Gulf was supported by a statement that the United States and the United Kingdom were powerful peacekeepers. This argument, however, is seriously undermined by the fact that the prudence and economy of US/UK threats against Iraq did, in fact, ultimately precipitate military intervention.

CONCLUSIONS

It would appear that the practice of states in modern international relations is clearly supportive of the threat of force in certain circumstances as an aid to diplomacy. The peaceful resolution of the stand-off in the Gulf in February 1998 in relation to weapons inspections is testament to the positive role that the threat of force can play in the maintenance of international peace and security. On the other hand, clearly the threat of force is a dangerous tool in the hands of diplomacy, as is illustrated by the actual resort to force by the United States and the United Kingdom in December 1998. Thus, the threat of force when played out to its full has the potential as much to precipitate military intervention as it has the potential to stop it.[52] For this reason, the *opinio juris* of states, in spite of state practice to the contrary would appear to be in favour of restricting rather than permitting the threat of force.

It may be possible to conclude therefore that the prohibition on the

---

52. The threat of force was unable to prevent the January 1993 attack on Baghdad by the United States, the legitimacy of which is discussed above.

threat of force is yet another example of the weakness of international law and its lack of enforceability. Thus states are able to pay lip service to the illegality of the threat of force while resorting to the threat of force in cases where they consider their vital national interests to be at stake. This would be particularly so in the case of the more powerful states and it is indeed to protect against this that states in a legal sense generally support the prohibition on the threat of force.

If one is to square the circle between international law and what states actually do, it is important for international law to be able to set the standards of state behaviour in this field. The opportunity exists for the United Nations and, in particular, the Security Council, to square that circle. The recent crisis in the Gulf should be used as a precedent, not only for states to be allowed to threaten force in pursuit of a diplomatic objective but, more importantly, for the Security Council to take upon itself the role of arbitrator between what is a 'diplomatic' threat of force and what is an 'undiplomatic' threat of force.

It is accepted that, given the past record of the Security Council, the analysis outlined above can be criticized for being too idealistic and, perhaps, naïve. However, without the existence of an independent legal body capable of determining the greyness of states' action, it is left to the Security Council to act in the way in which it was envisaged that it would act. If the Security Council fails to take on this role, claims of international society as an anarchic society will prevail. If, however, the United Nations takes on such a role, increased possibilities for greater world order will undoubtedly follow.

CHAPTER 6

EXTRADITING PINOCHET

INTRODUCTION

The South American State of Chile has been plagued throughout the twentieth century by struggles for political dominance between the left and the right.[1] In spite of an edifice of constitutional legality and commitment to democracy, underlying class and economic divides made for a 'precarious state of balance' in the period up to 1970.[2] The election of Dr Salvador Allende as president in 1970, the first-ever democratically elected Marxist head of state, brought with it the promise of social justice by constitutional means.[3] However, the lack of a revolution did not pacify those outside Chile who were opposed to the advancement of socialism in South America.[4] The United States, in particular, was concerned at the

---

1. The first major success of the left had occurred in 1938 but serious in-fighting during the 1940s led to the outlawing of the Communist Party in 1948. Throughout the remainder of the century, there was popular support for both left and right as, for example, in 1958 when the Marxist Salvador Allende polled over 28 per cent of the vote and lost only narrowly to the conservative candidate. See Whitehead (1974), p. 3.
2. See Roxborough, O'Brien and Roddick (1977), Chapter 1.
3. 'The logical culmination of this tradition of constitutional development, in my eyes, was Popular Unity's attempt to initiate a peaceful, constitutional road to socialism' (*idem*, p. 14).
4. According to one author, 'the Unidad Popular brought social reforms not socialism to Chile, and the impact of these reforms was comparable, in the American context, to that of the social measures of Franklin Roosevelt's New Deal' (Yglesias, 1974, p. 14). On the other hand, Allende's Marxist credentials were well established and the social redistribution envisaged by his government was far-reaching. Indeed, the Allende Government was regarded by many as a test case examining whether it is possible 'for a democratic government to undertake a general and massive redistribution of income, wealth and power without resort to extensive repression directed against the losing classes' (Whitehead, 1974, p. 1).

process of nationalization of industry, instigated by Allende, which included the expropriation of US-owned copper mines.[5] Indeed, the US Government quickly identified Allende as a pro-Cuban communist and encouraged and assisted opposition against him.[6] Subsequently, the US Government and, most notably, the CIA, were heavily involved in the 1973 military coup, which resulted in the death of President Allende and the investiture of General Augusto Pinochet Ugarte as president.[7]

In the years that followed, Pinochet's government pursued a policy of extremism against political opposition both inside and outside Chile. Opponents in Chile were tortured, killed or simply 'disappeared'. The ferocity of the initial purge cannot be denied. An Amnesty International report published in September 1974 noted that: 'A vast but unknown number of people – estimates range from 5,000 to over 30,000 – have lost their lives in Chile since the military coup. Though official executions are no longer announced, disappearances continue ... More than 2,000 people are now known to have been executed in custody between 11 September and the end of December 1973.'[8] Much of the repression was centrally organized and coordinated, particularly after the creation, in June 1974, of the Directorate of National Intelligence (DINA). According to one observer, 'the DINA ... was directly responsible for the purging of all the political opponents of the military regime. Between 1973 and 1977 the DINA was responsible for the "disappearance" of over 2,000 Chileans. They were kidnapped from their homes, in the street or at their place of work, and taken to secret detention centres for interrogation under torture. Most were never heard of again.'[9] Outside Chile, many exiled opponents of the Pinochet regime were pursued and assassinated. The overall position was summed up by Lord Browne-Wilkinson in the House of Lords where he remarked that: 'There is no real dispute that during the period of the Senator Pinochet regime appalling acts of barbarism were committed in Chile ... '[10]

---

5. See further, Petras and Morley (1974), who note at p. 119 that: 'The US government long ago gave up the idea that a parliamentary facade is a necessary accompaniment of capitalist development in Latin America.'

6. It is reported, for example, that the US State Department, surprised by Allende's victory, gave their Ambassador in Chile, Edward Korry, 'maximum authority to do all possible ... to keep Allende from taking power' (O'Brien and Roddick, 1983, p. 31).

7. According to O'Brien and Roddick, the coup was, in fact, masterminded by a group of '*laissez-faire* economic technocrats known as the "Chicago Boys", many of whom had studied in the Economics Department at the University of Chicago' (*idem*, Chapter 4).

8. Amnesty International (1974), p. 31.

9. Barnes (1983), p. 110.

10. *Reg. v Bow Street Metropolitan Stipendiary Magistrate, Ex p. Pinochet Ugarte (No. 3)* (1999) (hereinafter *Pinochet No. 3*), p. 833.

As the human rights abuses continued, Chile became increasingly isolated in the international community, with even the United States agreeing to ban all military aid to Chile in 1976.[11] Nevertheless, Pinochet's power base in Chile remained and in 1980, a plebiscite approved the so-called 'Constitution of Liberty'. The new Constitution provided for a transition to democracy in 1989. In the meantime, however, Pinochet was to continue as president and all political activity was declared illegal. Even after 1989, the Constitution gave the military junta the power to name the president. Thus, as one commentator has noted, 'the new constitution guaranteed Chile 24 years of Pinochet in power, a one-man dictatorship until 1997'.[12] As we now know, the grand designs of the new Constitution did not come to fruition, although it was to be a further eight years before Pinochet was completely removed from power. The collapse of the Chilean banking system in 1983 led to the emergence of mass opposition to the Pinochet regime in Chile, which encompassed not only the working classes but also the Catholic church and the military. Eventually, in October 1988, Pinochet's proposal that he should remain in power for a further eight-year term was defeated in a plebiscite. Constitutional changes followed, leading to the election as president, in December 1989, of Patricio Aylwin, leader of the moderate Christian Democratic Party. President Aylwin formally took power in March 1990.

The peaceful transfer of power away from Pinochet came with a price. As part of the agreement to give up power, Pinochet negotiated an amnesty guaranteeing constitutional and legal impediments to any proceedings against him in Chile in respect of the abuses which had been carried out during his regime.[13] Accordingly, in 1991, when the official report of the Chilean National Commission on Truth and Reconciliation revealed that there had been 2,279 deaths during Pinochet's time in office of which over 2,115 were executions carried out by the secret police, no charges were brought against Pinochet. Indeed, Pinochet remained head of the armed forces in Chile until 1997 and continues as a Senator in the Chilean Parliament.

In spite of the Chilean amnesty, a number of international human rights organizations, including, in particular, Amnesty International, have been seeking to bring Pinochet to justice for many years. Amnesty have argued that the widespread and systematic human rights violations

---

11. O'Brien and Roddick (1983), p. 111.
12. *Idem*, p. 87.
13. See generally Mera (1995), p. 171, pp. 180–3.

in Chile during the Pinochet regime amount to crimes against humanity. Such crimes, say Amnesty, are subject to universal jurisdiction which not only gives any state the ability to prosecute such crimes but, in fact, *obliges all* states to prosecute and punish such crimes.[14] One state which appears to have more direct interest in the activities of the Pinochet regime than most is Spain. In particular, it was alleged that as many as 50 of the victims of the Pinochet purge had been Spanish nationals.[15] A high-level investigation into the activities of the Pinochet government had been continuing in Spain for some time under the direction of Judge-Magistrate Garzon who eventually issued an international warrant for Pinochet's arrest. The warrant was in fact challenged by the Spanish authorities who raised the question as to whether Spain had jurisdiction over activities which had essentially occurred in Chile. The jurisdiction was confirmed on 5 November 1998 by the National Court Criminal Division, ironically on the basis of universality rather than the Spanish nationality of certain of the victims. Thus, the Court held that Spain 'had jurisdiction to try crimes of terrorism and genocide even committed abroad, including crimes of torture which are an aspect of genocide, and not merely in respect of Spanish victims ... by virtue of the principle of universal prosecution for certain crimes – a category of international law – established by our internal legislation'.[16] Accordingly, a formal request for extradition was forwarded by the Spanish government to the British authorities.[17] In the meantime, a British official had issued a provisional warrant for the arrest of Pinochet which had been served on him as he recovered from a back operation in a private clinic in London. So began the legal process in the English courts aimed at bringing to justice, in Spain, an individual in respect of crimes committed in Chile, the state of which he was head, by the regime of which he was, ultimately, in charge.

---

14. Amnesty International News Service 216/98, United Kingdom/Chile, 3 November 1998. See http://www.amnesty.org/news/1998/23nov98.htm (emphasis added).
15. See the decision of the Spanish National Court Criminal Division of 5 November 1998 reported by Lord Slynn in *Reg. v Bow Street Metropolitan Stipendiary Magistrate, Ex p. Pinochet Ugarte* (1998) (hereinafter *Pinochet No. 1*), at p. 1463.
16. *Idem.*
17. According to Lord Bingham, Lord Chief Justice in the Divisional Court, 'Extradition is the formal name given to a process whereby one sovereign state, "the requesting state", asks another sovereign state, "the requested state", to return to the requesting state someone present in the requested state, "the subject of the request", in order that the subject of the request may be brought to trial on criminal charges in the requesting state.' The decision of the Divisional Court in *Ex p. Pinochet* has not been reported.

THE ISSUES

In making its first decision, on 25 November 1998, that Pinochet should be extradited to Spain to face charges there of torture, hostage-taking and murder, the Judicial Committee of the House of Lords, the highest court of criminal appeal in England and Wales, decided that the crimes of which Pinochet was accused were crimes against humanity which could be tried by any state and that such crimes did not attract head of state immunity. This decision was welcomed by human rights lawyers and activists as a great step forward in the development of international human rights law. More generally, the implications of the decision on the future enforcement of international law could not be overlooked. As Damrosch had noted in her Hague Lectures, there is a problem with 'penalising the State in its entirety for actions committed only by its ruling echelon'.[18] Perhaps actions such as those brought against Pinochet would signal the way forward in this regard.

However, as politicians and international lawyers around the world were contemplating the full implications of the ruling, rumours began to circulate about the involvement of one of the judges, Lord Hoffmann, and his wife, with Amnesty International[19] which had been allowed to intervene in the case when it had reached the House of Lords. Concern was quickly raised as to the possibility of bias, or at least the appearance of bias. Eventually, in a wholly unprecedented move, a new panel of the House of Lords was convened to consider the allegations against Hoffmann and their effect on the decision in *Pinochet No. 1*. The new panel decided on 15 January 1999 that 'in order to maintain the absolute impartiality of the judiciary there had to be a rule which automatically disqualified a judge who was involved, whether personally or as a director of a company, in promoting the same causes in the same organisation as was a party to the suit'.[20] The effect of the decision was to vitiate and vacate the judgment, although all their lordships were careful

---

18. Damrosch (1997), p. 30.
19. Specifically, Lady Hoffmann was found to have held various administrative posts within Amnesty's international secretariat in London since 1977. Lord Hoffmann himself was a director and chairperson of Amnesty International Charity Ltd, an associate company of Amnesty International Ltd. See further Lord Browne-Wilkinson in *Reg. v Bow Street Metropolitan Stipendiary Magistrate, Ex p. Pinochet Ugarte (No. 2)* (1999) (hereinafter *Pinochet No. 2*), pp. 276–8.
20. *Pinochet No. 2*, p. 272.

to point out that they had not found that Lord Hoffmann had been biased, rather that the possibility of bias had existed.[21] As a result, the judgment in *Pinochet No. 1* has no effect in English law but may have persuasive authority both inside and outside the United Kingdom.

A new bench of seven judges was convened to rehear the original case. On this occasion, Amnesty International was again allowed to intervene but so too were a number of other parties, including the state of Chile, which had not had any direct involvement in any of the previous hearings. In the meantime, the Spanish authorities had presented an extended list of charges in respect of the extradition request. The House of Lords heard the case in the last week of January but did not deliver its decision until 23 March 1999. It held by a majority of six to one that Pinochet's extradition should go ahead. However, the charges on which Pinochet was to be allowed to stand trial were fundamentally reduced. The reasoning of their lordships in *Pinochet No.3* was lacking in a number of respects, not least in respect of the two matters which had been central to the decision in *Pinochet No. 1*, that is the issue of universal jurisdiction over crimes against humanity and the matter of head of state immunity. Furthermore, the case seemed to turn on the issue of 'extraditable crimes' which had not been at issue before the court in *Pinochet No. 1*.

THE DECISION IN *EX PARTE PINOCHET*

Extraditable Crimes

In terms of UK law, by virtue of the Extradition Act 1989, if an individual is to be extradited from the United Kingdom to stand trial in another country for an alleged offence, the authorities of the State seeking extradition are required to fulfil a number of requirements. For example, the offence must be sufficiently serious, carrying a potential sentence of at least six months' imprisonment. There must also be sufficient evidence that the offence has been committed, this latter requirement is known as the *prima facie* case requirement. The most important requirement for present purposes, however, is that the offence constitutes an offence under the law of both the United Kingdom and the state seeking extradition, in this case, Spain. This is known as the double criminality rule. More particularly, as is made clear by section 2 of the 1989 Act, if the

---

21. See, for example, Lord Goff at p. 287 and Lord Hutton at p. 294.

offence is an extraterritorial offence in the state seeking extradition, it must also be an extraterritorial offence in the United Kingdom.[22]

The crimes of murder, hostage-taking and torture have long been recognized as offences under UK law when those offences are committed on the territory of the United Kingdom. The right to prescribe the criminality of such acts lies in the principle of territorial jurisdiction which is the primary basis of criminal jurisdiction in international law and highlights the fundamental concept of territorial sovereignty of states. However, it was not previously clear whether murder, hostage-taking and torture constituted crimes under UK law when committed outside the territory of the United Kingdom. In other words, are they extraterritorial offences? Recognizing the limitations of territorial sovereignty in this regard, international law has sought to establish the individual criminal liability of individuals in respect of certain crimes through the jurisdictional principle known as universality. According to this principle, a state has jurisdiction over a particular crime regardless of the place of commission of the crime. It works essentially on the basis that states are required to prosecute individuals accused of such crimes or, where it is not willing or able to prosecute, to extradite the accused to a state which is willing or able to prosecute.

The origins and development of the principle of universality were highlighted in Chapter 2 above. In particular it was noted that recent attempts to provide for universal jurisdiction against crimes which are regarded as crimes against humanity have had to overcome the fundamental obstacle of the territorial jurisdiction of the state in which the alleged crime has been committed. In such cases, it would appear imperative for states specifically to consent to the exercise of a jurisdiction which has the effect of overriding its own territorial jurisdiction. Accordingly, the creation of such jurisdiction has only been possible through the creation of international treaty regimes which provide for a form of universal jurisdiction to be exercised on the basis of specific consent of the states involved in the regime, through their ratification of the relevant treaty instrument. Three such treaty regimes

---

22. According to section 2 of the Extradition Act:
    (1) In this Act, except in Schedule 1, 'extradition crime' means – ...
        (b) an extra-territorial offence against the law of a foreign state ... which satisfies –
            (i) the condition specified in subsection (2) below ...
    (2) The condition mentioned in subsection (1)(b)(i) above is that in corresponding circumstances equivalent conduct would constitute an extra-territorial offence against the law of the United Kingdom.

are relevant for the purposes of this analysis of the Pinochet litigation. First, the International Convention against the Taking of Hostages 1979, in respect of the charges of hostage-taking and conspiracy to take hostages between 1 January 1982 and 31 January 1992; secondly, the European Convention on the Suppression of Terrorism 1977 in respect of the charges of conspiracy to commit murder between January 1976 and December 1992; and finally, the International Convention Against Torture and other Cruel Inhuman or Degrading Treatment or Punishment 1984 in respect of the charges of torture and conspiracy to torture between 1 January 1988 and 31 December 1992.[23]

All three treaties provide in principle for the possibility of extra-territorial jurisdiction over the relevant offences. However, this quasi-universal jurisdiction is not automatic. According to Lord Browne-Wilkinson in *Pinochet No. 3*: 'The jurisdiction being established here by the torture Convention and the hostages Convention is one where existing domestic courts of all the countries are being authorised and required to take jurisdiction internationally.'[24] This is not entirely correct. State parties to the relevant treaties are being given the power to designate the relevant offences as extraterritorial offences within their own domestic law. Accordingly, if an individual is to be found personally liable for such an extraterritorial offence, that can only occur where individual responsibility has been provided for under the municipal law of the forum state. This point is well illustrated by reference to the Convention on the Prevention and Punishment of the Crime of Genocide 1946. Although ostensibly a crime against humanity which is allegedly subject to universal jurisdiction at customary international law,[25] the relevant provision of the Convention dealing with the question of jurisdiction, Article 6, provides that jurisdiction can only be exercised by 'a competent tribunal of the state in the territory of which the act was committed, or by such international penal tribunal as may have jurisdiction'. Accordingly, where no such international tribunal exists, the only right to jurisdiction provided for by the Convention is the, admittedly inherent, right of territorial jurisdiction of the state where the offence was committed. Accordingly, the relevant provision of UK law provides jurisdiction only where the offence of genocide has been

---

23. The charges set out here were those contained in the provisional warrant of 22 October 1998 which was the basis of the hearing before the House of Lords in *Pinochet No. 3*. See further Lord Hope, *Pinochet No. 3*, p. 866.
24. *Pinochet No. 3*, p. 847.
25. See *Attorney-General of the Government of Israel v Eichmann* (1961), paras. 29–30.

committed in the territory of the United Kingdom.[26] The second provisional warrant issued against Pinochet did not include the charge of genocide or conspiracy to commit genocide. However, because the United Kingdom would not itself have had jurisdiction to try Pinochet for any alleged genocide in Chile, it would have been unable, as a matter of UK law, to extradite Pinochet to Spain in respect of these charges by virtue of the double criminality rule. The only state to which the United Kingdom could have lawfully extradited Pinochet in respect of any allegations of genocide is Chile, the state where the alleged offences might have occurred. Nevertheless, all three of the conventions referred to above have been incorporated into UK law by means of an Act of Parliament. The relevant enactments are respectively, the Taking of Hostages Act 1982, the Suppression of Terrorism Act 1978 and section 134 of the Criminal Justice Act 1988, all of which provide for extra-territorial jurisdiction in respect of the relevant crimes.

A further difficulty in respect of the assertion of quasi-universal jurisdiction by virtue of treaty regimes arises in respect of non-parties to the relevant Convention. In other words, can jurisdiction be asserted over a national of a state which is not party to the relevant Convention? This particular problem arose in the context of the Pinochet litigation in connection with the European Convention on the Suppression of Terrorism. Section 4 of the Suppression of Terrorism Act 1978 is quite clear that the jurisdiction of the United Kingdom in relation to the offence of murder and conspiracy to commit murder when committed outside the territory of the United Kingdom is available only where the offence took place in a Convention country or a country which has agreed to the application of the provisions of the Act.[27] As Lord Hope noted in *Pinochet No. 3*, 'Chile is not a Convention country for the purposes of [the] Act, nor is it one of the non-Convention countries to which its provisions have been applied by section 5 of the Act.'[28] Accordingly, the alleged murder of 'about four thousand persons of many nationalities murdered in Chile'[29] did not fall within the jurisdiction of UK law and, again by virtue of the double criminality rule, the United Kingdom was not entitled to extradite Pinochet to Spain in respect of those charges. However, one of the charges against

---

26. Genocide Act 1969, section 1.
27. See Suppression of Terrorism Act 1978, section 5. The only countries which have made such agreements are the United States and India.
28. *Pinochet No. 3*, p. 874.
29. *Idem*, p. 871.

Pinochet was that 'Senator Pinochet agreed in Spain with others who were in Spain, Chile and France that the proposed victim would be murdered in Spain.'[30] Spain is a party to the European Convention and the United Kingdom therefore had *prima facie* jurisdiction over Pinochet in respect of that one charge by virtue of section 4 of the 1978 Act.

With respect to the charges of hostage-taking and conspiracy to take hostages, the issue of Chile's ratification of the relevant treaty did not arise.[31] The problem with hostage-taking relates to the definition of the offence, in particular, the purpose for which any hostage is taken. According to section 1(1) of the Taking of Hostages Act 1982:

> A person, whatever his nationality, who, in the United Kingdom *or elsewhere* – (a) detains any other person ('the hostage'), and (b) in order to compel a state, international governmental organisation or person to do or to abstain from doing any act, threatens to kill, injure or continue to detain the hostage, commits an offence.[32]

The specific charge made against Pinochet in relation to the conspiracy to take hostages specified that the intention was to take hostages 'as part of a campaign to terrify and subdue those who were disposed to criticise or oppose Senator Pinochet or his fellow conspirators'.[33] The purpose was not, as required by the 1982 Act, directed against a particular state or international governmental organization. Thus, as Lord Hope noted:

> This does not seem to me to amount to a conspiracy to take hostages within the meaning of section 1 of the Act of 1982. The purpose of the proposed conduct, as regards, the detained persons, was to subject them to what can best be described as a form of mental torture.[34]

Again, because of the lack of jurisdiction over the specific extraterritorial offences, the House of Lords was unable to consider extradition of Pinochet to Spain in respect thereof.

As to the specific charges of torture, torture is an extraterritorial crime in the United Kingdom by virtue of section 134 of the Criminal Justice Act 1988 which provides in subsection 1 that:

> A public official or person acting in an official capacity, whatever his nationality, commits the offence of torture if in the United Kingdom *or*

---

30. *Idem*, p. 872.
31. Chile became a party to the treaty on 3 January 1980, ratified it on 12 November 1981, and it took effect in Chile's domestic law from 3 June 1983.
32. Emphasis added.
33. *Pinochet No. 3*, p. 870. No details of actual hostage-taking were provided to the court.
34. *Idem*, p. 871.

elsewhere he intentionally inflicts severe pain or suffering on another in the performance or purported performance of his official duties.[35]

There is no difficulty fitting the allegations against Pinochet within this definition and, as Chile is party to the Torture Convention, there is, in principle, no difficulty in relation to the assertion of jurisdiction in respect of offences committed in Chile. It may well seem, therefore, that, in respect of the allegations of torture at least, the requirements of double criminality were satisfied in the case of Pinochet, presuming, of course, that Spanish law made similar provision for the extraterritoriality of these crimes.[36] Unfortunately a further difficulty arose.

In the Divisional Court, it was held that the offence need only satisfy the double criminality rule at the time of the extradition request. The matter was not considered by the House of Lords in *Pinochet No. 1*. However, in *Pinochet No. 3*, where the issue of double criminality again became an issue, it was held that double criminality must exist at the time of the commission of the alleged offence, not just at the time of the bringing of the extradition proceedings. This is one of the most controversial aspects of the decision of the House of Lords in *Pinochet No. 3* and appears to go against established judicial precedent in the United Kingdom.[37] Nevertheless, the effect of the decisions was devastating on the specific allegations of torture brought against Pinochet, particularly as section 134 of the Criminal Justice Act only came into force on 29 September 1988. As crimes of torture committed outside the territory of the United Kingdom can only be tried in the United Kingdom after 29 September 1988, the double criminality rule ensures that Pinochet could be extradited to Spain only in respect of the alleged crimes torture in Chile which occurred after that date. While the issue of double criminality was central to the decision of the House of Lords in *Pinochet No. 3*, the actual question on appeal to the House of Lords concerned the question of what immunity from the jurisdiction of the UK courts, if any, was Pinochet entitled to claim.

---

35. Emphasis added. It should be noted that torture is specifically defined as being 'public torture'. In other words, torture for personal gratification is not covered by this definition.
36. See further the decision of 5 November 1998 of the National Court Criminal Division, Note 15 above.
37. See *R v Home Secretary, ex parte Gilmore* (1998). For a criticism of this aspect of the House of Lord's decision see Warbrick, Salgado and Goodwin (1999).

Head of State Immunity

International law recognizes two primary forms of immunity from jurisdiction, state and diplomatic immunity. Diplomatic immunity has existed in one form or another since ancient times and perhaps even before then. However, the modern law of international immunities developed out of the so-called 'representative character' theory which was dependent upon the personal sovereignty of the early European monarchs. According to Sir Arthur Watts: 'In many respects the State could almost be seen as the property of its ruler, and it was to a considerable degree the ruler's personal attributes of sovereignty which gave his State the quality of being a sovereign State, rather than the other way round.'[38] The basis for the granting of international immunities was, accordingly, based upon the Latin maxim *par in parem non habet imperium*; specifically, 'no state can be expected to submit to the laws of another'.[39] The effect of the dictum was summed up by Chief Justice Marshall in the celebrated case of *The Schooner Exchange v McFaddon*.[40] The case concerned a vessel belonging to two American citizens, which, it was argued, had been illegally seized by forces acting under the authority of the Emperor of France. The United States Attorney argued that even if the vessel had in fact been wrongfully seized from the appellants, property therein had passed to the Emperor of France and the vessel was therefore immune from process. According to Chief Justice Marshall:

> The jurisdiction of the nation within its own territory is necessarily exclusive and absolute. It is susceptible of no limitation not imposed by itself ... All exceptions, therefore to the full and complete power of a nation within its own territories, must be traced up to the consent of the nation itself. They can flow from no other legitimate source ...
>
> This full and absolute territorial jurisdiction being alike the attribute of every sovereign ... would not seem to contemplate foreign sovereigns nor their sovereign rights as its objects. One sovereign being in no respects amenable to another, and being bound by obligations of the highest character not to degrade the dignity of his nation by placing himself or its sovereign rights within the jurisdiction of another, can be supposed to enter a foreign territory only under an express licence or in the confidence that the immunities belonging to his independent sovereign station though not expressly stipulated, are reserved by

38. Watts (1994), p. 35.
39. Higgins (1994), p. 79.
40. (1812) 7 Cranch 116.

implication, and will be extended to him.

The perfect equality and absolute independence of sovereigns and this common interest compelling them to mutual intercourse, and an interchange of good offices with each other, has given rise to a class of cases in which every sovereign is understood to waive the exercise of a part of that complete and exclusive territorial jurisdiction, which has been stated to be the attribute of every nation.[41]

One commentator has observed that 'for Chief Justice Marshall, the overriding consideration appeared to be "the perfect equality and absolute independence of sovereigns" which rendered it improper for a State to exercise the plenitude of its territorial jurisdiction by subjecting a foreign sovereign or the "sovereign rights" exercisable by him to that jurisdiction'.[42] Although recognizing that states can and do cooperate with one another, Marshall's dictum is strongly supportive of the realist paradigm that state sovereignty is supreme and can be limited only by consent. The result was that every state was entitled as a matter of right to absolute immunity from the jurisdiction of every other state.

Nevertheless, the idea that the sovereignty of a state necessarily precludes the possibility of another state exercising jurisdiction over its acts has been strongly criticized by, among others, Professor Sir Hersch Lauterpacht who, in a seminal article in 1951 argued that:

> No legitimate claim of sovereignty is violated if the courts of a state assume jurisdiction over a foreign state with regard to contracts concluded or torts committed in the territory of the state assuming jurisdiction. On the contrary, the sovereignty, the independence and the equality of the latter are denied if the foreign state claims, as a matter of right – as a matter of international law – to be above the law of the state within the territory of which it has engaged in legal transactions or committed acts entailing legal consequences according to the law of that state.[43]

Lauterpacht's argument is firmly based on the primacy of the territorial jurisdiction of the state where the legal consequences have occurred and may not be applicable to extraterritorial consequences. However, states have accepted that, in respect of commercial transactions and certain torts, immunity can be limited through the application of the so-called restrictive theory of state immunity which allows for the exercise of jurisdiction over such legal relations. Clearly states do interact with one

---

41. *Idem*, pp. 135–6.
42. Sinclair (1980), at p. 122.
43. Lauterpacht (1951), at p. 229.

another and in doing so they will enter into legal relations with individuals in one another's states. A realist approach to the enforcement of such relations would allow the state simply to exert its power and deny the right of any other state exercising jurisdiction over it, if not, indeed, the existence of legal obligation. Certainly this was the case under the absolute theory of state immunity. However, more structured approaches to international relations such as institutionalism and regime theory have recognized that in cases such as these, legal obligation can and does exist, particularly where the relevant rule of international law has been internalized.[44] Nevertheless, in spite of the development of the restrictive theory of state immunity, it remains possible for states to assert that truly public acts, often referred to as acts *jure imperii*, should not be subject to the jurisdiction of another state's courts and, in some respects, international tribunals. One illustration of this relates to the immunity of heads of state.

The position of international law on the immunity of heads of state, both serving and former, is unclear.[45] It would appear that there are two aspects to the immunity of a serving head of state. First, there is immunity *ratione personae*. This immunity attaches to the person of the head of state and is analogous to diplomatic immunity. It brings with it wide immunity from the civil and administrative and criminal jurisdiction of a foreign state.[46] It applies regardless of where the head of state is. According to Watts: 'A head of state's immunity is enjoyed in recognition of his very special status as holder of his state's highest office ... his position as head of state is one which he has *erga omnes*, at all times wherever he is.'[47] However, immunity *ratione personae* exists only as long as the recipient remains in office. In other words, it is not available to former heads of state. Former heads of state are, nevertheless, entitled to some immunity in respect of the acts undertaken by them while serving

---

44. See further, Byers (1999), p. 31 and pp. 57–8. On the internalization of rules of international law see Koh (1997), pp. 2645–59.
45. See generally, Bass (1987), Mallory (1986), Watts (1994).
46. By analogy with the position of the diplomatic agent, immunity from criminal jurisdiction is absolute. Immunity from civil and administrative jurisdiction is subject to three minor exceptions in respect of real actions relating to private immovable property, actions relating to succession and actions relating to any professional or commercial activity. See Vienna Convention on Diplomatic Relations 1961, Article 31(1). As with diplomatic agents, heads of state are not exempt from the law of a foreign state which they have an obligation to obey (Vienna Convention, Article 41(1)).
47. Watts (1994), p. 40.

as a head of state. This is the second form of immunity and is known as immunity *ratione materiae* and attaches to the official acts of the head of state. Crucially, the acts in question are deemed not to be the personal acts of the head of state. Rather they are the acts of the state for which an individual cannot be held personally responsible.[48]

The international law position is reflected in the United Kingdom in terms of section 20(1) of the State Immunity Act 1978 which provides that heads of state are entitled to the same privileges and immunities to which diplomats are entitled under the Diplomatic Privileges Act 1964. The 1964 Act was enacted to bring into UK law the provisions of the Vienna Convention on Diplomatic Relations 1961. Article 39(2) of the Vienna Convention provides that diplomatic agents are entitled to immunity after their functions have ceased but only in respect of official acts. In both *Pinochet No. 1* and *No. 3*, it was argued on behalf of Pinochet that section 20(1) of the State Immunity Act and, as a result, Article 39(2) of the Vienna Convention could apply only to a head of state present in the United Kingdom and further, it could apply only to official acts undertaken in the United Kingdom, in the same way as it would apply to diplomatic agents. In both cases, their Lordships examined the negotiating text of the State Immunity Act and all agreed, bar one,[49] that it had been intended that it should apply to heads of state whether or not they were, or indeed ever had been, present in the United Kingdom.[50]

By attaching immunity to the official acts of a head of state, international law may simply be reasserting the realist assumption that the official or public acts of a state are beyond the jurisdiction of foreign states, if not, indeed, the jurisdiction of international law. However, there are two approaches which can be taken in order to avoid this, rather

---

48. For a discussion of the effect of immunity *ratione materiae* in respect of diplomatic agents, see Dinstein (1966) and Denza (1998), p. 361.

49. Only Lord Phillips took the view that 'section 20 of the Act of 1978 has [no] application to a conduct of the head of state outside the United Kingdom. Such conduct remains governed by the rules of public international law' (*Pinochet No. 3*, p. 927).

50. The examination revealed that an amendment to the original State Immunity Bill had changed the original wording of the relevant section which had limited the provision to heads of state physically present in the United Kingdom so as to cover all heads of state whether present in the United Kingdom or not. Lord Browne-Wilkinson was of the view that the 'correct way in which to apply Article 39(2) to former heads of state is baffling' (*Pinochet No. 3*, p. 845). However, as a matter of construction of UK law, the position stated by the House of Lords, while difficult to follow and extremely untidy, must nevertheless be correct.

pessimistic, assumption. First, it may be possible to argue that certain acts of a head of state are not official acts and, accordingly, no immunity will attach to those acts. Alternatively international law itself recognizes that certain official acts are justiciable, either before municipal courts or international tribunals. In both cases, the development of the principle of international criminal responsibility is again the key. Both approaches are apparent in the decision of the House of Lords in *Pinochet No. 3*. Thus, while, on the face of it, six of the seven judges who sat in *Pinochet No. 3* agreed that Pinochet was not entitled to immunity as a former head of state in respect, at least, of the crime of torture, the majority were equally divided on the question of whether the acts in question were official acts.

Persuasive arguments to the effect that acts designated as crimes under international law cannot be official conduct and so not covered by immunity *ratione materiae*, had previously been put forward by the majority in *Pinochet No. 1*.[51] According to Lord Steyn:

> Negatively, the development of international law since the second world war justifies the conclusion that by the time of the coup d'état, and certainly ever since, international law condemned genocide, torture, hostage-taking and crimes against humanity (during an armed conflict or in peace time) as international crimes deserving of punishment. Given this state of international law, it seems to me difficult to maintain that the commission of such high crimes may amount to acts performed in the exercise of the functions of a head of state.[52]

Similarly, Lord Nicholls pointed out that:

> International law recognises, of course, that the functions of a head of state may include activities which are wrongful, even illegal, by the law of his own state or by the laws of other states. But international law has made plain that certain types of conduct, including torture and hostage-taking are not acceptable conduct on the part of anyone. This applies as much to heads of state or even more so, as it does to everyone else; the contrary conclusion would make a mockery of international law.[53]

In *Pinochet No. 3*, three of the judges, specifically Lords Browne-Wilkinson, Hutton and Phillips, agreed with that position. In particular, Lord Browne-Wilkinson posed the following question: 'Can it be said that the commission of a crime which is an international crime against

---

51. The primary basis of the majority decision in *Pinochet No. 1* was that 'the crimes of torture and hostage-taking fell outside what international law would regard as the functions of a head of state' (*Pinochet No. 1*, p. 1457).

52. *Idem*, p. 1506.

53. *Idem*, p. 1500.

humanity and *jus cogens* is an act done in an official capacity on behalf of the state?'[54] Accordingly, it was the nature of the act, not only as a criminal act but, particularly, as a crime against humanity, which was the determinative factor in the decision as to whether or not the acts were official.

There are a number of problems with this approach. First, while it is not difficult to agree with the assertion of Lord Nicholls that 'it hardly needs saying that torture of his own subjects, or of aliens, would not be regarded as a function of a head of state',[55] a similar statement could be made in relation to the murder by a head of state of his own subjects or of aliens. Yet by this test, murder would not fall outside the functions of a head of state because murder, as such, is not recognized as an international crime. Indeed, Lord Browne-Wilkinson specifically held in *Pinochet No. 3* that: 'As to the charge of murder and conspiracy to murder, no one has advanced any reason why the ordinary rules of immunity should not apply and Senator Pinochet is entitled to such immunity.'[56] Murder is not, in the words of Lord Steyn, a 'high crime'. The issue becomes where to draw the line.

Such high crimes by their very nature can often only be carried out by public officials. Indeed, with regard to the offence of torture, it has already been noted that the offence requires that the torture be carried out by an official or with their consent or acquiescence. To deny the official character of such offences is to fly in the face of reality. As a matter of international law they are official acts. As a matter of UK law, they are official acts. As Collins J stated in the Divisional Court: 'There is in my judgement no justification for reading any limitation based on the nature of the crimes committed into the immunity which exists.'[57] Finally, and perhaps most importantly, to deny the official character of such acts would be to remove any liability which the state itself might have under international law for the acts of its officials.

This does not, of course, mean that there can be no individual responsibility for heads of state in respect of such crimes. However, it is first necessary to draw a distinction between the personal responsibility of an individual for a crime under international law and their responsibility under municipal law. Particularly in *Pinochet No. 3*, considerable reliance was placed on the following passage from Sir

---

54. *Pinochet No. 3*, p. 846.
55. *Pinochet No. 1*, p. 1500.
56. *Pinochet No. 3*, p. 848.
57. Unreported.

Arthur Watt's Hague Lectures:

> While generally international law ... does not always directly involve obligations on individuals personally, that is not always appropriate, particularly for acts of such seriousness that they constitute not merely international wrongs (in the broad sense of a civil wrong) but rather international crimes which offend against the public order of the international community. States are artificial legal persons: they can only act through the institutions and agencies of the state, which means, ultimately, through its officials and other individuals acting on behalf of the state. For international conduct which is so serious as to be tainted with criminality to be regarded as attributable only to the impersonal state and not to the individuals who ordered or perpetrated it is both unrealistic and offensive to common notions of justice. The idea that individuals who commit international crimes are *internationally* accountable for them has now become an accepted part of international law. Problems in this area – such as the non-existence of any standing international tribunal to have jurisdiction over such crimes and the lack of agreement as to what acts are internationally criminal for this purpose have not affected the principle of individual responsibility for international criminal conduct.[58]

Any observer of the Nuremberg and Tokyo trials or, more recently, the work of the International Criminal Tribunals for Rwanda and the former Yugoslavia, cannot deny the existence of the principle of international individual responsibility. Indeed, the new International Criminal Court is premised on the very notion of such responsibility and its Statute and those of the Rwandan and Yugoslav Tribunals recognize this by expressly denying immunity attaching to the official capacity of a person accused of the relevant crime. In the case of the Rome Statute of the International Criminal Court, Article 27 is entitled 'Irrelevance of Official Capacity' and reads as follows:

> 1. This Statute shall apply equally to all persons without any distinction based on official capacity. In particular, official capacity as a Head of State ... shall in no case exempt a person from criminal responsibility under this Statute, nor shall it, in and of itself, constitute a ground for reduction of sentence.
> 2. Immunities or special procedural rules which may attach to the official capacity of a person, whether under national or international law, shall not bar the Court from exercising jurisdiction over such a person.[59]

---

58. Watts (1994), p. 82.
59. (1998).

The crimes covered by the Rome Statute include the crimes of genocide, crimes against humanity, including torture, war crimes and crimes of aggression.[60] Were it not possible for such crimes to be committed in an official capacity there would be no need for the specific inclusion of Article 27 of the Statute.[61]

The alternative approach to providing for the individual criminal responsibility of heads of state in respect of official acts is to look for specific exclusions to immunity provided by international law. Such an exclusion will exist generally for cases brought before the International Criminal Court by virtue of Article 27 of its Statute as stated above. However Article 27 does not apply to cases brought before national courts. Nevertheless, in relation to torture, it was argued by three of their lordships in the majority that such an exclusion does exist in the form of the Torture Convention.

The first step in this approach is to make clear that the acts were indeed official acts. Thus, Lord Millett in *Pinochet No. 3* noted that: 'These were not private acts. They were official and governmental or sovereign acts by any standard.'[62] He later continued:

> The offence can be committed *only* by or at the instigation of or with the consent or acquiescence of a public official or other person acting in an official capacity. The official or governmental nature of the act, which forms the basis of the immunity is an essential element of the offence.[63]

Similarly, according to Lord Saville:

> To my mind it must follow in turn that a head of state, who for state purposes resorts to torture, would be a person acting in an official capacity within the meaning of this Convention. He would to my mind be a prime example of an official torturer.[64]

Lord Hope reached a similar decision,[65] as did Lord Goff, albeit while dissenting from the position of the majority regarding the removal of immunity.[66] If the acts in question were official acts Pinochet was *prima facie* entitled to immunity *ratione materiae* in respect of them. If immunity *ratione materiae* were to be refused there would have to be some

---

60. *Idem*, Articles 5–9 (as amended).
61. See further Sarooshi (1999).
62. *Pinochet No. 3*, p. 907. See also Lords Saville and Hope below.
63. *Idem*, p. 913.
64. *Idem*, p. 903.
65. *Idem*, p. 881.
66. *Idem*, pp. 849–50.

provision of the law expressly removing immunity in respect of those acts.

It is at this point that the reasoning of their lordships becomes rather muddled. Lord Goff, of course, found that there was no express removal of immunity, nor indeed was immunity impliedly removed by the terms of the Torture Convention.[67] However, Lord Millett found the express removal of immunity in the form of customary international law which provided for universal jurisdiction over the acts in question.[68] Lord Hope argued along the same lines but apparently required the express consent of the United Kingdom and Chile to the Torture Convention in order to 'crystallize' the removal of immunity.[69] Lord Saville held, quite simply, that the terms of the Torture Convention had expressly removed immunity *ratione materiae*.[70] All that can be said for definite is that those judges in the majority who found that Pinochet had committed official acts were agreed that international law itself had provided an exception to Pinochet's immunity *ratione materiae* in respect of torture at least.

CONCLUSIONS

The limitations of the decisions in *Ex parte Pinochet* are all too apparent. First, the decision in *Pinochet No. 1* has no binding authority whatsoever. Even in the United Kingdom, the reasoning of the four judges who stated reasons is persuasive only. Furthermore, while the decision in *Pinochet No. 3* serves as a legal precedent in the United Kingdom, no other state's courts are bound by it. The best that can be said is that a decision of the highest court of criminal appeals in the United Kingdom is persuasive authority for courts in other jurisdictions, particularly Commonwealth states and, perhaps, the United States, all of which share a common legal heritage with the United Kingdom. Even this possibility, however, may be exaggerated. *Pinochet No. 3* is a decision which is substantially limited to its facts. It applies only to former heads of state and only in respect of the crime of torture as defined in the Torture Convention. Indeed, the reasoning of the judges over the two substantive cases has been shown to be lacking in a number of ways and the failure to agree on the crucial matter of whether Pinochet was acting in the course of his official duties

---

67. *Idem*, pp. 855–63.
68. *Idem*, p. 915.
69. *Idem*, pp. 886–7.
70. *Idem*, p. 904.

will appear puzzling to many and will limit the persuasiveness of both decisions around the world.

Furthermore, the decisions in *Pinochet* cannot stand as a precedent for international tribunals and international law in general. At best, the decisions stand as evidence of the practice of the United Kingdom in relation to the application and interpretation of the Torture Convention 1984. It is likely that the decisions will be used by those pushing for stricter enforcement of the Torture Convention who may ratify the decisions incorporating them into their own state practice either by similar decisions where the circumstances arise, or, simply, through statements supporting the decisions. In such a way a rule of customary international law may emerge, may indeed already be emerging, which will confirm the operation of the Torture Convention as overriding the existence of state immunity in relation to official torture as defined in the Convention.

The cases further illustrate that international law remains essentially positivist. Thus, the House of Lords was clear that if universal jurisdiction were to exist in this case, there had to be an international treaty to that effect to which Chile was a party. Of course, had the House of Lords found, as it did in *Pinochet No. 1*, that the universality of the crime of torture was part of customary international law, that would have been binding on Chile unless it had persistently objected to the development of that rule of customary international law. However, the difficulty of arguing the existence of rule of customary international law in this regard derives from the concept of exclusive territorial sovereignty on which much of international law is premised.

Nevertheless, the cases do illustrate the ways in which international law has developed during the second half of the twentieth century. In particular, they illustrate the potential for increased cooperation of states in areas including the protection of human rights. Thus, fifty years ago, the possibility of a case such as this occurring would have seemed impossible. The reason that Pinochet, at this time,[71] continues to face

---

71. At the time of writing, Pinochet remains in the United Kingdom where further legal steps have been taken by him to prevent his extradition. However, it is apparent that his health is deteriorating and there is some indication that he may be allowed to return to Chile on health grounds.

extradition to Spain to face criminal charges is because states have been able to create relevant treaty regimes which not only provide for the protection of international human rights but also, in appropriate circumstances, provide for the individual criminal responsibility of individuals who interfere with those rights. The creation of the International Criminal Court is a further development in this direction and should generally be welcomed.

CHAPTER 7

THE ABUSE OF DIPLOMATIC PRIVILEGES AND IMMUNITIES: A NECESSARY EVIL?

International lawyers attempting to illustrate how international law plays a central role in the relations of states would do well to point to the example of the law governing diplomatic privileges and immunities as an example of how well international law can work. In terms of enforcement, the law is wholly dependent on the principle of reciprocity and, as a result, the law in this area clearly illustrates the potential benefits of close interdependence amongst states. Nevertheless, the law of diplomatic privileges and immunities is open to abuse by states and by individual diplomats. The most notorious example of abuse of the law by a state concerned the Iranian seizure of the US embassy in Tehran in 1979. A leading example of abuse by an individual diplomat is undoubtedly the shooting, in London, of WPC Yvonne Fletcher by an unknown Libyan diplomat in April 1984. This case study will use this latter incident as a focus for the explanation of the reasons for diplomatic privileges and immunities and the efficacy of the law in this area. Reference will also be made where necessary to the former incident.

THE FLETCHER INCIDENT

The sequence of events leading up to and immediately following the shooting of WPC Fletcher have been documented by the Foreign Affairs Committee of the UK House of Commons in the following terms:

At about midnight on 16 April [1984] two members (recognised diplomats) of the Libyan People's Bureau came to the Foreign Office. They told the duty officer that they had come to protest against a demonstration to be held the next morning and to say that the Libyans 'would not be responsible for its consequences'. That the message did not emanate from a local decision is emphasised by the fact that a similar one was delivered to Her Majesty's Ambassador in Tripoli after midnight.

The demonstration the next day was peaceful and gave rise to no problems of public order. Shooting, now believed to have come from two windows in the Bureau, caused the death of WPC Fletcher, who was on duty in the Square. The Libyan authorities in Tripoli were immediately asked to instruct those inside the Bureau to leave the building and to allow it to be searched for weapons and explosives. The request was refused. The British Embassy in Tripoli was the scene of hostile demonstrations and certain British citizens were unjustifiably arrested and detained.

Her Majesty's Government proposed 'as a basis for terminating relations by agreement' that:

(1) The occupants of the Bureau and all other Libyan diplomatic staff in the country should have safe conduct out of the country ...
(2) Our own diplomats were to leave Libya in safety.
(3) We should be satisfied that all weapons and explosives were removed from the Bureau and that it could no longer be used for terrorist acts.

These proposals were refused.

On 20 April, a bomb exploded in the luggage hall of Heathrow Airport injuring 25 people. The Government have reserved their position as to whether it was connected with the incidents [outside the Libyan embassy] though there was wide press speculation that this was in fact the case. On 22 April the Libyans were notified that diplomatic relations would terminate at 6.00 p.m. that day and that all diplomatic staff and other persons in the Bureau were to leave by midnight 29–30 April. Two Libyans (not at the Bureau) were deported after the shooting of WPC Fletcher. Various measures were announced by the Home Secretary for tightening the exercise of his discretionary powers in respect of Libyans already in the country or wishing to enter.

The Bureau was evacuated on 27 April 1984. Those leaving were questioned and electronically searched. Diplomatic bags that left the Bureau were not searched or scanned. The Bureau was sealed and on 30 April 1984 was entered by British authorities, in the presence of a representative of the Saudi Arabian Embassy, and searched. Weapons and relevant forensic evidence were found.[1]

What should be noted from this official statement of events is the meticulous observance of the Vienna Convention on Diplomatic Relations 1961 by the British authorities. This occurred in the face of

---

1. Foreign Affairs Committee (1984–5), paras. 73–7.

widespread calls for a breach of the Convention requirements by the press and public in the United Kingdom. In order fully to understand why the United Kingdom acted in this way requires an analysis of the development and rationale behind the granting of diplomatic privileges and immunities as codified in the 1961 Vienna Convention.

THE DEVELOPMENT AND RATIONALE OF DIPLOMATIC PRIVILEGES AND IMMUNITIES

The law of diplomatic privileges and immunities has developed over many thousands of years. Reference has already been made to the probability that 'diplomatic' inviolability was one of the earliest principles of international law. Indeed, it is clear that the principle of the inviolability of the diplomatic envoy was observed among very many different and, often, unconnected empires within the ancient world. Thus, the Greeks and Romans in the West and the Indians and Chinese in the East generally adhered to the principle that a messenger from a foreign territory was allowed to complete his mission without the fear of interference. As with the development of international law generally, religion played an important part in the early practice of such civilizations and early ambassadors were often cloaked with religious sanctity. Thus, Gentili, one of the early classical writers on international law, informs us that in the court of Alexander, for example, no one could 'perform the functions of an embassy unless he had first washed his hands in water poured over them by heralds, and had made a libation to Zeus from goblets wreathed with garlands'.[2] Similarly De Martens has argued that, amongst the ancients, the basis of the inviolability of the diplomatic envoy was essentially religious and not dependent upon the idea of the ambassador representing a sovereign nation nor upon the character of the envoy himself.[3]

However, while religion may be used to explain the sanctity of ambassadors within and between empires having similar religious beliefs and understandings, it does not suffice to explain the inviolability of ambassadors sent between empires whose religious beliefs and tolerances were not only different but also diametrically opposed. Thus, according to Ganshoff, writing on the role of religion in the Middle Ages: 'The personal immunity of the envoys was a generally accepted rule in

---

2. Gentili (1585), Vol. II, p. 58.
3. De Martens (1866), p. vi.

the Moslem as well as in the Western and Eastern Christian worlds.'[4] Thus, it is likely that the cloak of religious sanctity was used as a form of guarantee against harm being done to persons who were regarded as fulfilling an essential role in society. Certainly, however, religion has very little if any relevance to the modern law of diplomatic privileges and immunities.

As the establishment of permanent diplomatic relations became a necessity, three secular bases of diplomatic law were advanced. These were the representative character theory, the exterritoriality theory and the functional necessity theory. The representative character theory attracted most favour in the early development of diplomatic privileges and immunities following the establishment of permanent diplomatic relations. The essential basis of the theory is that it 'ultimately traces immunity to the sovereignty of the state which sends the agent'.[5] This theory was developed by the classical writers, including Grotius, who noted that: 'Ambassadors as if by a kind of fiction, are considered to represent those who sent them.'[6] Accordingly, the early development of the theory required that ambassadors were to be given all the privileges and respect which would be accorded to the sovereign himself. The representative character theory did not die out with the emergence of the modern state system. Rather, the development of the theory of the absolute sovereignty of states ensured that the privileges and immunities of the ambassador continued unchallenged by these developments.

Nevertheless, the development of the exclusive territorial jurisdiction of states, while not directly challenging the, by then established, rules of diplomatic law, did result in certain misgivings among writers about the apparent contradiction between the granting of diplomatic privileges and immunities and the jurisdiction of the territorial state over all matters within its territory. These misgivings apparently led to the emergence of the exterritoriality theory. According to this theory, the ambassador is considered, by a legal fiction, not only to be outside the jurisdiction of the territorial state but actually physically outside that territory. Thus, according to Bynkershoek, writing in 1721, 'ambassadors are thought of as being outside the territory of him to whom they are sent as ambassadors'.[7] As the theory developed, the fiction of exterritoriality came to be applied not only to the person of the ambassador but also to

---

4. Ganshoff (1970), p. 134.
5. Ogdon (1936), p. 105.
6. Grotius (1625), Bk. II, Ch. XVII, p. 443.
7. Bynkershoek (1721), Ch. VIII, p. 43.

his residence. As a result, immunity from jurisdiction was extended not only to members of the ambassador's family and his official staff but also to unofficial members of his household and any hangers-on. In practice, the effect of reliance on the exterritoriality theory soon got out of control. Thus, a situation quickly developed in practice whereby not only the premises of the embassy and private residences of diplomatic personnel were considered to be foreign territory but also vast areas of the surrounding cities, making those areas havens for outlaws and criminals. The position has been vividly summed up by Anderson who has noted that:

> By the eighteenth century, the position in Rome had become so impossible (since not merely considerable areas around foreign embassies but also churches and the houses of cardinals offered refuge to criminals) that the papal police had to be equipped with special maps to show them which streets they were permitted to pass through.[8]

The excesses associated with the exterritoriality theory and, to a lesser extent, the representative character theory resulted in the emergence of a third juridical explanation for the granting of diplomatic privileges and immunities to ambassadors, that is the functional necessity theory. While the necessity of the diplomatic function had been recognized since ancient times, the theory of functional necessity did not truly emerge until the time of Vattel in the middle of the eighteenth century. Vattel was the first of the classical writers to place emphasis on the need to ensure that ambassadors could function properly noting that '[ambassadors] can not accomplish the object of their appointment unless they are endowed with all the prerogatives necessary to perform the duties of their charge safely, freely, faithfully and successfully'.[9] Vattel, indeed, was the first of the classical writers to attempt to limit the apparently absolute privileges and immunities which had emerged in practice under the lead of the representative character and exterritoriality theories. Thus, according to Vattel:

> The independence of the foreign minister must not be converted into unrestrained licence; it does not release him from the duty of conforming in his external conduct to the customs and laws of the country in all that does not relate to his character as an ambassador; he is independent but he has not the right to do whatever he pleases.[10]

---

8. Anderson (1993), p. 56.
9. Vattel (1758), Bk. IV, Ch. VII, p. 376.
10. *Idem*, p. 377.

As the law of diplomatic privileges and immunities developed into the twentieth century, the exterritoriality theory was abandoned and the functional necessity theory came to dominate theoretical justifications in this area. The representative character theory, while remaining relevant, has nevertheless become of secondary importance. Accordingly, when the International Law Commission began its work on the codification of the law of diplomatic privileges and immunities in the mid-1950s, it was guided primarily by the functional necessity theory in areas where state practice was unclear. It did note, however, that it continued to bear in mind the representative character of the head of the mission.[11] This juridical basis of diplomatic law was confirmed in Paragraph 4 of the Preamble to the Vienna Convention on Diplomatic Relations of 1961 in the following terms: 'Realising that the purpose of such privileges and immunities is not to benefit individuals but to ensure the efficient performance of diplomatic missions as representing states.'

It should be noted, however, that the Vienna Convention was the culmination of a process of development of diplomatic privileges and immunities which had been occurring through the mechanism of customary international law over many hundreds of years. Accordingly, many of the rules concerning diplomatic privileges and immunities which developed on the basis of the representative character and exterritoriality theories remain valid insofar as they were regarded as reflecting state practice and accepted as such in the terms of the Convention.[12]

THE SUBSTANTIVE LAW OF DIPLOMATIC PRIVILEGES AND IMMUNITIES

The basic privileges and immunities of diplomatic missions and their agents are contained in Articles 20–36 of the Vienna Convention. Included among the privileges are the exemption of the diplomatic agent from dues and taxes,[13] social security provisions,[14] personal, public and military service[15] and customs duties, taxes and related charges,[16] as well as the exemption of the sending state and the head of mission from dues

---

11. UN Doc. A/3623, 1957 *YBILC*, Vol. II, p. 136.
12. Barker (1995), pp. 609–10.
13. Vienna Convention, Article 34.
14. Vienna Convention, Article 33.
15. Vienna Convention, Article 35.
16. Vienna Convention, Article 36.

and taxes in respect of the premises of the mission,[17] and the exemption of the mission itself in respect of dues and taxes payable on any fees and charges levied by it in the course of its official duties.[18] While many reasons have been put forward to explain why such privileges are granted, it seems clear that 'the interference with the functions of a mission and the loss of independence which may by caused by attempts to collect dues or taxes, or in the enforcement of social security provisions or provisions governing military service, for example, provide a more than adequate basis on which to ground these exemptions'.[19] Essentially, privileges grant specific exemptions from local jurisdiction.

Where no such exemptions exist, the diplomatic agent is required to 'respect the laws and regulations of the receiving state'.[20] However, where a diplomatic agent does break the law in the receiving state, he cannot be arrested or otherwise detained. Nor can he stand trial, be sued or be made to testify before the judicial authorities of the receiving state. Essentially, a diplomatic agent is both inviolable[21] and, except in respect of a few minor exceptions, immune from the legal process of the receiving state.[22] Similarly, the premises of the diplomatic mission,[23] its archives[24] and official documents[25], as well as the private residence,[26] papers and correspondence and, subject to a few minor exceptions, the personal property of the diplomatic agent,[27] are all inviolable. Furthermore, the family of a diplomatic agent is entitled to the same privileges and immunities extended to the diplomatic agent.[28] In all cases, inviolability and immunity from jurisdiction are clearly justified on the basis of functional necessity. Thus, inviolability is essential for maintaining the independence of the diplomat and the mission and

---

17. Vienna Convention, Article 23.
18. Vienna Convention, Article 28.
19. Barker (1996), p. 70.
20. Vienna Convention, Article 41.
21. Vienna Convention, Article 29.
22. Vienna Convention, Article 31. A diplomatic agent is immune from the criminal jurisdiction of the receiving state and from its civil and administrative jurisdiction except in connection with real actions relating to private moveable property, actions relating to succession and actions relating to any professional or commercial activity (Vienna Convention, Article 31(1)). See further Barker (1996), pp. 77–8.
23. Vienna Convention, Article 22.
24. Vienna Convention, Article 24.
25. Vienna Convention, Article 27(2).
26. Vienna Convention, Article 30(1).
27. Vienna Convention, Article 30(2).
28. Vienna Convention, Article 37(1).

ensuring their protection from interference by the receiving state and by third parties. The immunity of diplomatic agents and, indeed, their families can be justified for similar reasons.[29]

DEALING WITH ABUSE

It may seem from this brief survey of the provisions of the Vienna Convention that diplomatic agents have an unrestrained licence to do whatever they wish and get away with it. Certainly, the facts of the Fletcher incident would seem to bear out this initial impression. However, as the ICJ pointed out in the *Tehran Hostages Case*, the Vienna Convention constitutes a 'self-contained regime which, on the one hand, lays down the receiving state's obligations regarding the facilities, privileges and immunities to be accorded to diplomatic missions and, on the other, foresees their possible abuse by members of the mission and specifies the means at the disposal of the receiving states to counter any such abuse'.[30] Nevertheless, there is, and always has been, a fundamental dichotomy between the granting of diplomatic immunity and the exercise of jurisdiction over diplomats by local authorities. Thus, according to Grotius, 'on the one side stands the utility of punishment against grave delinquents, [even if they be ambassadors] and on the other, the utility of ambassadors, the sending of whom is facilitated by their having all possible security ... the Law of Nations makes an exception in favour of ambassadors and those who come under the public faith. Hence to put ambassadors under accusation is contrary to the Law of Nations, which permits many things which Natural Law forbids.'[31] Accordingly, while the Vienna Convention on Diplomatic Relations 1961 is unequivocal that the duty of diplomatic agents is to 'respect the laws and regulations of the receiving State,[32] this duty is subordinate to the long-established rights of inviolability and immunity.[33]

---

29. See further, Barker (1996), pp. 70–81.
30. *Tehran Hostages Case* (1980) ICJ Rep. para. 86.
31. Grotius (1625), Bk. II, Ch XVIII, Sec IV, paras. 2–3.
32. Vienna Convention, Article 41.
33. See, for example, the view of the International Law Commission that ' ... in the final analysis the absolute principle of inviolability must have overriding force' ([1957] 1 *Yearbook of the International Law Commission* 148). See also the view of the UK's Foreign Affairs Committee which noted that: 'it is not correct that when a diplomat violates this duty he loses his immunity. Such a reading is inconsistent with the immunities given, which operate precisely in respect of such alleged violations, and which, in the case of diplomatic agents, apply even to unofficial acts ... a person remains an accredited diplomat until the receiving State requires him to be withdrawn' (Foreign Affairs Committee (1984–5), para. 42).

The primary mechanism available to the receiving state as a response to the abuse of diplomatic privileges and immunities by an accredited diplomat or a member of his family is to declare the individual *persona non grata* and request his recall or dismissal in terms of Article 9 of the Vienna Convention. The sanction of *persona non grata* is long established in customary international law and is recognized as the primary deterrent against abuse of diplomatic privileges and immunities by diplomatic staff. Thus, according to Hill, writing in 1931, 'recall, dismissal and expulsion are effective sanctions in two ways. They deter gross violations of the laws of the receiving state and they prevent repeated infractions of the law of the receiving state by removing the offender from the country.'[34] On the other hand, states have always been reluctant to overuse this provision. This was the case even before the enactment of the Vienna Convention. Again, according to Hill:

> Request for recall and in a higher degree dismissal and expulsion are used with great caution by governments since states have shown great reluctance in granting to the receiving state the right to terminate the function of a diplomatic representative unless a serious charge is brought against him and adequately proved ... Second, these sanctions have been limited in application to offences committed against the receiving state such as conspiracy, infraction of neutrality laws, or interference with the internal affairs of the receiving state, or discourteous or unfriendly conduct.[35]

While the Vienna Convention makes it clear that states are entitled at any time and without having to give reasons to declare any member of the diplomatic staff of a mission *persona non grata*, it remains a remedy which states resort to only very rarely. The United Kingdom, prior to the Fletcher incident, for example, would only consider the declaration of *persona non grata* in cases of serious criminal offences.[36] Even after its review of the Vienna Convention in the aftermath of the Fletcher incident, the UK Government took the view that: 'As a general rule, espionage and incitement to, or advocacy of, violence require an immediate declaration of *persona non grata*. Those involved in drug trafficking are also declared *persona non grata* unless a waiver of immunity is granted.'[37]

---

34. Hill (1931), p. 257.
35. *Idem*, pp. 256–7.
36. Foreign Affairs Committee (1984–5), Minutes of Evidence, p. 8.
37. UK Government (1985), para. 69.

That these offences constitute serious offences cannot be disputed and the impression is that the commission of lesser crimes would not result in the declaration of *persona non grata*. This impression is borne out by the British Government's official figures which indicate that even in the years after the Fletcher incident, the number of diplomats expelled by the United Kingdom for the commission of serious offences remained comparatively small. Thus, in 1993, for example, 33 alleged serious offences were committed by diplomatic personnel which resulted in only eight diplomats being withdrawn from their posts.[38] The most plausible reason for this apparent reluctance among states to use the sanction of *persona non grata* to the fullest extent possible is the possibility of reciprocal action. Thus, even though there is no need to give a reason for a declaration of *persona non grata*, the fear or expectation of reciprocal action by the sending state ensures that the declaration of *persona non grata* will only be used in the most clear-cut cases of abuse where there is no other option.

Other remedies for abuse of diplomatic privileges and immunities are envisaged by the Vienna Convention. Thus, Article 31(4) ensures that immunity from the jurisdiction of the receiving state does not exempt the diplomat from the jurisdiction of the sending state. In other words, a diplomat can, in principle, be sued in the courts of the sending state for any matter which occurred while serving in the receiving state. However, this provision is extremely limited. As this author has noted previously:

> The 1961 Convention contains no positive obligation on the sending state to allow its diplomatic personnel to be sued or tried in its own courts, nor even to delegate a court in which such actions could take place. Even if such actions were possible, the cost to an individual of attempting to sue in a foreign state would be prohibitive ... in practice, there are severe limitations on the possible reliance on the civil and criminal jurisdiction of the sending state.[39]

A further provision which envisages the possibility of legal action being taken against a recalcitrant diplomat but which does not directly challenge the immunity of the diplomatic agent is found in Article 39(2) of the Vienna Convention. According to this provision, which was central to the case against Pinochet as highlighted in the previous

---

38. Marston (1993), p. 627.
39. Barker (1996), pp. 118–19.

chapter, a diplomat is no longer entitled to privileges and immunities at the moment he leaves the country except in respect of his official acts for which immunity continues. Accordingly, in respect of non-official acts committed whilst serving as a diplomat, an individual loses his immunity and can thereafter be sued or even criminally tried. Again, however, the full effects of this provision are limited in the sense that a diplomatic agent or other person entitled to diplomatic privileges and immunities must be allowed to leave the territory of the receiving state. Accordingly, in order for proceedings to be brought that person must return to the territory of the receiving state.

The final possible deterrent against the possibility of abuse by diplomatic personnel is waiver of immunity. Article 32 of the Vienna Convention provides that the sending state is entitled, by express provision, to waive the immunity from jurisdiction of diplomatic agents, and other persons enjoying immunity in terms of Article 37 of the Convention. This provision would appear, on its face, to be the solution to both the problem of deterring the abuse of diplomatic privileges and immunities and the perceived lack of justice inherent in the system of diplomatic privileges and immunities. Yet the waiving of diplomatic immunity by a sending state even in cases of serious abuse is very rare indeed.

The negotiation of Article 32 of the Vienna Convention was focused to a considerable degree on the questions of who was entitled to waive immunity and whether a distinction should be made between the waiver of civil and criminal jurisdiction. The conclusion was that the right to waive immunity is a right of the sending state alone. Thus, Article 32, paragraph 1 makes it clear that 'immunity from jurisdiction ... may be waived by the sending State'. Paragraph 3 requires that waiver must always be express. Paragraph 4 of Article 32 makes it clear that in relation to civil and administrative matters, waiver of immunity in respect of proceedings shall not be held to imply waiver from immunity in respect of execution for which a similar waiver is required.

The wording of Article 32 makes it clear that there is no obligation on states to waive diplomatic immunity in any circumstances. It enunciates a right which a state is entitled to exercise according to its own determination. Thus, even the earliest drafts of the Article in question refer to the fact that a state 'may' waive immunity. It is worth noting that an attempt was made at the Vienna Conference to hold states responsible for damage caused by diplomatic personnel by including a requirement that states make fair compensation for such damage. The proposal, which was put forward by the Holy See, was intended to ensure the accountability of states for the actions of their representatives in cases where the immunity of those representatives was not waived.[40] However, the proposal was soundly rejected by the vast majority of states, who made clear their opposition to there being any sense of obligation to waive immunity or to pay damages *in lieu*.

It would seem that the general attitude of states against there being an obligation to waive immunity is reflected in the current practice of states generally to refuse to waive diplomatic immunity. The UK Government noted in 1985 that: 'The main abuse lies not so much in the comparative number of alleged offences (which is small) or in their relative gravity, but in the reliance on immunity to protect individuals for offences without any obvious connection to the efficient performance of the functions of a diplomatic mission.'[41] As the decision whether or not to waive diplomatic immunity lies with the sending state and not the individual, it would appear that the UK Government was of the view that the primary abuse of diplomatic privileges and immunities lay in the refusal of states to waive diplomatic immunity in appropriate cases. On the other hand, the UK Government was unwilling to pursue any mechanism by which the waiving of diplomatic immunity could be more easily achieved. It concluded that, even if it was objectively justifiable to impose an obligation to waive immunity, in appropriate circumstances, there was no support for such a move, not even on a limited basis amongst close allies:

> We have found ... no support within the European Community or elsewhere for the idea of bilateral or limited mutual agreements to waive immunity either generally or in specific cases. There would, in any case, be a risk that a restriction on immunity could in certain countries be exploited for political or retaliatory purposes against British diplomats and communities overseas.[42]

Essentially, the decision as to whether or not to waive immunity is not a legal one. Rather, it is a political decision based upon a number of factors which take account of the possibility of retaliatory measures being taken against diplomatic personnel, most obviously in the form of trumped-up or fabricated charges, but which also take account of the wider general interests of the state in question. The political nature of the decision as to

---

40. The proposal was intended to ensure states had regard to 'the moral and humanitarian principles which imposed upon the sending State an obligation to ensure justice for persons who have suffered loss or damage through the act of a diplomat' (UN Doc. A/Conf.20/C.1/L.292).
41. UK Government (1985), para. 62.
42. *Idem.*

whether or not to waive diplomatic immunity in any particular instance is apparent in the US Department of State's 1986 Guidance to the Foreign Service. The Guidance noted that:

> the individual, who ultimately benefits from the immunity, has no power to waive immunity even in cases where he or she believes that it would be in his or her personal or commercial interest to do so. Rather, the sending State must waive immunity when it judges that to do so *is in the national interest*.[43]

In the same note, the Department of State made clear its policy against the waiving of immunity: 'While the power to waive immunity is always available, it is the usual practice of the Department of State to waive only in benign circumstances.'[44]

It would seem, accordingly, that matters of justice in the receiving state are very much of secondary consideration to the national interests of the United States in making such a determination. A particular example of this policy at work was the case of James Myres Ingley, the clergyman husband of an American diplomat stationed in London, who was accused of 'gross indecency' against a female minor. The United States refused to waive immunity in this case in spite of the good relations between the United Kingdom and the United States and the fact that the standard of justice in the United Kingdom was not in question. According to McClanachan: 'The American Embassy had declined to waive immunity "after due consideration of the case and consistent with the long-standing US Government policy on such issues".'[45] It would seem that this attitude prevails throughout the world.

One recent exception which may well prove the rule was the incident which occurred in January 1997 involving Mr Gueorgui Makharadze, a Georgian diplomat accredited to the United States. Makharadze was accused of killing a 16-year-old girl in Washington, DC, by hitting her with his car. It was also alleged that he was drunk at the time of the accident. What makes the Makharadze case stand out from others is the decision by Georgian authorities, on the personal intervention of President Eduard Shevardnadze, to take the 'highly unusual'[46] step of

---

43. McClanachan (1989), pp. 138–9.
44. *Idem.*
45. *Idem*, p. 138.
46. Mr Nicholas Burns, State Department spokesman, noted that the decision by the Georgian President was 'a courageous step' which was 'highly unusual in modern diplomacy' (reported in Myres, 1997).

waiving the immunity of Mr Makharadze on 'moral and ethical' grounds.[47] Undoubtedly, part of the motivation behind the decision to waive the immunity of Mr Makharadze must have been the developing political and economic relations between Georgia and the United States, thus highlighting the fact that decisions such as these have as much to do with political reality as the rule of law. Indeed, the decision to waive immunity in Mr Makharadze's case led his lawyers to conclude that the diplomat was 'an unwitting political pawn in an international chess game'.[48]

A NECESSARY EVIL?

The public perception of diplomatic immunity is that it is 'a basic principle of foreign relations that flies in the face of justice'.[49] Many proposals have been put forward aimed at reducing such immunity, particularly immunity from criminal jurisdiction. Proposals have ranged from the introduction of a Permanent International Diplomatic Criminal Court to the forfeiture of immunity in cases of espionage. Specific attempts have been made in the United States to introduce legislation aimed at reducing diplomatic immunity in certain situations. It seems likely that legislators in many other jurisdictions have also considered amending their law so as to provide for the arrest and punishment of diplomats who have seriously abused their privileges and immunities. Yet no attempt by academics or legislators to amend the law of diplomatic privileges and immunities has brought about an amendment to the Vienna Convention. Does that mean, accordingly, that the abuse of diplomatic privileges and immunities is simply a necessary evil which has to be accepted so as not to undermine the broader process of international diplomacy?

Undoubtedly the primary aim of the law of diplomatic privileges and immunities is to ensure the efficient functioning of the diplomatic process. Thus, privileges and immunities are granted to the families of diplomatic personnel who, while they perform few, if any, official diplomatic functions, are nevertheless entitled to immunity in order to

---

47. See statement issued by the Georgian Embassy in Washington, DC, on 9 January 1997 which indicated the willingness of the Republic of Georgia to waive immunity in the particular case, although it stopped short of formally waiving immunity (*idem*).
48. Myres (1997).
49. *Idem.*

secure the independence of the diplomatic agent. Furthermore, it is clearly accepted that any type of legal action against a diplomat personally can impede the diplomatic process whether it is intended to or not. Thus, according to Ogdon:

> As long as states are agreed that diplomatic immunity exists for the purpose of safeguarding the performance of the diplomatic function, the test is not whether acts are public, private or professional, but whether the exercise of jurisdiction over the agent would interfere with the performance of his official functions.[50]

It is worth noting that the development of diplomatic law has, in fact, recognized that the granting of full diplomatic privileges and immunities to all diplomatic personnel is not 'necessary' for the efficient functioning of the diplomatic mission. Thus, members of the administrative and technical staff of a mission enjoy full immunity from criminal jurisdiction but are entitled to immunity from the civil and administrative jurisdiction of the receiving state only in respect of acts performed in the course of their official duties.[51] Members of the service staff of the mission enjoy immunities from both criminal and civil and administrative jurisdiction only in respect of their official functions,[52] while private servants of members of the mission enjoy immunity only to the extent admitted by the receiving state.[53]

Crucially, however, diplomatic privileges and immunities are necessary not only to ensure the efficient functioning of the diplomatic process but also to ensure the fullest protection is given to diplomatic personnel. Thus, the inviolability of the diplomatic agent has always been regarded as the fundamental principle of diplomatic law. According to the ICJ when making an Order for Provisional Measures in the *Tehran Hostages Case*:

> Whereas there is no more fundamental prerequisite for the conduct of international relations between states that the inviolability of diplomatic envoys and embassies, so that throughout history nations of all creeds and cultures have observed reciprocal obligations for that purpose; and whereas the obligations thus assumed, notably those for assuring the personal safety of diplomats and their freedom from prosecution, are essential, unqualified and inherent in their representative character and their diplomatic function.[54]

---

50. Ogdon (1936), p. 180.
51. Vienna Convention, Article 37(2).
52. Vienna Convention, Article 37(3).
53. Vienna Convention, Article 37(4).
54. (1979) ICJ Rep. 7, para. 38.

In this respect, the Vienna Convention provides not only for the inviolability of diplomatic agents and missions but imposes a special duty of protection on the receiving state in respect thereof. Thus, Article 22(2) of the Convention states: 'The receiving state is under a special duty to take all appropriate steps to protect the premises of the mission against any intrusion or damage and to prevent any disturbance of the peace of the mission or impairment of its dignity.' Similarly, the special duty of protection in respect of the diplomatic agent is to be found in Article 29 of the Convention which, having declared the inviolability of the diplomatic agent, continues: 'The receiving state shall treat him with due respect and shall take all appropriate steps to prevent any attack on his person, freedom or dignity.'

According to Rozakis, writing in 1974: 'The current flood of terrorism has reached an unprecedented peak in all its manifestations and has resulted in a dramatic increase of incidents against international officials.'[55] Similarly, a conference in the wake of the Tehran hostage crisis on the subject of 'International Terrorism: The Protection of Diplomatic Premises and Personnel' drew attention to the vulnerable position of diplomatic representatives. It noted that: 'The protection of diplomats merits special attention because diplomats are especially vulnerable symbolic targets of political violence.'[56] As one British former diplomat, himself the subject of a failed kidnapping attempt, has noted, 'it is the special status of the diplomatic agent which renders him unsafe'.[57]

As symbolic figures, diplomatic representatives can become the targets for all types of political violence, most often by those objecting against the policies of the state of which the diplomat is a representative. However, diplomats can also be targeted by those protesting against the policies of the receiving state, as was apparently the case in respect of the Lima hostage crisis. Many highly publicized attacks against diplomatic establishments have occurred in recent years, including, most notably, the siege of the American embassy in Tehran in 1979–80, the siege of the Iraqi embassy in London in 1991, the bombing of the Israeli embassy in London in 1994, and the siege of the Japanese embassy in Lima, Peru in 1997. More recently, terrorist bomb attacks on the United States' Embassies in Kenya and Tanzania in August 1998 have had the effect of reminding the citizens of the United States of the dangers faced by their

---

55. Rozakis (1974), p. 32.
56. Hevener (1986), p. 5.
57. Jackson (1981), pp. 92–3.

diplomats on a daily basis throughout the world.

Far from providing an argument in support of reducing diplomatic privileges and immunities, incidents such as these simply serve to reinforce the need to observe the diplomatic privileges and immunities of all diplomatic personnel. Thus, developments since the entry into force of the Vienna Convention regime have seen increased attempts to secure greater protection of diplomatic agents and other internationally protected persons. These include the 1970 Organization of American States Convention to Prevent and Punish the Acts of Terrorism Taking the Form of Crimes Against Persons and Related Acts of Extortion That Are of International Significance and the Convention on the Prevention and Punishment of Crimes Against Diplomatic Agents and Other Internationally Protected Persons 1973.

It is generally accepted that the removal of the cloak of diplomatic privileges and immunities is not the solution to the problem of abuse. All states are both sending states and receiving states. While acting as a receiving state, the natural inclination would be to pursue policies which would favour the reduction of privileges and immunities. However, every state benefits as a sending state from the independence of and protection of its own diplomatic personnel abroad. The incidence of abuse has been shown to be very small indeed. However, the risks involved in a reduction of diplomatic privileges and immunities and the consequent exposure of diplomatic personnel to interference and loss of independence is very real indeed.

Examined objectively, the law of diplomatic privileges and immunities is required to balance the risk that diplomatic personnel will be able to hide behind the cloak of diplomatic privileges and immunities against the risk that the receiving state will harass and oppress such personnel. The more obvious risk is oppression by the receiving state. Individual diplomats without broad immunities could be seriously oppressed by a ruthless state with very little chance of effective recourse. Accordingly, broad diplomatic privileges and immunities are necessary, not only to allow individual diplomats to function freely and independently, but also to ensure the fullest protection of such individuals.

CHAPTER 8

CONCLUSIONS

Having outlined the theoretical basis of international law and examined four case studies illustrating how international law has been applied in recent years, it is now possible to draw certain conclusions about the role of international law and its relevance to the international relations of states. First, international law is not a system of static unchangeable rules. It is a common mistake to consider that once an international legal rule has been established, it is set in stone. Undoubtedly states can change rules by entering into new treaty arrangements or by engaging in contrary practice and developing a new *opinio juris* in relation to a new rule of law. However, even when a rule is firmly established it is still open to interpretation. The interpretation of international legal rules may occur through judicial or arbitral settlement. However, such settlement is subject to the consent of states. Accordingly, international law, in a way which is not typical of legal systems in general, leaves it up to the individual subjects of the law to develop interpretations of the law through their practice. Thus, according to Rosalyn Higgins:

> When . . . decisions are made by authorised persons or organs, in appropriate forums, within the framework of certain established practices and norms, then what occurs is *legal* decision-making. In other words, international law is a continuing process of authoritative decisions. This view rejects the notion of law merely as the impartial application of rules. International law is the entire decision-making process, and not just the decision to the trend of past decisions which are termed 'rules'.[1]

To many this may seem unacceptable. However, insofar as international law is created by states through their practice and agreement, it should not surprise anyone that the rules of international law are subject to change and interpretation in this way.

The case studies have illustrated how this process works. In particular, the first case study sought to illustrate the development of Chapter VII of

---

1. Higgins (1968), pp. 58–9.

the UN Charter through the practice of both the Security Council and individual states. It was emphasized in that chapter that the key to the development of international law lies in the reaction of states to asserted interpretations of the law. Similar assertions were made in relation to the development of the prohibition on the threat of force considered in Chapter 5. Certainly, it cannot be denied that this form of rule changing and rule interpretation is not centralized. However, if centralization were to be taken as the fundamental requirement of the relevance of law to international society, it is asserted that international law can never and, indeed, never will be relevant to the conduct of international relations.

This point leads directly to another conclusion regarding the relevance of international law, that is that states not only accept the existence of international law but consider it also to be binding upon them. Chapter 1 considered the binding nature of international law, concluding that it lies in the political acceptance by states that it is binding upon them. The veracity of that conclusion has been illustrated by each of the case studies considered. In particular, the examination of the *Pinochet* litigation in Chapter 6 highlighted the fact that, in the United Kingdom at least, the existence of international law is accepted by its municipal courts. While the various decisions of the UK courts can be criticized in many ways, arguments supporting or criticizing these various decisions are concerned specifically with disputing the content of various rules of international law and their interpretation in the particular case, not with the existence of those rules in the first place.

The *Pinochet* case study also serves to illustrate a third conclusion. That is that international law remains primarily a law between states and, further, that that law remains essentially positivist. Thus, the majority decision of the House of Lords in *Pinochet No. 3*, while agreeing that Pinochet could be extradited to Chile to stand trial for the offences of which he was accused, limited the relevant offences only to those deriving from the Torture Convention, a Convention to which Spain, the United Kingdom and Chile were all parties. This serves to illustrate that state consent remains crucial to legal obligation in international law. It further illustrates that there is, as yet, no overriding concept of natural law deriving from the protection of human rights which is capable of bypassing the lack of consent in such circumstances. The positivist nature of international law is also aptly illustrated by the *prima facie* illegality of the NATO intervention in Kosovo considered in Chapter 4. This example sought to highlight the fact that, while international law may be developing a rule of 'humanitarian intervention' in the face of gross violations of human rights, no such right currently exists, and, indeed, no such right will develop unless states specifically consent to its development through the express amendment of the UN Charter or through their state practice in the interpretation of the relevant provisions of the Charter.

A fourth conclusion must recognize that international law is only one factor in the wider political, social and economic framework of the relations of states. This is perfectly illustrated by the final case study in Chapter 7 focusing on the legal regime surrounding the exchange of diplomatic personnel. Thus, even if it is the case that the Vienna Convention on Diplomatic Relations is one of, if not *the*, most rigorously observed international legal instruments, the observance of many of its provisions rely specifically on political rather than legal considerations. This is explicitly the case in relation to the question of whether or not states should waive diplomatic immunity. However, it is more implicitly the case in relation to the observance of the Convention as a whole. Thus, the success of the Convention is derived almost entirely from the reciprocity inherent in the exchange of diplomatic relations.

To assert that international law is capable, in and of itself, of determining the actions of states in their international relations is to do a major disservice to the subject of international law. The role of international law is quite simple. That is, to provide a framework in which states can cooperate. Insofar as international relations theory discounts the possibility of inter-state cooperation, international law has no role to play. However, as international relations theory develops towards a fuller acceptance of the possibility of international cooperation and, ultimately, the existence of an international society of states, the role of international law in providing a framework for such developments will continue. Crucially, international relations theorists and international lawyers are now much more able to work together to develop workable rules which are subject to rational interpretation and enforcement.

BIBLIOGRAPHY

Akehurst, Michael (1974–5) 'Custom as a source of international law', 47 *British Yearbook of International Law* 1.

American Law Institute (1986) *Restatement of the Law Third: The Foreign Relations Law of the United States* (St Paul, MN: American Law Institute Publishers).

Amnesty International (1974) *Chile, An Amnesty International Report*.

Anderson, M. S. (1993) *The Rise of Modern Diplomacy* (London: Longman).

Arend, Anthony Clark (1998) 'Do legal rules matter: international law and international politics', 38 *Virginia Journal of International Law* 107.

Arend, Anthony Clark and Robert Beck (1993) *International Law and the Use of Force* (New York: Routledge).

Austin, John (1995) *The Province of Jurisprudence Determined*, Wilfrid E. Rumble (ed.) (Cambridge: Cambridge University Press).

Barker, J. Craig (1995) 'The theory and practice of diplomatic law in the renaissance and classical periods', 6 *Diplomacy and Statecraft* 593.

—— (1996) *The Abuse of Diplomatic Privileges and Immunities: A Necessary Evil?* (Aldershot: Dartmouth).

—— (1999) 'The future of former head of state immunity after *Ex parte Pinochet*', 48 *International and Comparative Law Quarterly* 937.

Barnes, Jon (1983) 'Human rights and the Pinochet decade', in Philip J. O'Brien and Jackie Roddick (eds), *Chile: The Pinochet Decade: The Rise and Fall of the Chicago Boys* (London: Latin America Bureau).

Bass, Peter Evan (1987) 'Ex-head of state immunity: a proposed tool of foreign policy', 97 *Yale Law Journal* 299.

Beck, Robert J., Anthony Clark Arend and Robert D. Vander Lugt (eds) (1996) *International Rules: Approaches from International Law and International Relations* (Oxford: Oxford University Press).

Bedjaoui, Mohammed (1979) *Towards a New Intenational Order* (Paris: UNESCO).

Bentham, Jeremy (1996) *An Introduction to the Principles of Morals and Legislation* (eds James Burns and Herbert L. A. Hart) (Oxford: Clarendon Press) (First published London, 1780).

Bishop, William W. (1971) *International Law: Cases and Materials* (3rd edn) (Boston, Toronto: Little, Brown & Co.).

Boutros-Ghali, Boutros (1992) *An Agenda for Peace* (New York: United Nations).

Bowett, Derek William (1958) *Self-Defence in International Law* (Manchester: Manchester University Press).

Breasted, James H. (1927) *A History of Egypt from the Earliest Times to the Persian Conquest* (2nd rev. edn) (London).

Brierly, James L. (1928) 'The "*Lotus*" case', 44 *Law Quarterly Review* 154.

—— (1932) 'International law and the resort to armed force', 4 *Cambridge Law Journal* 308.

—— (1954) *The Law of Nations: An Introduction to the International Law of Peace* (5th edn) (Oxford: Clarendon Press).

—— (1958) *The Basis of Obligation in International Law* (Oxford: Clarendon Press).

Britton, Roswell S. (1935) 'Chinese interstate intercourse before 700 BC', 29 *American Journal of International Law* 616.

Brownlie, Ian (1963) *International Law and the Use of Force by States* (Oxford: Oxford University Press).

—— (1981) 'The reality and efficacy of international law', 52 *British Yearbook of International Law* 1.

—— (1998) *Principles of Public International Law* (5th edn) (Oxford: Clarendon Press).

Brunnee, Jutta and Stephen J. Toope (1997) 'Environmental security and freshwater resources: a case for international ecosystem law', 90 *American Journal of International Law* 384.

Bull, Hedley (1995) *The Anarchical Society: A Study of Order in World Politics* (2nd edn) (Basingstoke: Macmillan).

Byers, Michael (1997) 'Taking the law out of international law: a critique of the "iterative perspective"', 38 *Harvard International Law Journal* 201.

—— (1998) 'The right ruling for humanity', *The Times* (London), 26 November, p. 24.

—— (1999) *Custom, Power and the Power of Rules: International Relations and Customary International Law* (Cambridge: Cambridge University Press).

Bynkershoek, Cornelius van (1721) *De Foro Legatorum*, in J.B. Scott (ed.), *Classics of International Law Series* (1964) (New York: Oxford University Press).

Carr, Edward H. (1939) *The Twenty-Years' Crisis, 1919–1939: An Introduction to the Study of International Relations* (London: Macmillan).

Cassesse, Antonio (1986) *International Law in a Divided World* (Oxford: Oxford University Press).

—— (1999) '*Ex iniuria ius oritur*: are we moving towards international legitimation of forcible humanitarian countermeasures in the world community?', 10 *European Journal of International Law* 23.

Charlesworth, Hilary, Christine Chinkin and Shelley Wright (1991) 'Feminist approaches to international law', 85 *American Journal of International Law* 613.

Chatterjee, H. (1958) *International Law and Inter-State Relations in Ancient India* (Calcutta: Firma K.L. Mukhopadhyay).

Chayes, Abram and Antonia Handler Chayes (1993) 'On compliance', 47 *International Organisation* 175.

—— (1995) *The New Sovereignty: Compliance with International Regulatory Agreements* (Cambridge, MA.: Harvard University Press).

Chen, Lung-Chu (1989) *An Introduction to Contemporary International Law: A Policy-oriented Perspective* (New Haven and London: Yale University Press).

Cheng, Bin (1965) 'United Nations resolutions in outer space: instant international customary law?', 5 *Indian Journal of International Law* 23.

Cooley (1991) 'Pre-war Gulf diplomacy', 33 *Survival* 125.

Corbett, P. E. (1925) 'The consent of states and the sources of international law', 6 *British Yearbook of International Law* 20.

D'Amato, Anthony A. (1971) *The Concept of Custom in International Law* (Ithaca, NY: Cornell University Press).

Damrosch, Lori Fisler (1997) 'Enforcing international law through non-forcible means', 269 *Hague Recueil* 13.

Dannreuther, Roland (1992) *The Gulf Conflict: A Political and Strategic Analysis, Adelphi Papers*, No. 264, Winter 1991/2 (London: International Institute for Strategic Studies).

De Martens, C. (1866) *Le Guide diplomatique* (ed. E. Geffenken) (Leipzig).

de Vitoria, Francisco (1557) *De Potestate Civile*.

Denza, Eileen (1998) *Diplomatic Law: A Commentary on the Vienna Convention on Diplomatic Relations* (2nd edn) (Oxford: Clarendon Press).

Dias, R. W. M. (1954) 'Mechanism of definition as applied to international law', 12 *Cambridge Law Journal* 215.

Dinstein, Yoram (1966) 'Diplomatic immunity from jurisdiction *rationae materiae*', 15 *International and Comparative Law Quarterly* 76.

Dixon, Martin (1993) *Textbook on International Law* (2nd edn) (London: Blackstone Press).

Fitzmaurice, Gerald (1956) 'The foundations of the authority of international law and the problem of enforcement', 19 *Modern Law Review* 1.

—— (1958) 'Some problems regarding the formal sources of international law', *Symbolae Verzijl* 153.

Foreign Affairs Committee (1984–5) *The Abuse of Diplomatic Immunities and Privileges*, HC Paper 127.

Franck, Thomas Martin (1970) 'Who killed Article 2(4)?', 64 *American Journal of International Law* 809.

—— (1988) 'Legitimacy in the international system', 82 *American Journal of International Law* 705.

—— (1990) *The Power of Legitimacy Among Nations* (Oxford: Oxford University Press).

—— (1995) *Fairness in International Law and Institutions* (Oxford: Clarendon Press).

Freeman, Michael D. A. (1994) *Lloyd's Introduction to Jurisprudence* (6th edn) (London, Sweet & Maxwell).

Friedmann, Wolfgang Gaston (1964) *The Changing Structure of International Law* (London: Stevens).

Ganshoff, F. L. (1970) *The Middle Ages: A History of International Relations* (trans. R. I. Hall) (New York: Harper & Row).

Gentili, Alberico (1585) *De Legationibus Libri Tres,* text trans. Gordon J. Laing, *Classics of International Law Series 12,* 1924 (New York: Oxford University Press).

Geny, Francois (1919) *Methode d'interpretation et sources en droit prive positif* (2nd edn) (Paris: Librairie Generale de Droit et de Jurisprudence).

Ghandhi, P. R. (1998) *The Human Rights Committee and the Right of Individual Communication: Law and Practice* (Aldershot: Ashgate).

Glennon, Michael J. (1991), 'The Constitution and Chapter VII of the United Nations Charter', 85 *American Journal of International Law* 74.

Goodrich, L., E. Hambro and A. Simons (1969) *Charter of the United Nations* (3rd edn). (New York: Columbia University Press).

Gray, Christine (1994) 'After the ceasefire: Iraq, the security forces and the use of force', 65 *British Yearbook of International Law* 135.

Greig, D. W. (1991) 'Self-defence and the Security Council: what does Article 51 require?', 40 *International and Comparative Law Quarterly* 366.

Grotius, Hugo (1625) *De Jure Belli ac Pacis: Libre Tres; Prolegomena,* reprinted in Robert J. Beck, Anthony Clark Arend and Robert D. Vander Lugt (eds) (1996) *International Rules: Approaches from International Law and International Relations* (New York and Oxford: Oxford University Press), pp. 38–53.

Grotius, Hugo (1625) *De Jure Belli ac Pacis: Libre Tres,* in J.B. Scott (ed.), *Classics of International Law Series* (1925) (New York: Oxford University Press).

Hall, William Edward (1924) *A Treatise on International Law* (ed. A. Pearce Higgins) (Oxford: Clarendon Press).

Hamilton, Bernice (1963) *Political Thought in Sixteenth-Century Spain: A Study of the Political Ideas of Vitoria, De Soto, Surarez and Molina* (Oxford: Clarendon Press).

Harris, David John (1998) *Cases and Materials on International Law* (5th edn) (London: Sweet & Maxwell).

Hart, Herbert L. A. (1961) *The Concept of Law* (Oxford: Clarendon Press).

—— (1994) *The Concept of Law* (2nd edn) (Oxford: Oxford University Press).

Henkin, Louis (1979) *How Nations Behave* (2nd edn) (New York: Columbia University Press).

Henkin, Louis, Richard C. Pugh, Oscar Schachter and Hans Smit (1987) *International Law: Cases and Materials* (St. Paul, MN.: West Pub.).

Hevener, Natalie Kaufman (1986) *Diplomacy in a Dangerous World: Protection for Diplomats under International Law* (New York: Westview Press).

Higgins, Rosalyn (1963) *The Development of International Law Through the Organs of the United Nations* (London: Oxford University Press).

—— (1968) 'Policy considerations in the international judicial process', 17 *International and Comparative Law Quarterly* 58.

—— (1978) 'Conceptual thinking about the individual in international law', 4 *British Journal of International Studies* 1.

—— (1982) 'The identity of international law', in Bin Cheng (ed.), *International Law: Teaching and Practice* (London: Stevens & Sons).

—— (1994) *Problems and Process: International Law and How We Use It* (Oxford: Clarendon Press).

—— (1999) 'International law in a changing international system', 58 *Cambridge Law Journal* 78.

Hill, C. (1931) 'Sanctions constraining diplomatic representatives to abide by the local law', 25 *American Journal of International Law* 252.

Hillier, Tim (1998) *Sourcebook on Public International Law* (London: Cavendish Publishing).

Hobbes, Thomas (1651) *Leviathan* (Glasgow: Collins).

Hoffmann, Stanley (1968) 'International law and the control of force', in Karl Wolfgang Deutsch and Stanley Hoffmann (eds), *The Relevance of International Law: Essays in Honour of Leo Gross* (Cambridge, MA: Schenkman).

Hurd, Douglas (1997) *The Search for Peace* (London: Warner).

Hurrell, Andrew (1993) 'International society and the study of regimes: a reflective approach', in Volker Rittberger and Peter Mayer (eds), *Regime Theory and International Relations* (Oxford: Clarendon Press).

Jackson, Geoffrey (1981) *Concorde Diplomacy* (London: Hamish Hamilton).

Jessup, Philip Caryl (1949) *A Modern Law of Nations: An Introduction* (New York: Macmillan).

Kaplan, Morton A. and Nicolas de Belleville Katzenbach (1961) *The Political Foundations of International Law* (New York: Wiley).

Kelsen, Hans (1966) *Principles of Public International Law* (2nd edn) (ed. Robert W. Tucker) (New York: Rinehart).

Kemp, Geoffrey (1990) 'The Gulf crisis: diplomacy or force', 32 *Survival* 507.

Kennan, George Frost (1984) *American Diplomacy* (Chicago: University of Chicago Press).

Keohane, Robert Owen (1988) 'International institutions: two approaches', 32 *International Studies Quarterly* 379.

—— (1989) *International Institutions and State Power: Essays in International Relations Theory* (Boulder, CO: Westview Press).

—— (1997) 'International relations and international law: two optics', 38 *Harvard International Law Journal* 487.

Kocs, Stephen A. (1994) 'Explaining the strategic behaviour of states: international law as system structure', 38 *International Studies Quarterly* 535.

Koh, Harold Hongju (1997) 'Why do nations obey international law?', 106 *Yale Law Journal* 2599.

Krasner, Stephen (1982) 'Structural causes and regime consequences: regimes as intervening variables', 36 *International Organisation* 185.

Lauterpacht, Hersch (1933) *The Function of Law in the International Community* (Oxford: Clarendon Press).

—— (1946) 'The Grotian tradition in international law', 23 *British Yearbook of International Law* 1.

—— (1947) 'The subjects of the law of nations', 68 *Law Quarterly Review* 438.

—— (1951) 'The problem of jurisdictional immunities of foreign states', 28 *British Yearbook of International Law* 220.

Lobel, Jules and Michael Ratner (1999) 'Bypassing the Security Council: ambiguous authorizations to use force, ceasefires and the Iraqi inspection regime', 93 *American Journal of International Law* 124.

Lowe, Vaughan (1983) 'Do general rules of international law exist?', 9 *Review of International Studies* 207.

McClanachan, G. V. (1989) *Diplomatic Immunity: Principles, Practices, Problems* (New York: Hurst & Co.).

Mallory, Jerrold L. (1986) 'Resolving the confusion over head of state immunity: the defined right of kings', 86 *Columbia Law Review* 169.

Marston G. (1993) 'United Kingdom materials on international law 1993', 64 *British Yearbook of International Law* 579.

Mearsheimer, John (1994/5) 'The false promise of international institutions', 19 *International Security* 5.

—— (1995) 'A realist reply', 20 *International Security* 82.

Mera, J. (1995) *Chile: Truth and Justice under the Democratic Government in Impunity and Human Rights in International Law and Practice* (ed. Naomi Roht-Arriaza) (New York, Oxford: Oxford University Press).

Moravcsik, Andrew (1992) *Liberalism and International Relations Theory* (Center for International Affairs, Harvard University, Working Paper No. 92–6).

—— (1997) 'Taking preferences seriously: a liberal theory of international politics', 51 *International Organisation* 513.

Morgenthau, Hans Joachin (1973) *Politics Among Nations: The Struggle for Power and Peace* (5th rev. edn) (New York: Knopf).

Myres (1997) 'Georgia prepared to waive immunity of a top diplomat', *New York Times*, 11 January.

Nardin, Terry (1983) *Law, Morality and the Relations of States* (Princeton and Guildford: Princeton University Press).

Nicolson, Harold (1954) *The Evolution of Diplomatic Method* (London: Constable).

Nussbaum, Arthur (1962) *A Concise History of the Law of Nations* (rev. edn) (New York: Macmillan).

O'Brien, Philip J. and Jackie Roddick (1983) *Chile, The Pinochet Decade: The Rise and Fall of the Chicago Boys* (London: Latin America Bureau).

O'Connell, Daniel Patrick (1971) *International Law for Students* (London: Stevens).

Ogdon, Montell (1936) *Juridical Bases of Diplomatic Immunity* (Washington, DC: John Byrne & Co.).

Olson, William C. and Groom, Arthur J. R. (1991) *International Relations Then and Now: Origins and Trends in Interpretation* (London: HarperCollins Academic).

Pennington, Kenneth (1993) *The Prince and the Law, 1200–1600: Sovereignty and Rights in the Western Legal Tradition* (Berkeley: University of California Press).

Petras, James F. and Morris H. Morley (1974) *How Allende Fell: A Study in US–Chilean Relations* (Nottingham: Spokesman Books).

Phillipson, Coleman (1979) *The International Law and Custom of Ancient Greece and Rome* (reprint edn) (Arno Press Inc.).

Pogson Smith, William G. (1909) *Hobbes' Leviathan* (Oxford: Clarendon Press).

Rama-Montaldo, Manuel (1970) 'International legal personality and implied powers of international organisations', 44 *British Yearbook of International Law* 111.

Ratner, Steven (1998) 'International law: the trials of global norms', 110 *Foreign Policy* 65.

Reisman, Michael (1990) 'Sovereignty and human rights in contemporary international law', 84 *American Journal of International Law* 866.

Rostow, Eugene V. (1991) 'Until what? Enforcement action or collective self-defence?', 85 *American Journal of International Law* 506.

Roxborough, Ian, O'Brien Philip J. and Jackie Roddick (1977) *Chile: The State and Revolution* (London: Macmillan).

Rozakis, C. L. (1974) 'Terrorism and the internationally protected person in light of the ILC's draft articles', 23 *International and Comparative Law Quarterly* 32.

Sadurska, Romana (1988) 'Threats of force', 82 *American Journal of International Law* 239.

Sarooshi, Danesh (1999) 'The Statute of the International Criminal Court', 48 *International and Comparative Law Quarterly* 387.

Schachter, Oscar (1984) 'The right of states to use force', 82 *Michigan Law Review* 1620.

—— (1989) 'Self-defense and the rule of law', 83 *American Journal of International Law* 259.

—— (1991) 'United Nations law in the Gulf conflict', 85 *American Journal of International Law* 452.

Schelling, Thomas C. (1966) *Arms and Influence* (New Haven: Yale University Press).

Schuman, Frederick Lewis (1948) *International Politics: The Destiny of the Western State System* (4th edn) (New York: McGraw-Hill Book Co.).

Schwarzenberger, Georg (1972) 'Historical models of international law: towards a comparative history of international law', 25 *Current Legal Problems* 219.

—— (1976) *The Dynamics of International Law* (London: Professional Books).

Setear, John (1996) 'An iterative perspective on treaties: a synthesis of international relations theory and international law', 37 *Harvard International Law Journal* 139.

Shaw, Malcolm Nathan (1997) *International Law* (4th edn) (Cambridge: Cambridge University Press).

Shearer, Ivan A. (1994) *Starke's International Law* (11th edn) (London: Butterworths).

Simma, Bruno (1999) 'NATO, the UN and the use of force: legal aspects', 10 *European Journal of International Law* 1.

Sinclair, Ian (1980) 'The law of sovereign immunity: recent developments', 167-II *Hague Recueil* 113.

Slaughter, Anne-Marie (1994) 'The liberal agenda for peace: international relations theory and the future of the United Nations', 4 *Transnational Law and Contemporary Problems* 377.

—— (1995) 'International law in a world of liberal states', 6 *European Journal of International Law* 503.

—— (1997 'The real new world order', 76 *Foreign Affairs* 183.

Slaughter, Anne-Marie, Andrew S. Tulumello and Stepan Wood (1998) 'International law and international relations theory: a new generation of interdisciplinary scholarship', 92 *American Journal of International Law* 367.

Slaughter Burley, Anne-Marie (1993) 'International law and international relations theory: a dual agenda', 87 *American Journal of International Law* 205.

Starr, Harvey (1995) 'International law and international order', in Charles W. Kegley Jr. (ed.), *Controversies in International Relations Theory: Realism and the Neoliberal Challenge* (New York and Basingstoke: St. Martin's Press).

Thirlway, H. W. A. (1972) *International Customary Law and Codification: An Examination of the Continuing Role of Custom in the Present Period of Codification of International Law* (Leiden: Sijthoff).

Tunkin, Gregory (1958) 'Coexistence and international law', 3 *Human Rights* 1.

UK Government (1985) *Diplomatic Immunities and Privileges*, Report on Review of Vienna Convention on Diplomatic Relations, Cmnd. 1419.

Vattel (1758) *Le Droit des gens*, in J.B. Scott (ed.), *Classics of International Law Series* (1916) (New York: Oxford University Press).

Viswanatha, Sekharipuram V. (1925) *International Law in Ancient India* (Bombay/New York/London: Longmans, Green & Co.).

Walzer, Michael (1992) *Just and Unjust Wars: A Moral Argument with Historical Illustrations* (2nd edn) (New York: Basic Papers).

Warbrick, Colin, Salgado, Elena and Goodwin, Nicholas (1999) 'The Pinochet cases in the United Kingdom', 2 *Yearbook of International Humanitarian Law* 91.

Watts, Arthur (1994) 'The legal position in international law of heads of states, heads of governments and foreign ministers', 247-III *Hague Recueil* 9.

Wendt, Alexander (1992) 'Anarchy is what states make of it: the social construction of power politics', 46 *International Organisation* 185.

—— (1994) 'Collective identity formation and the international state', 88 *American Political Science Review* 384.

—— (1995/6) 'Constructing international politics', 20 *International Security* 71.

Westlake, John (1894) *International Law* (Cambridge: Cambridge University Press).

Weston, Burns H. (1991) 'Security Council Resolution 678 and Persian Gulf decision making: precarious legitimacy', 85 *American Journal of International Law* 516.

White, Nigel (1995) *Keeping the Peace, the United Nations and the Maintenance of International Peace and Security* (Manchester: Manchester University Press).

Whitehead, Laurence (1974) *The Lessons of Chile* (London: Fabian Society).

Whyte, Frederick (1928) *China and Foreign Powers: An Historical Review of Their Relations* (2nd rev. edn) (London: Oxford University Press).

Williams, Glanville L. (1945) 'International law and the controversy surrounding the word "law"', 22 *British Yearbook of International Law* 146.

Wright, Quincy (1955) *The Study of International Relations* (New York: Appleton-Century-Crofts, Inc.).

Yglesias, Jose (1974) 'Introduction' in Judy White (ed.), *Chile's Days of Terror: Eyewitness Accounts of the Military Coup* (New York: Pathfinder).

Young, Eileen (1964) 'The development of the law of diplomatic relations', 40 *British Yearbook of International Law* 141.

Young, Oran Reed (1986–7) 'International regimes: towards a new theory of institutions', 39 *World Politics* 116.

—— (1989) *International Cooperation: Building Regimes for Natural Resources and the Environment* (Ithaca, NY: Cornell University Press).

Official websites

American Political Science Association *www.apsanet.org*
American Society of International Law *www.asil.org*
European Court of Human Rights *www.echr.coe.int/*
European Union with links to sites on European Union Law *www.europa.eu.int/*
International Court of Justice *www.icj-cij.org*
International Criminal Court *www.un.org/law/icc/index/htm*
International Law Association *www.ila-hq.org*
International Law Commission *www.un.org/law/ilc/index/htm*
North Atlantic Treaty Organisation *www.nato.int*

Other useful websites

www.law.cam.ac.uk/RCIL/ILCSR/Stateresp.htm website on developing law of state responsibility containing all latest information from James Crawford, Special Rapporteur ro the International Law Commission

http://jurist.law.pitt.edu/kosovo.htm legal guide to the Kosovo crisis.

www.law.ecel.uwa.edu.au/intlaw/ University of Western Australia containing in excess of 90 links to international law topics.

www.abacom.com/innomagi/online/law/interna.htm private website with numerous links to international law topics

INDEX